I DON'T WHETHER MYSELF

JOANNA SORRENTINO

THE PAPER HOUSE
PUBLISHING

*To all of those who were there, helping us through this adventure.
You are in this book, and in my heart – always.
Thank you.*

CONTENTS

PROLOGUE

"Tom, touch your nose!"

Tom sits there. He does not touch his nose. He does nothing.

"Tom, look! Like this." The therapist touches her nose. "Touch your nose."

Tom just sits. He looks attentive, as if he is concentrating, his eyes focused on the woman's face, but he does not touch his nose.

"You try it, Tom. Do what I do. Touch your nose. Your nose, Tom! Touch your nose."

Tom never moves.

"Try this, Tom. Stick out your tongue." The therapist sticks out her tongue and wags it around like a worm on a fish hook.

The rest of us laugh, but Tom sits there.

Valiantly, the plucky woman goes through her entire repertoire. She touches her nose, her eyes, her teeth; she sticks out her tongue and pats the top of her head with broad, exaggerated gestures, always urging Tom to copy her actions. To us it looks pretty comical, like an out-of-control Marx brother, but there is no response from Tom other than a fixed stare. He clearly does not understand her at all; he has no way to interpret the little drama being acted out with such fervor just inches in front of him.

Outside the window, the late afternoon sun brings out a flat polish on the heaps of old snow. Inside, the little room is stuffy as we sit in and among our sweatshirts and winter jackets. Like the audience of a bad off-Broadway play, we maintain an embarrassed silence as the therapist, a thoroughly determined woman, goes bravely through her little performance.

There is still no sign of understanding or appreciation from Tom; the therapist decides to make this group theater.

"C'mon, we'll all do it." She waves us up and we all face Tom and touch our noses upon command. We stick out our tongues, pat our heads, stamp our feet. We show an outstanding knowledge of our body parts, and a wonderful ability to move them about.

Tom does nothing.

The therapist does not surrender, but eventually her time is up, her matinee concludes. She looks directly into Tom's face and tells him, "That's all for today, Tom. We'll work again tomorrow." Smiling at him and at us as if she were thoroughly satisfied, she leaves the room.

We sit on with Tom, trying to continue her work. We point and pat, stick out and stamp, but there is no reaction from Tom and we begin to feel a bit foolish ourselves. Finally, Tom ends the agony for all of us by closing his eyes and either sleeping or feigning sleep in his chair.

Tom is forty-six years old. He has a Master's Degree in Educational Technology and eleven teaching and supervisory certificates. But he cannot touch his nose.

PART I

Forgive, O Lord, my little jokes on Thee
And I'll forgive Thy great big one on me.

– Robert Frost

CHAPTER 1

1970 − 1993

T om raised his hand and I called on him. "Yes, Mr. Sorrentino?"

"Are you going to discuss the significance of the hornets?" he asked.

The students in the classroom looked from him to me. By now they were accustomed to seeing Mr. Sorrentino, a history teacher, drop into our English class from time to time with his sandwich and coffee, and unobtrusively take a seat in the back row of desks to eat his lunch.

I thought I was quite cool with his occasional visits − I just went on teaching. The kids were cool with it, too. This was the 70s, and everything was cool.

However, this was the first time he had participated and his question took me by surprise. I had taught Camus' *The Stranger* for several years but had never considered that the hornets might have had some kind of symbolism. In fact, I could not even recall anything at all about hornets.

"Would you care to explain your question, Mr. Sorrentino?" I asked. "I'm not sure what you mean."

I think we were all impressed that this history teacher, known for his encyclopedic retention of facts, was also able to discuss an esoteric piece of literature. I know I certainly was.

He took a sip of coffee, a dramatic pause before his reply. "When Mersault is in his cell, he notices the hornets buzzing around the light fixture on the ceiling." His tone of voice implied a deep significance in that little scene.

"Ah," I said. I waited, but he was finished with his line of inquiry. I had clearly missed the significance but I was equal to the task. In a totally uncool moment, I agreed with and even elaborated on his construction. Teachers learn to think on their feet.

"Perhaps the significance of the hornets and the light fixture is that they symbolize freedom. Mersault in his prison cell has lost his freedom. The insects, also imprisoned within a building but drawn to the light, may be searching for a way out. Light has always been a symbol of liberty, or freedom."

He smiled and saluted me with the half sandwich he held. The students dutifully recorded the significance of the wasps in their notebooks.

Years later, Tom confessed to making the whole thing up.

MY GENERATION JUDGED A WOMAN'S SUCCESS BY HER ABILITY to attract men. I was spectacularly unsuccessful. Short, a little dumpy, ethnically sallow, and myopic in my world view (through Coke-bottle-bottom glasses), I was never the classic All-American Girl Next Door. Despite my mother's ceaseless efforts at forcing my hair to curl, it always remained stubbornly straight which in my youth was a sin. This condition won me countless roles in elementary school plays as an Indian or a Gypsy, but never even once as the fairy princess, a part I coveted. I had my father's nose, which looked fine enough on him but was rather discordant on a young girl's face. I had few if any socially endearing qualities. I was not pretty, not funny, not athletic, not artistic or musical, not a cheerleader, and not a party girl. To make matters worse, I loftily disdained both makeup and fashion trends as being "phony". (A very big word in the 50s was "phony." It was the excuse for "unattainable.")

My older cousin told me, "You have to suffer to be beautiful." Suffering held no appeal. Sure, it would have been nice to be beautiful, but I knew a hopeless case when I saw one. And protracted agony didn't make any sense at all.

There was one thing I had going for me: intelligence. Alas, in my day intelligence was not recognized as a boon to young ladies, certainly not young ladies in Italian American families.

"Don't let the boys know how smart you are," was my mother's advice. "No boy wants to marry a girl who's smarter than he is."

She meant well. She had found her happiness through marriage and a family and she wanted the same happiness for my sister and me. Perhaps blinded by a mother's love, she could not see that intelligence was all I had. If I hid my one talent, I had nothing.

Assuming I was doomed to be single, I ploughed through my teens and twenties immersed in books, Girl Scouts – including Mariners – college, a stint in the Peace Corps, summer study at Oxford, and a teaching career. My family, of course, despaired that I would ever marry and thus, to their way of thinking, never find true happiness. I wallowed in my loneliness, writing some cringe-worthy but soulful poetry, proud of my isolation and determined to find a degree of happiness on my own.

And then I met Tom.

Tom noticed me long before I noticed him.

Well, not entirely accurate. I had noticed him, of course. Who could miss him? He was over six feet tall, darkly handsome, with a serious, intelligent cast to his face. He had a reputation for dating beautiful girls; I assumed I had no chance.

And then he started showing up in my classroom.

We barely knew each other, but he continued to drop in with his lunch, stay a few minutes, and leave. I was flattered, but also puzzled. Why was he spending his lunchtime in my classroom?

"It was more fun than sitting in the faculty lunchroom," was the best explanation he later gave me. Could it be he was checking me out without the burden of making a commitment?

Tom had been a Boy Scout and still loved camping. I had been a Girl Scout with a lot of camping experience. He read and studied constantly. He was sweet and gentle, but most of all, he was intelligent, and he valued intelligence in others. Others like me, for instance. At last I was vindicated. I could show the world (meaning my family) that it was possible to be intelligent and still attract a fine, decent man.

We never dated much because we knew we wanted to be with each other. Instead of dating we scandalized – and embarrassed – our families by moving in together. In our time such a situation was referred to as "living in sin." (I hope I don't sound like a refugee from the Middle Ages.)

When my mother finally agreed to meet Tom, she was struck

by his handsome appearance and therefore certain he was an opportunist. (Notice the implication: how could such an attractive man possibly be interested in me?) One of the things she said to him was, "How can I be sure you won't just walk away and break my daughter's heart?"

He replied, "How can I be sure she won't walk away and break mine?"

This was unfathomable to my mother. Men were the breakers of hearts; women were the breakees.

Tom's parents were polite, but distant. Our living arrangements offended their Catholic sense of morality. We were the first couple in both families to *live in sin*. After us, it happened all over the place but for us it was tough. There were even family members who would not have us in their homes until after we were married. It's not easy to be a pioneer.

The school was abuzz. We tried to low-key the whole thing, but word was out. The kids thought we were great.

Just about all the teachers assumed it would not last. Why? I can sum it up by quoting one faculty member who told another (who subsequently told me), "I'm surprised Tom is going out with her. She isn't very pretty."

But Tom was the man plain girls dream about. He saw through the exterior and right into the soul. He thought I was the "nicest person" he had ever met, and he enjoyed my company. And I guess he figured I would be in it for the long run, because he sat down and wrote up a Thirty-Year Financial Plan shortly after we met.

We had a good run for over twenty years. We divided our responsibilities in a mutually satisfactorily way and we stuck to The Plan with a bit of compromising (owing chiefly to my career restlessness). Tom took charge of the finances, which was probably a good thing. Had I controlled them, we'd have had a really exciting life spent mostly in Boston – a city I love – and Italy – where my heart resides, but we would not have had steady work or anything saved for the future.

I've always been a Gypsy at heart. In fact, when I was only four I tried to become one in body as well. We lived in Newark. Around the corner, a group of Gypsies had settled into a vacant store. Probably my family had told me the usual legends about Gypsies, principally that they stole children and traveled around a lot. True or not, the legends were all I needed to hear. I stood on the street corner for an entire afternoon, waiting to be kidnapped and begin my travels. They never came for me. I knew the pain of rejection at a tender age.

Years of adventure were all behind me when I met Tom. (So, were the thick glasses, exchanged for contact lenses.) Although I had traded excitement and wanderlust for security and a safe future when we married, Tom compromised as well. I convinced him early in our relationship that the world would not fall apart and our (his) Financial Plan would still be relatively intact if he did not work in the summers so we could camp across the country every July and August.

Consequently, we lived in a tent in almost every state of the Union and every province in Canada for many summers. Eventually, we bought a cabin deep in the Idaho wilderness, which became our summer escape and was to be our retirement headquarters for half of each year. The other half, when the cabin was snowed in, was going to be spent in travel and study. They were relatively simple plans, but we sacrificed many of the day-to-day luxuries through the years to buy the cabin and provide for our future. Tom was very happy with the plan; he loved our home in Idaho and was looking forward to early retirement so we could spend more time there. He used to say, "We work in New Jersey, but we live in Idaho."

We lived to the tune of doo-wop music. Tom had a smooth and sweet tenor voice. He loved to accompany recordings by the 50's groups. I can say without contradiction that he was indistinguishable from the other Platters. His voice won him the role of Perchik in a local production of *Fiddler on the Roof*, and a ruggedly handsome, utterly convincing Perchik he was.

Our son Bill, whose diapers were changed on campground picnic tables and who backpacked his own tent for forty-two miles when he was only eight years old, loved our summers and Idaho. Altogether, things were working out well and we were quite pleased with ourselves.

Our marriage had lasted twenty peaceful and faithful years. We respected each other's independent interests and shared an intellectual life that brought us both pleasure. Tom no longer worried about financial security. I no longer worried about not being pretty. It was all going so well...

...too well.

That should have been my first clue, huh?

Thus far we'd not been asked to endure any sufferings or grievances of the type that afflict less fortunate families. We were healthy; our son was healthy. We worked steadily and lived within our means. It was a safe, secure, fortunate, and rather ordinary life. Of course, it did not provide any material for the sad and soulful poems I used to write, but I could live with that.

I studied for my teaching certificate in Art and was very happy with my position at Coastal Learning Center as an art teacher for emotionally disturbed students. Tom was close to early retirement, just a year-and-a-half away from the completion of his Thirty-Year Plan. Bill had begun college at the University of Idaho. Life for all of us was good.

And then, on a mild December day, a perfectly ordinary day in 1993, Tom drove out to the supermarket.

CHAPTER 2

DECEMBER 2, 1993

You know the scene; you've watched it played out dozens of times on television or in the movies. You even know all the words. It's the one where the policeman comes to the door. He makes sure he has the right house, the right people. And then he says, "I'm sorry to have to tell you this, but there's been an accident..." That's the scene; you know how it goes.

My turn to play the scene came on Thursday, December 2, 1993, in the early evening of what had been a pleasant, ordinary day. My mother had stopped by in the late afternoon when Tom and I were both back from school. We all had coffee in the living room while Tom laid the fire in our woodstove – our usual afternoon routine. It was a warm day and he did not need to light the fire, but the stove was his baby and he loved attending to it. My mother brought over two pairs of earrings from which I was to choose one pair as my Christmas gift. Tom told us something funny that had happened at school and we had a laugh over it. A comfortable, happy afternoon. My mother left about four-thirty; I began supper; Tom tended to his wood. Just an ordinary day.

At what point did this ordinary day turn around and begin its wild descent into a nightmare? My mother held herself responsible – if only she had stayed later or left earlier, she claimed, the timing would have been different and Tom would not have been in the accident. But of course that's absurd. If blame is to be placed anywhere, let's drop it where it clearly belongs – in the salad bowl. Tom decided he wanted to transform our plain supper salad into an antipasto; he went out to the store for salami and cheese. He left at five o'clock with a small grocery list, bound for the supermarket less than three miles away. He never got there.

And, in a sense, he never returned. For the next eight years, our lives were spent helping the man who had been Tom come back from his "quick trip to the supermarket."

At home, I was keeping supper warm and gradually becoming aware that he was delayed. At first I thought he had run into a friend or colleague and was talking. He could get carried away with a discussion if the topic interested him. However, no subject, no matter how intriguing, could ever keep Tom from his next meal. When he was still missing after an hour, I began some serious worrying.

I paced between the window, which looked out on to the street, and the stove, where supper was slowly drying up. While preparing our food I had been listening to a cassette of classical music; one of the selections was the *Hallelujah Chorus*. I cued the tape to the beginning of the piece; my plan was to press "Play" when Tom finally stepped through the door to be greeted by a shout of triumph.

Of course I was worried, but as I think back now, I believe a kind of protective numbness began to set in during the two hours I waited. Obviously, something was wrong. On the other hand, this was Tom. Tom – intelligent, capable, organized. (Also very handsome. That has nothing to do with it, but I thought he'd be pleased if I mention it one more time).

Tom had been at the helm through most of our voyage. Although I rearranged his master plan on several occasions, it was his steadfastness of purpose that had gotten us to the near completion in only twenty-two years of the original thirty-year plan! It was Tom who, after a year of reading books on the subject, built our house, a geodesic dome. It was Tom who drafted a letter to the *Guinness Book of World Records* inquiring about a category for "Most Certified Teacher in the World." He already had a Master's Degree and eleven teaching and supervisory certificates and was planning to acquire two more through correspondence courses the following summer. Things did not happen to Tom; Tom made things happen.

It just wasn't possible that something had happened to him now. It certainly wouldn't be fair this close to the goal. I convinced myself that he was trapped in snarled traffic, or had gone to a second store, or encountered car trouble. Nothing else made sense.

When I finally saw headlights turn off the main road and travel slowly down our street, I was relieved. I ran to the stove, turned up the heat, and placed my finger on the Play button.

A car door slammed, but even then I knew it didn't have the right sound. Footsteps crunched on the gravel driveway, but they did not sound like Tom's. You get used to the familiar sounds of your own household, don't you, and these were not right. Sure enough, instead of the door being opened, there was a knock,

Two raps on the door, echoed by *Uh-oh* in my head.

I turned around and the scene began, just like in the movies. A policeman stood outside the glass door. Mechanically, I opened it. I don't think I said anything; I had no lines yet. But the numbness had already begun to set deep inside. I remember thinking, *Just do this thing; just walk through it.*

"Mrs. Sorrentino?"

I nodded. The policeman stepped inside.

"I'm sorry to tell you this, but there's been an accident. Your husband has been taken to Jersey Shore Medical Center."

My first thought: *Why Jersey Shore?* We lived only a couple of miles from Paul Kimball Hospital. I asked over a dozen questions at once, at least four of which were, "Why Jersey Shore?" Also, "What happened?" and "What's wrong with him?" My words rushed out in a torrent; I had no control over them. Unbidden, they poured out into our kitchen, rising to fill the open space. Words, questions, took up the air and gobbled all the breathing room, weighing down and suffocating the stranger I suddenly became. I was oddly out-of-body, even as I spoke my part. But the curtain had been raised; the play had to go on.

The policeman stood patiently until I finished my frenetic monologue. As I recollect the scene, it seems more dramatic in memory than it probably had been in reality. I may be confusing it with all the variations of the same scene I knew from the movies. I do know the policeman waited for me to take a breath and then said, "I don't know what happened, ma'am. I was in the patrol car and got the call to come over here."

"What should I do? And why Jersey Shore? What should I do?" I was walking in circles around in my kitchen. While all this was happening, while I was totally thrown off base by the news, there was still a tiny part of my brain saying, "Look at you – you really are turning in circles. This really is what people do."

At the time, it seemed natural. I certainly didn't choreograph it. I was shaking my hands as well, as if to get rid of the whole thing, like dirty water. At least that is my recollection.

"What should I do?"

"You should secure your house and go up there," he said. And he left.

Now I ask you – was that right? Here I had just enacted a crazed carousel in my kitchen, turning circles, wringing my hands, spewing out panicky questions, and he left! He never offered to drive me up to the hospital. Wouldn't you have thought he could tell I was in no condition to drive, and do the gallant thing? Didn't he realize I do not see well at night, and besides, I had no idea where Jersey Shore was? But no – like a premonition of the years to come, I was suddenly alone and forced to make by myself the kind of decisions Tom and I had made together for the past twenty years. I was a teacher and I had just cooked a delicious meal, which was somewhat desiccated by now. That was my reality. How was I expected to go off careening into the night to an unknown destination? (Ironically, that was to become a metaphor for the next eight years – careening off in the dark to uncharted waters.) This was unreal; the whole last scene was unreal. Tom would be home any moment and reality would snap back into place.

Of course, it didn't. You know that.

It suddenly felt still and sobering to recall the officer's words: "Secure the house." The big winds had blown over and now I had to deal with the wreckage. I knew I could never get to the hospital by myself. Tom had taken my sub-compact Toyota to the supermarket, leaving his big Blazer truck at home, and it was too big for me to handle easily, even were I not too distraught to drive in the first place.

Now please, don't go thinking I was some kind of helpless female who was completely dysfunctional in the absence of her husband. It wasn't like that at all. I consider myself a very independent person. I even have the results of my Peace Corps psychological profiles to prove it. However, through the years we had worked out a delegation of responsibilities. He took care of finances, the house and grounds, and the vehicles while I did all the housework, cooking, and shopping. We both raised our son, Bill, and we always consulted each other before making important decisions. The system had worked quite well, but it was one of interdependence. Stranded now on his side of the yard, facing night driving and a suspenseful situation, I was momentarily lost.

It took several phone calls before I found someone to drive me. Chuck, a family friend, was home and knew how to get to the hospital and that was all I needed.

It seemed like I waited interminably for Chuck as I paced our deck on that mild December evening. I was in a vacuum; it was a bottom-of-the-well feeling. Everything around me dissolved into blackness as I waited. I was completely unaware of my surroundings and only vaguely aware of the fact that I still didn't know what had happened. Pictures of car wrecks drifted through my mind. Part of my thinking went this way: how serious could an accident possibly be right here on our own quiet streets? I thought of broken bones, maybe cuts and bruises. Nothing ever happened around here.

Then, with a mental thud that clunked down in my brain, the other thought finally landed. *They've taken him to Jersey Shore, the regional trauma center.*

All the way to the hospital, Chuck assured me everything would be fine. We all had the same idea about Tom. He was too sensible, too practical, too organized. He was not the type to end up in any kind of crazy predicament. Not Tom.

But we were wrong.

They were waiting for us in the emergency room. As soon as I gave my name, the woman behind the Reception window stepped out and put her arm around me. An alarm clanged dully somewhere deep within me, penetrating the numbness. *This is trouble*, I thought. *This is what trouble feels like.*

"Your husband was brought here by helicopter," she said gently. "He's had a head injury. He is still in the emergency operating room. We'll let you know as soon as he's up in the Intensive Care Unit. Meanwhile, please wait here."

She led us into a small, private room off the main ER waiting room. It held a sofa, two armchairs, and a little table with a lamp and a telephone on it. The lamplight was low, lending a soft, but solemn air to the little room, especially in comparison to the bright white light of the main ER waiting room, a light that pushed itself through the window in the door of our little room, a harsh outer brightness which contrasted with our inner dusk. When she left us and I looked out on to the floor where little knots of people buzzed around their own victims – those with swollen ankles or bits of bloody rags stuck to various bodily locations, the ordinary cuts and bruises of everyday life – when I realized we had been sequestered from these people, I began to understand something dreadful had really happened, and it had happened to Tom.

"This isn't good, this little room," I said to Chuck. It was easy to picture a kindly doctor, talking softly on the upholstered chair, breaking the bad news to the family. How much grief had this small sofa seen? How many trembling hands had reached out to that telephone? How many families walked into the little room from one life, and walked out of it into another?

If you're ever given a sofa to sit on instead of a plastic chair, chances are you won't be getting up to dance. Trust me.

To pass time until I found out what dreadful thing had happened and to hold onto a piece of sanity before it eroded completely, I decided to make some phone calls and begin the dissemination of this horrible news, to thin it out by spreading it around so it wouldn't rest solely with me.

First, I called a colleague from school to tell her I would not be in tomorrow. It was already nine o'clock and I had no idea what kind of night was ahead. Even in the best possible scenario where Tom might have a gash across the forehead and a couple of broken limbs and could be left to the hospital's care, I would not be ready to go to school in the morning. I had no car, for one thing and the evening's drama had already exhausted me. Surely I deserved a day to rest after all this. But we did not know if we would be presented with my best-case scenario.

Tom's mother Helen had just driven up to North Jersey in the afternoon to stay a few days with her daughter, Pat, to help her prepare for a big family birthday party on Sunday. For a while I hesitated calling them. I had so little information. It was difficult to know whether they ought to drive down or wait. I briefly considered putting off the call until there was something more concrete to tell them. However, the solemnity of the little room convinced me to make the call. Because both Pat and Helen were nurses, I was sure they would have more technical questions than I could answer, therefore, when Pat picked up, I asked to speak to Dennis, her husband, and I gave him the news.

Doctor Sori from the trauma team arrived in our waiting room and explained a bit of what had transpired. I heard "massive brain damage... closed head injury...no need yet to operate...ICU..." None of it made sense. The doctor seemed calm and serious, but I was having trouble relating what he was saying to the Tom I knew. This man was speaking to me so earnestly, telling me words that could not possibly pertain to us, using unfamiliar terminology. I felt instinctively that I ought to be polite because he was so sincere, and all this information was obviously important to him, yet I listened as I might to a well-intentioned uncle who had what he believed to be useful advice for me, while all the time, inside, I was replying, *But you don't understand. We're different; this isn't Tom you're talking about. This is what happens to Other People, not us. You've got the wrong party here.*

Having explained the situation to me, or so he must have believed, Dr. Sori left. We waited until Tom had been brought up to the Intensive Care Unit, and then we went up to see him.

You know what I expected. You've seen the movies. You hear "head injury" or "brain damage" and you think turban, right? I expected Tom to look something like a mummy with bandages swathed around his head like a fat headdress, with two little eye slits cut out. The least I thought we would see was a gauze cap over his hair. Wouldn't you think the same thing?

So, as soon as I saw Tom in the ICU, my spirits soared. I thought, *They've made a mistake! There's nothing wrong with him!*

There was Tom without a scratch, not so much as a Band-Aid. No cuts, no bruises. True, he was in a coma, and he was hooked up to about a dozen machines. Tubes were going in and out of every part of his body. He was on a respirator. But he was here, up in the ICU, not dead, and he looked fine. How hurt could he be?

I thanked Chuck and sent him home. There did not seem to be any danger here, nothing I couldn't handle. The hospital had it all under control and Tom looked great. I was immensely relieved.

Now all I had to do was wait for the scene where the comatose person wakes up and says, "Get all this stuff off me and let's go home."

Looking back now, I suppose my reaction upon seeing Tom in the ICU was naïve and a measure of my ignorance. Maybe it was also a protective device, a kind of psychological armor that fell automatically into place to shield me from the true horror of the situation. Whatever the reason, the reaction sustained and supported me through what was to come, possibly too well. When I finally faced reality, it was enormously overwhelming. I had been perhaps too naïve, too ignorant, too well-protected.

Dr. Becker, another member of the trauma team, came in to see me. He explained that this was a closed-head injury. The CAT scan had revealed a subdural hematoma. So far there was no need to operate, but an additional CAT scan the following morning would help the team make a more informed determination. I asked no questions. The situation did not seem critical to me. I assumed they would have told me had it been otherwise. Besides, in the presence of all the complicated machinery, the tubes, the light, the gauges, I felt intimidated. The hospital was in charge. The impression I had was that they knew what they were doing and I was satisfied to let them do it. Besides, how badly hurt could he be? There wasn't a scratch, not a Band-Aid.

I think this might be a good time to tell you that I deliberately did not choose medicine as a career. While I have nothing but admiration for those who did, I always knew I was constitutionally unable to enter the field. Let's just say the "yuck factor" discouraged me. Therefore, I approached this situation as a bystander. My trust was in the doctors, the technicians, and their machinery. There was no foundation in my background knowledge from which to draw intelligent questions or form meaningful conclusions. Apart from having earned my Girl Scout Home Nursing Badge eons ago, I had no medical skills whatsoever. (I can, however, create a nifty pair of emergency slippers out of newspaper and fashion a dirty-tissue receptacle to hang off the bed. That's about it, sickroom wise.)

I vaguely recalled having read something rather recently indicating that, contrary to traditional belief, brain cells do regenerate; a brain injury did not necessarily mean the death of the brain. New pathways might be formed to replace the damaged ones. And there was Tom looking so good. I was sure his brain cells were already getting back into action. I felt very optimistic, under the circumstances. I did not know how ignorant I was.

Later, Tom's mother arrived with Dennis. They had left right after the phone call. My nephew Danny Radel came for a while; Tom's sister Andrea and her husband Joey Kiernan came. There was little any of us could do but stand and stare at Tom and his machinery. As a former ER nurse, Helen understood the equipment and she looked distressed. We all stood around and worried – except me, who was certain everything was going to be fine. Eventually they all went home to worry separately. I had decided to stay one night in the hospital because the part of my mind that was remotely in touch with reality sensed this was a critical time. Also I knew I would not be able to sleep. Besides, I had no car.

The night was spent chiefly in pacing. I formed a nodding acquaintance with members of other families who were also spending the night on the unit. Like flotsam, we were washed up on the shore – Jersey Shore, in this case – dazed and stunned by the circumstances that had carried us there. We wandered the halls, each of us wrapped in a cloak of silence, still too shell-shocked from our own private tragedies to communicate with each other.

The nurses either wanted me off the floor for a while - I imagine I annoyed them with my incessant circling the ward — or they took pity on me, and somewhere in the early hours of morning they let me in on the secret existence of the private hospital dining room, strictly off-limits to visitors. Down there, in a vast room with a sparse population, I had a cup of coffee at two or three o'clock. The room was forlorn, with clusters of wooden tables and chairs, each set of which looked as if it had been hastily abandoned when the diners dashed off to save lives. I felt very isolated and lonely, still numb, still cocooned. At six, when the public coffee shop opened down on the first floor, I had coffee and toast. All the while I tried not to think, just to wait. To stay numb. At seven-thirty Friday morning I retrieved a little note pad from my purse and began my journal:

> Comatose or unconscious...What is he thinking? ...And what happened? I still don't know. Was here all night, pacing...Bill? ...The doctor this morning says he's not getting worse, which is a good sign... All his plans, his hopes, Idaho...I want to say something, be brave, but I haven't the strength or whatever it takes to keep my voice from breaking and the tears from running...

A crazy jumble of thoughts tumbled through my mind.

Picture yourself sitting in front of a front-loading clothes dryer, the kind with the round glass window. All the clothes are tumbling around together in a big, wet mass, all tangled. Then the red shirt passes before the window and you see it and recognize it and then it's gone and the blue denim shorts whiz by. Then the green dish towel – you have a momentary awareness of each thing and quickly it's supplanted by something else. That's how my mind was working. Serious thoughts tumbled through: An awareness this was probably the most important thing that ever did or ever would happen to us flashed by along with trivial thoughts, the least of which was, would I be able to maintain my diet, through which I had recently lost twenty-five pounds, during whatever was to come? Let's not strain the dryer metaphor, but do let me say it was a long, long time before I was able to sort out that particular load of laundry!

CHAPTER 3

DECEMBER 3 - 5

In the beginning, there were things to do. On Friday over a dozen friends and family members stopped by throughout the day to look at Tom and comfort me. None of us knew yet what had happened.

My sister Paula came. Standing by his bed, she said, "This is a nightmare." That was the right word for the moment: nightmare. It was a dream, a bad dream, but just a dream and one awakens from a dream.

Remembering the purpose of Tom's trip to the supermarket, she wagged her finger at him and said, "You see, salami *is* bad for you!"

Threading in and out among our visitors were the staff – the doctors, nurses and technicians who dealt with Tom's machinery and bodily functions. I learned there was no change in his condition, but no worsening, either. CAT scans revealed the swelling had gone down. His eyes, when held open, were tracking light. There were no more abnormal muscular contractions.

These were good signs. However, he still could not open his eyes on his own, nor respond to our requests to squeeze our hands, lift a finger, blink, give us a sign.

I had heard that sometimes after people awakened from a coma they reported they had been able to hear everything anyone said to them while comatose, but they had been unable to reply. Accordingly, I stationed myself beside Tom as much as I could and repeated, "Tom, you're going to be fine. You've been in a car accident and you're in a hospital now, but you will be fine."

How many times did I say that over the next month? Maybe a million. At least my little recital convinced *me* that all would be well.

A small coterie of helpers paraded by and introduced themselves; their names and functions blurred in my mind. Among them were a social worker, an insurance representative, a rehab director – all would come and go within the next month, some before I'd ever sorted out what purpose they served, and others who became very helpful, indeed.

I said to Dr. Becker, "We have a son at school in Idaho. Should I send for him?"

"You're asking me if your husband is going to live or die," Dr. Becker replied. "I can't answer that. I can only tell you that if it were me, I'd have him here."

A most sobering response. Apparently Dr. Becker did not share my optimism that in the absence of even a Band-Aid, Tom would be fine. His suggestion that I contact Bill was the most serious – and depressing – intimation we'd had thus far that all might not be quite as fine as I wanted to believe.

Reaching Bill at the University of Idaho in Moscow was a complicated affair, taking into account his class schedule, the time difference, and the probability of locating him while ticket agents were still open for business. This was Bill's freshman year in college, his first semester. Ever since we dropped him off in August, I had been fully prepared to work up a mighty anxiety attack over his flight home at Christmas. It would be the first time he had traveled such a distance by himself and like any mother, I planned to be nervous and fidgety until he landed safely. Now, after Tom's devastating car accident only blocks from our house, I realized it was futile to worry about Bill. He would probably – and statistically – be safer than Tom had been.

It was a very good thing I changed my thinking, because I did not learn until he told me years later that the only way he could get home in a hurry at the last minute involved a series of four separate flights: Spokane to Salt Lake, to California, to Chicago, and finally to Newark!

Paula drove me home Friday night. I spent most of the evening answering phone calls and marching around the house saying, "He's going to be fine; he's going to be fine." I told the callers, I told the furniture and I told myself.

On Saturday we had sixteen visitors at the ICU and nineteen on Sunday – an outpouring of concern from family and friends. Probably the only reason such crowds were allowed to visit was that the hospital nursing staff had just gone on strike. Tom, who was always deeply interested in the history of the labor unions, and who had been a strike captain himself when salary negotiations with the Board of Education broke down several years earlier, would have been excited had he known. Although some wards at the hospital were put on limited occupancy, and some patients were shuttled to other facilities, the ICU remained intact, staffed by teams of replacement nurses formed from a national pool. I saluted the strikers daily as I drove in, for Tom's sake, but I was also supportive of the temporary staff. I don't

31

know if I could have mustered enthusiasm equal to Tom's for striking workers had we been removed to the trauma center across the state from us in Camden, or handed off to another, less-equipped hospital.

Our brother-in-law Joey Kiernan picked up Bill at the airport. The poor child was exhausted from the journey and his anxiety, but I was happy to have him home.

Bill was becoming a delightful young man. Tall and handsome, witty and charming, a thoroughly pleasant person. I had no idea what effect this devastating situation would have on him. He seemed to take it in stride, but I suspect now that he was being brave for me. Through the years Bill has developed an almost Zen-like level temperament; he has the ability to see through situations that panic me, and to find the right words, the simplest solution. On that Saturday, however, many of those talents were still inchoate; he was an exhausted, confused boy trying his best to be brave and strong.

Many of our visitors thought Tom looked much better than they'd expected. They, too, had been anticipating a mummy wrap, bruises, traction bars, swelling – more serious outward signs. I guess we all had seen the same movies.

On Saturday, we finally learned what had happened to Tom. It was a blindingly simple, annoyingly stupid accident. There was neither drama nor heroics involved, just human error of the sort Tom worked all his life to prevent. "Better to err on the side of caution," was his personal creed; he raised our son on the same premise. And now someone else's stupid, incautious error had done Tom in. It was so unjust.

Tom had been stopped at a red light in my little Toyota, the second car in line. A driver coming along behind him in a large Blazer had seen the light, planned to stop, but applied his foot to the accelerator instead of the brake. When his vehicle failed to slow down, he thought his brakes had failed, and so pressed harder on the pedal. He plowed into Tom at high speed, compressing the Toyota's trunk and back seat; its own force caused the Blazer to turn upside-down. Meanwhile, Tom's car and the one ahead were both propelled across the intersection. The first car came to rest safely on the other side. Tom's car was shot out into the highway, where he was struck again by a vehicle traveling with the green light. Traffic immediately stopped, snarled, but an ambulance arrived quickly. The EMTs freed Tom and took him to Paul Kimball's helicopter pad, from where he was immediately flown to the trauma center at Jersey Shore. All the other participants were treated and released at Paul Kimball.

This is how it always happens, I know that. This is how, in a cool instant, lives are transformed. This is why religions and philosophies rise and fall, and this is how we learn that life was never designed to be fair. At the time, reading the newspaper account of the accident published on Saturday, I was overcome not with anger, but with a sense of weakness, of frustration, of the poor fragility of human beings. And yes, of the injustice and irony of this particular accident brought about by carelessness and stupidity, having happened to Tom, a model of careful intelligence.

In *The Open Boat,* Stephen Crane describes human helplessness in terms of the victim's desire to "throw bricks at the temple" followed by the hopeless realization that there are no bricks and there is no temple. That's where I was: no bricks and no temple.

On Saturday night I wrote in the journal:

How awful it was to come home and find his things where he left them, so normal... But worst of all was leaving him. He looks so forlorn, and lonely and miserable... I wanted to stay but I'm of no use, and exhausted... I hurt for him so... I'm so scared...

We saw a few changes on Sunday. Tom seemed to be struggling to open his eyes. His left hand roamed over his stomach and his face scrunched up as if in response to some discomfort. He began to look a little better, more like a sleeping person than a comatose one. The physicians described it as "lighter."

The various family members of the serious, long-term ICU patients began to form a little community. We were the all-day people; we got to know each other and each other's tragedies. We took telephone messages for one another on the phone in the waiting room. We comforted and encouraged each other. We learned that nearly every patient on the ward got there through the simple process of everyday living as Tom had. A Christmas shopping trip resulted in an irreversible coma for one woman; an outing to get pizza made a quadriplegic out of a vibrant young man. Tom's salami and cheese adventure was typical. Who ever thought ordinary life could be so tough?

Even out in Idaho, little dramas were unfolding for our benefit. Bill had notified a few family friends before he left, and from there the word spread. Lane and Verna, two of the most determined people on earth, called us.

Calling from Pocatello, they reached Paul Kimball and were

then directed to Jersey Shore. After a bit of verbal meandering through various locations within the hospital, they were put through to the phone in the ICU waiting room, and of all the people in the room, perhaps twenty-five in number, Tom's sister Andrea picked up the phone!

On Sunday there was a great deal of poking and prodding at Tom on the part of his technicians. Just about every tube was pulled, replaced, or put somewhere else. We were asked to be out of the room more than we could be in it. Bill was exhausted. He'd had no sleep from Friday, when he received our message, through nearly all of Saturday, and Saturday night a group of his friends had taken him out to the diner. He made up for his lack of sleep by stretching out beneath some chairs in the vestibule outside the ICU. No one objected, although I occasionally kicked him when he snored.

Dr. Becker, who seemed to speak wholly in metaphors, told me about Tom's condition. "Picture a shoe, just one shoe, inside a shoebox. Now, picture the shoebox kicked forcefully across the floor and slammed into a wall. What would happen to the shoe?"

"I guess it would get pretty tossed around inside the box," I said.

"Exactly! That shoe is the brain and the box is the head. Through all the motion of the accident, the brain gets kicked around inside the head, hitting all sides, and hard. That's what happened to Tom."

"But what does that mean?" I asked. It was a colorful analogy but what I needed to know was the extent of the damage. Could the shoe be worn again?

"We can't say yet. With a heart attack, we talk about days; with a stroke, weeks. With brain injury, we talk about trimesters."

"So it's going to be a long time."

"Yes, a long time," he answered. "And it's not a straight-line recovery. With brain injury you may have progress, then a plateau where nothing seems to be happening. You can even have regression. But then there will be a little more progress, and the whole process begins again. It's slow and it's not straight-line."

What Dr. Becker never told me, perhaps because he couldn't know at the time, was that it would also not necessarily be a full recovery. To my naïve way of thinking, the word "recovery" meant a complete restoration to the state of health that existed prior to the accident. I was prepared to put in the time, and to deal with the plateaus and the regressions if recovery, as I understood the term, was ahead. This assumption, added to the appearance of normality and the absence of bandages or bruises on his body, led me to believe that one day Tom would be returned to us as he had been. The shoe would be wearable! Accordingly, I began to write my journal in the second person, thinking Tom would enjoy reading it someday. I imagined he'd get a kick out of his own history:

You moved your arms today; you tried to open your eyes.

If the nightmare had ended, the deep sleep had begun. It would be years before I woke up. Tom woke up before I did.

Dr. Becker explained the necessity for removing and replacing Tom's tubing in another of his metaphors: "Those plastic tubes are like condominiums for bacteria," he said. "Those little bacteria come out, they gather together, they build houses, set out the picnic tables, put on the barbecues. They have a ball in there."

Metaphorically, Tom's body was a huge block party for bacteria; it was a cheerful image, nonetheless. At least somebody was enjoying this, even if it was a village of bacteria.

Because I felt optimistic about Tom, my heart broke for the young boy two doors down in the ICU, and for Norman and Elaine, his parents, and Robin, his girlfriend. Clark had been thrown from the passenger seat of the car Robin was driving when she took a sharp left turn. They were just going out for pizza. Clark had been put on a new medication when he was admitted to Jersey Shore, but because it was experimental, he might have been given the placebo. Even Dr. Becker did not know. Norman and Elaine, one an engineer and the other a chemist, used contacts in the industry to have the actual drug flown in from Switzerland, but there were delays in the delivery, hold-ups at the airport.

At one point I asked Norman if the drug had arrived. "It doesn't matter," he said. "His body is shutting down."

We all cried together for Clark. Norman, however, through all his misery, had nothing but praise for Dr. Becker. "The man's a genius!" he said. Dr. Becker was also a mechanical engineer who designed some of the equipment in use at the hospital. But, despite the best knowledge and the best equipment, Clark was not doing well. Mrs. Peterson across the hall was not coming out of her coma. We all suffered for each other, but I almost felt guilty. These people had serious, irreversible situations. We, on the other hand, had a temporary set-back in life that eventually would straighten itself out.

I was the walking, talking example of Ignorance is Bliss. I should have had it tattooed on my forehead. Time and work were needed, but we had plenty of time and we had always worked.

Hadn't Dr. Becker, the great man himself, used the word "recovery"? After all, this was still Tom, wasn't it?

Sunday night I wrote:

Please, Tom, fight to get out of this.

The longest weekend of our lives had passed, and with it a way of life we had shared for over twenty years, and a future we had planned and worked for during all those years.

There is a saying: "When you want to make the gods laugh, make plans."

The gods must have been howling that weekend.

CHAPTER 4

DECEMBER 6 – 11

T om was the star attraction in the ICU. Happily for us, the nurses' strike continued, which meant there was not enough replacement personnel to supervise the waiting room and that worked to our advantage. Tom had floods of visitors. An average of twenty people a day trooped in and out to look at him, and the phone in the waiting room rang for us throughout the day. Had we been able to sell tickets, this might have turned into quite a profitable venture, even though the show itself was not very moving – literally!

I wrote the names of all the visitors in my journal, knowing that one day Tom, who was a little bit of a ham, would be pleased to see how much attention he was getting.

Certain patterns began to emerge that would continue for the following six months as Tom traveled from hospital to hospital. Our good friends Rich and Susan MacFarland came nearly every day. Bernie and Roz Ressner were with us very frequently. My cousin Barbara and her partner, Tracy, came every Sunday, if not more often, and took me out to dinner. Family members were there constantly; my mother and Tom's mother came daily. The wedding and funeral crowd, every day.

I was a hostess who did not have to clean the house or prepare food, but still got to enjoy the company of family and friends. Dare I admit it was even pleasant? But please remember I was under the impression everything would soon be well, with Tom restored to us as his former self. We would both go back to work, share some good thoughts about all people who showed so much concern, and life would go on. I told anyone who would listen that I was certain he would return to school in September, and they were kind enough not to contradict me.

Friends from the high school worked up some wonderful food baskets for Bill and me. Who knows how this ever came up in conversation, but at some time in my life I must have mentioned to someone that Lorna Doone and Vienna Fingers were my favorite cookies; boxes of each showed up in every basket. Bill and I appreciated the food; however we fell into some pretty bad eating habits – grabbing snacks in the hospital coffee shop and raiding the food baskets at home. Need I mention the havoc this irregular eating pattern played with the diet I was trying to maintain? Lorna Doone, that lusty temptress, did me in. Over the next few years, all the lost weight came back. I wished I could be one of those people for whom adversity equaled emaciation. Elizabeth Taylor said she could only lose weight when she was happy. Me, too, Liz!

At this time, our confidence (and ignorance) grew. We insisted we saw progress; we had great hopes for Tom's recovery. And no one said a word otherwise.

As much as I appreciated concern, what I certainly didn't need were little melodramas such as one, among several similar events, enacted on a particular evening when a friend arrived to see Tom. As soon as she entered Tom's room, I left. She believed herself to be very spiritual, propelled by her own faith and beliefs and comfortable with "the other side". I believed her to be bound up in crippling superstition. I knew a "miracle" would take place that evening and frankly, I did not want to be there to witness it.

Sure enough, a few minutes later she returned to the waiting room, glowing with satisfaction. "You'll never guess what happened," she said.

"Tell me," But I knew. There had been a miracle.

"I was just talking to Tom, just telling him how much I loved him, and much God loved him, and how we all wanted him back, and I was holding his hand. I just know he heard me. He had a little smile for me."

Okay – he didn't rise up and walk, but she believed it was a miracle and I was pleased for her, as I was for all of those who took reassurance in this way. But, I ask you – he didn't smile for his mother, or his wife, or his son, but for her he was going to smile? If he grimaced at all, it was probably gas. However, I learned many people needed to create their own reality when dealing with Tom. What I never understood at the time was how I was doing the same thing.

There's a novel or at least a white paper here. Does the comatose patient, through his very presence at the brink of life and death, force out of us some inner, basic persona that lives within our beings, yet remains below the surface until brought out to confront the edge of existence? Is that persona our real self? Is the coma victim but a catalyst, a tool, whose function is to force us to see ourselves as we really are? An intriguing point, but not one I pursued.

On Monday, the nurse who had been on duty through the

night, and the doctor, and yesterday's nurse all spoke of Tom as looking lighter, less deep in the coma. We were thrilled, but unfortunately not everyone in the unit was doing as well. I saw Norman outside Clark's room, his arms leaning against the wall and his face buried in his hands. I thought his son had died.

"Norman," I said, running to him and hugging him.

"They want to pull the plug," he said. He was teary and the words were soft and sad. "They want to turn off the machines."

"What did you tell them?"

"To keep the machines running. My brother and I are both engineers. I told Dr. Becker to design whatever machinery he needs, and we'll make it."

"And?"

He just shook his head, and walked away.

Considering that, it seemed almost trivial to notice the issue with Tom's right arm. It did nothing and seemed not to want to do anything. But − the left was squeezing tighter than ever and moving around, and the fingers were even gripping the side railing of the bed. Best of all, Tom finally opened his eyes! These were little things, but very important to us. We still did not have the movie moment when the patient suddenly sits up and begins remembering everything, but we were inching closer.

Bill went to the junkyard to see the car, where it was referred to as "the accordion." He found the sight of it very upsetting. I was not yet ready to see it. Eventually, I caught a glimpse of it after it had been hauled off to our lawyer's driveway. It was covered in a bright blue tarp and I could tell the vehicle was two-thirds of its regular size. That was enough for me.

We were constantly exhausted. The strain of our own problem was overwhelming, and we were surrounded in the ICU by other people and their problems. It was a great deal to carry.

Helen seemed overwrought, brought down by her projections of Tom's prognosis based upon her familiarity with the machinery and the terminology. She offset her apprehension by attending Mass every day.

In Monday's journal I wrote:

I like all the little signs and I think we're on the way up. I really do.

Love can be expressed in so many ways. Many of our friends chose food. There were all those goody baskets from the high school. Two roasted chickens and a monstrous tray of baked ziti appeared at home, waiting for us on the deck. A colleague made a batch of pierogies. The Ressners bought Bill two huge Jersey Mike's subs, the Kirschners brought chicken and salad and cookies. The refrigerator was full.

Huge manila envelopes from the children at Tom's school were brought in. My favorite was a simple message from a young girl:

Dear Mr. Sorrentino
It was sad, but
get over it.

I posted that one in every hospital room Tom occupied for the next six months. How refreshing was the child's simple faith that we could overcome any difficulty by just making ourselves "get over it."

On Tuesday Tom had a tracheotomy, which was to help

prevent the incipient pneumonia from getting worse. Rich MacFarland kept a vigil by the bed, watching the monitors, watching Tom's movements, talking to him. And, while I don't mean to imply that she was nervous, Helen occupied herself by dusting the machines!

From Tuesday's journal:

> *We all love you so much and it hurts so much to see you so helpless; I know this is not your style. Keep on keeping on.*

What excitement on Wednesday! Tom was breathing almost entirely on his own. The respirator moved along from "Mandatory" to "Assist" to "Spontaneous." It was a great step for us, but it made us feel even sadder for Mrs. Peterson's family; she was still deep in her coma, evidencing no lightening at all.

Tom's left hand continued to explore, to move, to grasp, but there was still no spontaneous movement from the right side. Since Tom was left-handed, I was pleased to see he was gaining some control of his dominant hand.

I had a few bad moments at home sitting at his desk. Everything was still as he'd left it, all very organized and efficient. His checkbook was missing and I mentioned it to him several times. I figured if anything could snap him out of the coma, his missing money would be the thing to do it. My bad moment passed, because I wrote:

> *I know you're going to come out of this soon...*

Robert, the nurse, called me at home at eight o'clock in the morning on Thursday, one week after the accident. I gasped as soon as he identified himself. He must have heard me because he immediately said, "It's good news, don't worry."

"What is it?" My mind soared from despair to a vision of Tom up, out of bed, and demanding to be sent home.

"He opened his eyes again, and kept them open for a short time."

"He did? He really did?"

"Yes. He opened them, looked around, then closed them."

"That's a good sign, isn't it?"

"Yes, it is."

How many people can you call at eight in the morning to tell that your husband opened his eyes? Many – and I did!

We had even more excitement later in the day. Tom's left hand became very active, grasping tighter and reaching higher than before. Some people thought he was searching for a hand to hold (the romantics) and others believed his hand motions were random (the pragmatists). There were latent philosophers constantly emerging around Tom's bed.

Tom was placed in a chair! True, it was more of a cruise ship lounge chair, but still, a chair. I was buoyed by his progress. In addition, color seemed to be returning to his face; the ashen pallor was now tinged with a little ruddiness. Even for Clark it was a better day. His family spread a Hanukah table in the waiting room for all of us. Optimism was in the air. That night's entry:

This was a great day for us, Tom. You made tremendous strides and we all feel confident and optimistic. All of us except the very conservative doctors. They want measurable functions from the machinery; we are content with the flutter of an eyelid or the squeeze of a hand...It's been a real up day and as usual I'm exhausted, but also excited to see what tomorrow will bring.

Apparently there had been unspoken caution, even as early as a week after the accident, but I refused to acknowledge it. I did not know what kind of questions to ask; maybe once we knew he would survive, I simply assumed recovery, a full restoration of the former Tom, would soon follow. I might have been afraid to know more, but I don't think that was the case. A week after the accident I know I was excited and optimistic; I believed Tom would be back in school by the following September. As it turned out, I was just about as out of touch with reality as Tom was, but no one was monitoring me.

Friday was a day of wild excitement. For three different periods of about forty minutes each, Tom opened his eyes and kept them open. The first time, he seemed a little scared; his eyes were flying up, down and to the left – but not to the right. He seemed to be surveying his situation. We kept talking to him, telling him it was all going to be all right, and explaining what had happened. In those early days I must have said over a thousand times, "You're fine, Tom. You're going to be fine. You were in a car accident and now you're in the hospital, but you will be all right." It was a mantra I repeated constantly, although I had no indication Tom could hear or understand it.

I had not yet returned to school, but the school was coming to me in bits and pieces through visitors, cards, and phone calls. I taught art in a small school for emotionally disturbed youngsters.

Some of our children had been treated quite roughly by life; most of them learned to give back the kind of treatment they'd received, which led to the type of uncontrolled behavior that resulted in placement in our school. Those who did not act out often retreated into special worlds of their own, also necessitating removal from the public school systems. Few of these youngsters were free enough from their own injuries to show any interest in the injuries of others, therefore I was surprised and pleased when three of them appeared on Friday afternoon. They all lived near the hospital and had walked over.

The interesting thing about their visit was that these three, each of whom was easily – and often – capable of disrupting the entire school, now hung back in the doorway of Tom's room. This was a lot bigger than they'd expected. They showed remarkable restraint and patience. I think they finally found something they couldn't face down.

I hugged them all. "I'm so happy you came," I told them. "Don't be afraid. He's wrapped up in a lot of machinery now, but he's going to be fine, eventually. Some of his tubes have even been removed. You should have seen him last week."

After a few nearly catatonic minutes in the door frame, Henry mustered up his courage and asked, "Can I see him?"

"Of course, Henry." I kept my arm around his shoulders and led him up to the bed. Henry stood there for a few minutes, looked at Tom, at the tubes and machines, and, for the first time since I'd known him, was absolutely quiet. He backed away.

"Sholanda?" I asked. Sholanda was one of many students who found refuge in the art room just about every day. She could be difficult, but we had moments when we connected, and I took a special interest in her. On this day she remained in the doorway. "I'm okay from here," she said.

47

Josh, the third student, looked like a choirboy but was often the devil itself. He hung around after the other two children left, alternating between visits to the ICU and his grandfather on another floor. Josh was in the room one of the times Tom opened his eyes.

"Josh," I said, "Tom's mother is in the hospital chapel. Do you think you can find it and bring her up here while he still has his eyes open?"

"Sure!" and he was off. I had no idea where the chapel was, but I have an abiding faith in eleven-year-old boys .

A few minutes later they appeared while Tom's eyes were still open. "You won't believe this," Helen said, "but Tom opened his eyes while I was praying for him."

I was happy for her. This little miracle justified her faith in prayer.

Each time Tom opened his eyes, he seemed less frightened and more interested in focusing in the direction of voices. The effort exhausted him and he slept for a while following every attempt.

The medicine tube positioned in his mouth since the accident was taken away. Following its removal, Tom celebrated with some mouth and tongue exercising, as if to be sure the nasty thing was really gone.

Roz Gertner, the retired chairman of the high school History Department where Tom started his teaching career, came to see him. She and her husband David sat in stunned silence. They had endured overwhelming personal tragedies in their own lives, the deaths of both of their children, and truly understood the range of emotions we felt.

"Tom is the talk of the town," Roz told me. "Wherever I go, people are asking about him."

"So many people know him," I said, "or know the family. He has five brothers and sisters, his father worked for the church and his mother was a nurse at Paul Kimball. So he's well known."

"It's more than that," she said. "He's well loved."

There was much hugging and happiness in the unit on Clark's behalf; he had a good day. I was really happy, especially for his parents; they invested everything in this. The miracle drug made in Italy and shipped from Switzerland may have helped – his pancreas was now working. Norman told me he prayed and didn't question the whys and wherefores. We were all pulling for Clark.

There was a kind of balance in the ICU on Friday. To offset Tom's and Clark's progress, there were two deaths. One of them was an elderly man, a heart attack patient, whose daughter had been living in the unit for the past three weeks. She became very attached to Clark and his family, and they to her. After we all consoled her, Norman took me aside, tears in his eyes as he spoke. "I have to tell you," he said, "because it's hard to know how to feel about this."

I understood. Over the days as those of us on the unit became a family of our own, we had developed an unspoken form of communication. We said things on the surface, we went through motions but our deepest thoughts and most expressive words were tacit. I think it's perhaps because they were so tender that we could not bear to release them, to subject them to the rigors of life in the spoken world.

"Mary Ann just told me," Norman continued, "that she, too, had prayed for her father. But she asked God that if it came to a choice between her father and Clark, to take her father." Norman shook his head in bewilderment.

This ICU was no place for the faint-hearted, in or out of the beds.

Also on Friday, Tom's brother Joe, Bill and I met with a lawyer. The insurance companies were all in motion. Plans were being laid for rehabilitation. Various representatives came to see me or Tom, to leave information with us. The technical aspects of Tom's accident were moving along in a sphere of their own, a parallel existence that occasionally touched our own.

The parents of Bill's best friend invited us to dinner Friday night. I was almost too exhausted to eat. All the good news was every bit as tiring as the depressing days.

That night, I entered a thought for Tom to consider when he was able to read the journal.

> How can we leave all these good people, Tom? When it's time to retire to Idaho and to wander. I wonder whether we're going to be able to do it. Such a surround of love and care and good wishes and support - can we walk away from that?

My general optimism regarding his recovery was still in high gear, as I wrote to Tom, also in Friday's entry.

> People talk about a long road ahead, Tom, but you know what? I think you're going to fool them. I think you're going to pull out of this faster than they expect - I really do!

On Saturday, some little tendrils of reality crept into my day. I did laundry and because Bill had not brought many clothes home and needed more, I had to go to the bank for money. Because Tom had always overseen our finances I had not done any banking in over twenty years, which suited me just fine.

To get to the bank, I had to drive Tom's big Blazer – in the rain. But I did it, to my own amazement. At the bank I sat myself down at one of the desks and explained to the lady behind it, "My husband is in a coma and I haven't done any banking in twenty years. I need help."

She said, "Is he the teacher?"

We were off. She knew who Tom was, she knew all about the accident, and she handled all the banking for me.

After Tom's performance the previous day, I expected him to rise up and walk on Saturday, therefore I was a little troubled to find him in a sound sleep when we arrived at the hospital. I found a nurse and asked if he was all right.

"Don't worry," she told me. "It's quite normal for the brain to need long stretches of time to heal after exertion, especially such vigorous exertion as he experienced yesterday with those three long awake periods."

"Thank you," I replied, greatly relieved. "I really was worried. I guess I expected more of the same from him today."

"Sleep is important," she said. "Healing takes place during sleep."

No drama that day, but no cause for alarm, either.

As usual, I spent a good bit of time at Tom's bedside, telling him over and over about his situation. I guess I thought it would permeate his sleep like those language tapes people put under their pillows. Or possibly the sheer boredom of hearing me repeat the same stuff endlessly would prompt him to wake up if only to tell me, "Enough already. I got it."

"You shouldn't tell him about the accident," my mother said.

"You might upset him."

But he didn't ever look upset. My thinking was that if he could hear me and understand me, I wanted him to know what was going on around him, and not be frightened by it. As it turned out, Tom was not the coma patient you hear about occasionally, the one who later says, "I heard everything that was said; I just couldn't answer." Nor was he the coma patient in the movies who wakes up one day, sees and understands everything around him, and speaks full sentences.

Tom's mother was at the hospital most of every day. She assisted the nurse and an aide in bathing and shaving him. She was there for the Oak Street School Christmas Assault, which took place one afternoon. A local family, the Parkhursts, descended upon us carrying boxes and bags of cheer made by all the children at Oak Street, Tom's school. There were folders upon folders of letters and cards; there were huge posters made by the kids, and boxes of hand-made decorations for a Christmas tree.

"We wanted to bring a tree in," Mrs. Parkhurst explained, "but they stopped us down in the lobby. So we have a hundred decorations but no tree."

"But we do have a tree!" That was me. "There's a naked tree in the ICU vestibule! The nurses put up the tree before they went out on strike, and it's just been sitting there. You can decorate that."

"Shouldn't we ask Patient Representation?" That was Helen. She probably knew best, based on her own extensive hospital experience, but we didn't ask anyone for fear they might refuse us. We were, after all, just decorating a tree, not commandeering the OR for personal experimentation.

The Parkhursts put up dozens of hand-made ornaments from

every class in the school. The tree looked terrific and the nurses were thrilled. They said it was the best tree they'd ever had. Moreover, they told us that when Tom was moved to another ward, the tree had to stay.

In Tom's journal, I told him:

The cards are darling - so much love and caring, so honestly expressed. You'll really enjoy them when you are able to, and I think you'll be very impressed with how much the children love you.

At this point we were nine days into our adventure. Nine days during which the sun had risen and set, the tides had ebbed and flowed, the earth had spun and the people in the world had things to do. We were aware of none of this. The axis of our world was situated in a hospital room; our lives rotated around it. This was all we knew of life. The past had disappeared and the future seemed, despite all the optimism we could muster, very much uncertain.

PART II
STEPPING UP TO THE STEP-DOWN

*Life is what happens when you are
making other plans*

– John Lennon

CHAPTER 5

DECEMBER 12 – 29, 1993

Many people told us they were praying for Tom. Tom's name was popping up on prayer lists in churches all over town. I wanted to consider this because I do not pray and I was little enough in touch with reality, let alone harboring any inclination to go beyond. But many family members and friends thought it important to tell me they were praying for him, and I respected those people.

I understood these people prayed because they felt they were helping by doing so. Certainly, there was little else anyone could do.

Dozens of studies have demonstrated that there is little difference in terms of recovery between those people for whom prayers are said, and those for whom no one prayed. Yes, I am aware that for every such study, another will be brought forward claiming just the opposite. To those who believe in helpful prayers, I pose this question: What sort of theoretically all-good

God would deliberately choose not to heal certain people simply because they have no one to pray for them?

Further, I really wanted to ask the pray-ers: Where was God when this happened to Tom?

This led to the development of my concept of God-as-the-Neighborhood-Bully:

God is the toughest kid on the block, the one with all the power. He comes along, knocks you down, sits on you, pounds your head into the sidewalk, and then keeps you down while you beg for mercy.

No doubt religious people have a different explanation. For me, it was more practical not to bring God into the situation at all. After all, if God is supposed to be running everything, then he knew about the accident, knew it would happen, and allowed it to happen. And to Tom, of all people. Tom who, although disenchanted with the Church, still personified the ideals of all the religions that teach goodness, understanding, wisdom, and charity. Tom didn't deserve this. If God allowed this tragedy to happen to Tom, it would be asking a lot of me to beg him for mercy.

It doesn't work for me, and I certainly do not entertain theories about the devil or the forces of evil; that would mean the forces of darkness were more powerful than God at the time of the accident. Nor do I subscribe to the notion of God's inscrutable plan, one with meaning and purpose beyond our ability to understand. The concept represents an excuse offered by those who believe, who have faith, but no answers.

To ask why this happened or what purpose it served is only to invite conundrums, puzzles with no solutions. For me, it was not a question of God's will or divine purpose. It just happened.

Period.

That is not to say I did not appreciate other people's prayers. No doubt, they felt their petitions were a way to contribute to the overall direction of Tom's recovery. It happened not to be a source of comfort or consolation for me, but I understood its significance to others, and I realized it was their way to cope with an inexplicable situation. It's difficult to deal with catastrophe. I almost envy those who find solace through their prayers. We all need something to help us sort out tragedy. My strength comes from a conviction of the random nature of life: things happen, and humans are fragile. The most we can do is be good and do good work – and keep it all as simple as possible. That philosophy gives me direction.

As my nephew Dan Radel says, "Whatever floats your boat."

There was talk of miracles. It was a miracle that Tom survived and appeared to be intact. For those of us who waited, it would be a miracle if/when he awakened.

A miracle is something wonderful that isn't supposed to happen but happens anyway. But it is only one end of a continuum. At the other end is catastrophe. Many people pray for miracles, which presupposes someone or something has some control at that end. If nature is balanced, then there has to be some control at the other end as well – or none at either end: random, universal chaos within which we try our best to survive.

Praying for a miracle tips one end; it acknowledges a power on one side but fails to acknowledge a power on the other. Or it accepts the same two powers as equals. But it must set some sort of demon at the catastrophic end of the continuum. Then, as far as I'm concerned, we're back with the tree and sun worshippers ascribing mystic powers to all forms of experience.

Since we are being philosophical, I might mention that, truth be told, the primitive worship of nature and natural phenomenon makes more sense to me than the worship of an unseen, unknowable and purportedly good supernatural deity. After all, if the sun does not shine long enough, or the rainfall is not just right, we starve and die. Placating the forces of nature in order to survive seems like a rational practice on the part of our prehistoric ancestors.

Forgive my digression.

Throughout Tom's adventure, there would be pauses for reflection and opportunities for a good deal of philosophical contemplation. While I sat in the ICU, I was not yet aware of the depth of thought we would encounter along the route. Instinct and reaction alone kept me going. I thanked people for their prayers and kept my philosophy to myself.

Tom and I have the yin-yang on our wedding rings. We believe in the Balance, the Harmony achieved by balancing opposites. I believe in science and perseverance and hope.

And I believed in Tom.

The next two and a half weeks brought a great deal of progress. We moved up to the Step-Down Unit, the Progressive Care, which was on the floor below. Visitors dropped off, the effect of the holiday season and while not a lessening of interest, a sense that day-to-day changes were slow in coming, whereas weekly visits made them feel more encouraged. Those of us who were at Tom's bedside every day were often not as aware of his progress as those who saw him once a week.

The immediate family showed up daily – the two mothers,

Bill and I. Rich MacFarland was there every day, usually with Susan. Roz and Bernie Ressner and Tom's sister Andrea, often with her husband Joey, were frequent visitors. According to the women at the Information Desk in the hospital lobby, Tom was setting all kinds of records for guest passes. The ladies at the desk began to take an interest in his progress as if they knew him.

On the Progressive Care Unit, Tom was in a large room with four other patients. The nursing station situated in the center of the room provided constant monitoring of the four, but none of the patients needed the equipment and machinery of the Intensive Care Unit any longer. They had graduated. We often went upstairs to learn how Clark was doing, or to look at Tom's tree. The ICU family, solidified during the past few weeks, stayed in contact.

As I look back on some of the light-hearted entries in the journal, which was still being kept as if Tom would read it one day, it now seems that what I tried to do and what enthusiasm I mustered are signs of how naïve I was, and how ignorant. On December 12th, for example, I told him:

Today you were promoted to Progressive Care - you are off the ICU!!! Our space here is a lot smaller than it was upstairs, so we had to take much of the room décor down and bring it home - just when you get a place looking the way you want it, you have to move on! We put up the photos again so you can see them, and the cassette player is closer to you than it was before, and a few of the things the kids made

are on the door, but we had to take most of the rest
- cards, posters - back home.

Tom never seemed to notice the various items we had brought to his room, yet the photo montage followed him with every move, as did the cassette player with his favorite doo-wop music, and a bright neon poster signed by all the teachers at the high school. The little girl's card telling him to "get over it" was posted in each new location. Whether or not Tom paid any attention to these things, or if they made a difference, I thought it was necessary and important to surround him with as much that was familiar as possible. I still had the coma wake-up scene from the movies in my head: he would suddenly come awake, look around in confusion, then rest comfortably with a big smile as his familiar music played and family photos surrounded him. Perhaps he would even reach up, take down a photo from the wall, stroke it, and hold it to his chest as he fell asleep. And perhaps the picture would be of me, or Bill, or both of us. Of course, all this would happen at night with subdued lighting and a gentle rain scampering down the window. Of course.

Back in reality, when he did open his eyes now for brief periods, his facial expression was bewildered and somewhat frightened with perhaps a touch of quiet madness. His eyes had a haunted, searching quality conveying confusion, disconnection, perhaps – the look of a man who didn't know where he was or what had happened to him, which was, of course, precisely the truth.

However, I began to believe that the fog in his mind was breaking up:

For a minute or two I was experiencing our presence and words as you might be seeing them, I imagine you saw our faces hovering, maybe in darkness or as light spots in the darkness, and that you heard isolated words: hospital, accident, all right...

At times, he appeared to work out a very strained grin with closed, tight lips and crow's feet at his eyes. The effort put him right out again and he slept.

Bill was wrestling with conflicting emotions. He was in love with a girl in Idaho and wanted to share his happiness, but at the same time he was worried and upset about his father. He wanted to be in the hospital, but longed to be with his friends who took his mind off the hospital. His reaction to the turmoil was to try to do a little of everything, and then sleep. He slept at night when he got in after a few hours at the diner with his friends. He slept during the day either at home or at the hospital. He slept on the floor in the crowded waiting room and on two chairs with his head scrunched on one and his feet up over the back of the other. Even in that position, he snored.

I had to begin thinking about our next step, a rehabilitation facility. There were two reasonable choices, but one was closer to our home than the other. Since we were in the midst of a wicked winter, and because I knew we wanted to continue to make daily visits, I chose the closer of the two.

At this time, I was experiencing some very strange sensations. For example, I could not follow anything I read. After completing a page of a book, or a short article in the newspaper, I found that I had no idea what it was about. When Bill tried to talk to me and tell me a little incident from college or from his few days at home, my mind drifted away and when he finished I had no recollection of what he had said, nor did I know in any of these cases just where my thoughts had gone. Tom's sister Pat told me the whole phenomenon was quite normal and gave me a little booklet explaining it. It might have helped, had I been able to concentrate on it.

The little I did absorb from the booklet informed me that with head injury, the first six to 18 months were very important in determining the eventual extent of the patient's recovery.

In my mind, I replied, *But that applies to other people, not Tom.* There was a certainty within me which whispered, "No way is Tom going to take six to 18 months to get over this. He'll do it in two or three and be back in school in September."

In the journal for December 12th:

I know this is "Denial" and part of me (the intellect, not the emotions) knows that there's a Reality here I'm choosing to ignore. But last night the nurses told me to get some sleep, that we were in for the long haul, and today, in little whiffs when the fog cleared, something in my mind said, "This really happened. This is Tom and it really happened to him." Then a shadow comes over me like a cloak, and threatens to envelope me and I try to shake it off...At first this was all unreal and we walked in a cloud. Now that cloud is very gradually dissipating. Like an airplane in the mist, we are able occasionally to see patches of clear ground, and they are very strong and definite and firm compared to the ethereal quality of the cloud. And all across that clear ground is written: This is Real; This Really Happened. And then the clouds cover over again and I can breathe. And when I breathe, in the mist, I say we can do it, and we will do it, and faster and finer than anyone thinks it can be done.

I wish Tom had been alert for a few minutes on Monday, December 13. The nurses' strike was still on, which he would have supported because of his enthusiasm for labor movements. A temporary occupational therapist arrived at his bedside whose name was Molly Maguire. Yes, she had been named for *the* Molly Maguires. Tom would have loved it.

His right foot was beginning to twitch a little, which was the first bit of movement at all on his right side. His left hand was very busy rubbing his forehead. We wondered if he could feel the injury, or if he had a headache. Tom, who once prided himself on his communication skills, could tell us nothing.

He tried to pull off the NG tube and the catheter, but did not open his eyes all day. My brave aunt and cousin visited, and left in tears. I kept busy with various bits of work, dropping off papers at the lawyer's, consulting with the people at the Rehabilitation Hospital, filling out insurance papers. I sent out updates to our friends in Idaho and tried to figure out our finances. The doctor's report I had to mail out to the insurance company indicated that Tom might be out of school for a year. Naturally, I did not believe it, but I packed up a box of his current text books and lesson plans to give to his substitute.

On Tuesday I brought in two sensory stimulation kits I had put together at the suggestion of the speech therapist who had seen Tom the previous day. Apparently his ability to speak and to think could arise from gross stimulation applied in his comatose state. At best, the kits would awaken him and he would speak. At worst, I would be usefully occupied during the long hours by his bedside.

(Another movie scene: I would be rubbing sandpaper along his arm and he would suddenly sit up and say, "What do you think you're doing?" Then I would cry out of happiness and he, thinking he had hurt my feelings, would say all kinds of nice things about being sorry. I'd tell him what had happened and he would be amazed. Then we'd pack up his stuff and go home.)

Rubbing the sandpaper was about the only part of the scene that got to be played. In his tactile kit I assembled swatches of various textures for Tom to touch, or, to be more accurate, for me to rub on his arm and hands. There were little pieces of velvet, silk, sandpaper, leather, plastic, and so on. For the next several weeks, three or four times a day, I would press a swatch in his hand and identify it. "This is velvet, Tom. Velvet. It's soft and smooth. This is velvet."

He fingered a few of them listlessly and never really showed much interest, but I kept it up.

In the second kit, comprised of tiny bottles, I gathered things to smell – some extracts, soy sauce, spices, and so on. I dipped Q-Tips into each scented liquid and rested them briefly inside or just under his nose. Beyond a little bit of wrinkled nose motion at the scent of the soy sauce, there was little reaction. Still, I persevered in presenting the swatches several times a day. At least the procedure made me feel like I was making a contribution.

One day I was given a tour of the rehab hospital. When people leave a hospital, they are supposed to come home. Tom was leaving Jersey Shore only to go to another hospital. I found the whole thing a little depressing.

The facility seemed satisfactory, but I broke down when the admissions director began talking about some of the therapies Tom would receive, especially the ADLs (Activities of Daily Living). I kept thinking, *This isn't for Tom. This isn't Tom they're going on about. He doesn't need to learn how to turn off a stove. He can do that. He can do anything. He built our house!*

Bill tried to boost my spirits, even to the extent of corny jokes. He was being brave, but still coping by sleeping.

A gastrostomy tube was put in shortly after Tom's arrival in the Step-Down. Without the NG tube Tom's face was back to normal and he looked quite fine – regal, almost. He would now be fed through the stomach tube. His mother examined the tubing but I never went close. I'm something of a coward when it comes to dealing with innards. Have I mentioned that I deliberately did not choose medicine as a career?

In fact, although Helen readily helped with suctioning his trach tube, I had to leave the room when that little function was performed. The most I was able to note in the journal was how there was less "yick stuff" in the tube – such was my command of medical terminology. I found the procedures a bit repulsive and was relieved I did not have to take part. My mother-in-law let it be known at the hospital that she was an R.N. and could attend to his needs. Many of the nurses who were replacing the strikers and thus a bit overworked were happy to have her help. Others were not as receptive. She told them, "If there's no immediate

help when my son needs it, I'm not about to let him suffocate!"
She performed many suctions.

Upstairs, Clark was holding on and fighting. We visited with
Norman and Eileen – who were still there every day – and they
came down to check Tom's progress. One of Tom's new
roommates was a young man who either fell, jumped, or was
pushed from a third-floor window. I suspected he had attempted
suicide and now was bitter it hadn't work, but left him instead
with a severed spinal cord, which would probably result in total
paralysis of both legs. He was a whiner and a hypochondriac, and
had a flair for drama. Tragic as his situation was for him, dare I
admit that for us it was Comic Relief and we appreciated the
diversion? The day was punctuated with his cry, "Nurse! Nurse! I
can't breathe...I'm having an anxiety attack! Nurse...Nurse!"

At the two-week mark, I remembered what one of the
doctors had said to me the day before. "I know it's been the
longest two weeks of your life, but that's only like a minute
compared to the stretch of time yet ahead."

We had calls from all over the United States – all parts of
Jersey and Idaho, and also Connecticut, Chicago, Florida,
Colorado, Texas, and Pennsylvania, and soon Tom became an
international celebrity when my cousin in Italy called. So much
concern entailing so many repetitions of our status this far. Truth
to tell, it was exhausting, but we were grateful for all the interest.

One day Tom opened his eyes on three separate occasions,
each one for a full house of visitors. That night, Rich MacFarland
stood by his bed and said, "I've got a complaint, Tom. Every night
I bought a ticket for the evening performance and got no show,
and today you decide to give a matinee. That's not fair."

And then Tom opened his eyes again! We were thrilled.

More gifts arrived on Friday. Rich brought another food

basket from the high school. Tom's substitute brought four quarts of home-made minestrone. Jim Larkin made Tom a wooden reindeer with a bright red velvet bow. He and Marie set it up in the room. A plant arrangement arrived from former students. There was certainly enough activity around Tom, though very little *from* him. However, every time he opened an eye, or moved a finger, it was a gift he gave us and a cause to celebrate and we always had many, many people with whom to share the excitement. How very fortunate we were in such a terrible time not to be alone.

One Saturday we rode an emotional roller-coaster. When Helen and I arrived in the morning we learned Tom was running a fever of 102 degrees, which meant he would not be transferred to the rehab hospital the following Monday. He was being tested, cultured, and X-rayed for another form of pneumonia in addition to the staph infection he had at the time. His blood sugar count was high, so he was also being monitored for diabetic-type complications. He was lying in bed in a sweat.

I was quite depressed when Barbara and Tracy came and took Paula and me out to lunch. When we returned, Andrea greeted us with, "You missed it!"

"What?"

"He opened his eyes and kept them open for an entire hour!"

I was devastated that I had missed such a display, but later he repeated the performance, again for nearly an hour. While his eyes were open, he explored his face with his left hand and played little ballets with his right hand in the air, his arm resting on the elbow and his forearm straight up while he moved his fingers. We gave him a tissue and he held it, and seemed to wipe his face with it – a brief passage of the tissue across his face. He moved his thumb against the other fingertips. We believe he tried to speak

69

now that the doctor had capped the trach tube. Tom was mouth-breathing through closed lips; the breath came snorting out of the corners of his mouth. It looked as if he were trying to work his lips into shapes. Nothing more came of it but it was a refreshing finish to what had begun as a depressing day.

The next day was a good one as well. Tom's eyes were open nearly all day. His fever was down as well as the blood sugar level, and he had been given doses of antibiotics to combat the pneumonia.

During this week I had a bad dream, the first dream I was able to recall since the accident. The dream concerned Tom, his head, and his brain. What I remembered of it had to do with a doctor opening his head, removing and repairing the brain, putting it back, and sewing up his head. At one point in the dream, I was handling the brain and I put it back in his head, but backwards. There was "gunky stuff" on it. (My somewhat imperfect knowledge of medical terminology filtered through to my dreams.) It was an unpleasant experience altogether – a bad sleeping dream within the bad dream of our waking reality.

There were vague signs of intellectual advancement. Tom appeared less frightened when his eyes opened and a few times he almost reached for the items we held out to him. When an object was placed in his hand, he tried to focus on it as if to figure it out. He very definitely pushed his eyes over to the right several times, which might have been an indication that the swelling in his brain was going down. To us, these were hopeful signs and we rejoiced with each one.

One day I brought in some familiar objects – Tom's wallet, his Idaho key chain, a chess piece – and he handled each one in his left hand, fingering the object and focusing on it. After a while he got the idea of handing them back to me except for the pawn, which he wanted to hold. (Could there be a deep, hidden significance here? Did he think of himself as just a pawn in the Game of Life?)

We gave him a twenty-dollar bill and he stared at it, then rapidly and firmly moved his hand under the sheets, trying to tuck away the money! The old Tom was in there somewhere!

Later, he did something even more curious. He was seated in the lounge-type chair next to the bed. I gave him a set of keys. He held the keys, then selected one and, holding it flat, reached over to the bed and pressed that key flat against the bed. All the while he was frowning slightly. We wondered what he was thinking; what was the significance of that key, and why the frown?

That night I wrote:

> It's this kind of activity that makes me believe you'll get out of this fast. You're more alert each day and therefore probably more annoyed with your situation each day. All of which will help you rise from this. We want you back. We need you back.

Bill went to the high school Holiday Concert on December 22nd. Without knowing that Bill was present, the music director spoke to the audience about Tom, and asked for their thoughts and prayers.

Three weeks after the accident I tried to pick up a few little things in some of the stores. The constant, happy Christmas music made it difficult for me.

A little lady who appeared to be about 112 years old was moved into Tom's room. She cried constantly for her mother. All day she cried out, "Ma... Ma..." and sometimes, "I'm afraid." It tore at my heart. We knew Tom was off in some distant land, fighting his way back home; we wondered where she was.

The young man, the possible thwarted suicide, was moved out and sent on his way to Kessler for rehabilitation. Mrs. Peterson, who had been moved down to the unit, had still not awakened from her coma.

The Christmas season, emotionally charged as it is anyway, seemed to magnify to either extreme whatever happened in the hospital. The little triumphs seemed greater, more full of promise than they actually were; the little sadnesses seemed more profound, more hopeless. It was a time of exaggerated emotion, and it was difficult and enervating for us all.

On December 24th, Tom had a slow day, although we were certain he had been trying to form words. Rich even thought he heard "water." Overall, Bill and I found it difficult not to feel morose, melancholy, or just plain miserable. We stayed somewhat on the outskirts of Christmas, now and then peeking in on someone else's celebration.

Christmas Eve turned out to be a mechanical event for our family. Everyone at my sister's house tried to carry out our traditional dinner and gift-giving, but it was a subdued affair. I couldn't open any presents.

On Christmas Day the hospital was full of visitors. Little children ran around, everybody tried to make the best of the situation. Tom had fourteen guests. He was awake most of the day and kept all of us enthralled by his bizarre hand motions. He would stare, then point and shake his index finger, although none of us understood his meaning. He seemed to be listening, staring, trying to make sense of what was going on. The finger pointing appeared to be purposeful but its significance was still a mystery.

We had no Christmas dinner, but I remember a wonderful, huge chocolate-covered apple that Joey Kiernan brought to the hospital for us. We hacked at it all day. As I picture it from this distance, the piece of fruit has become in my mind's eye the size of a basketball. It was delicious, I remember, and apparently it sufficed until we got home and pulled things out of our food baskets.

In the evening Bill and I shared a few gifts, sitting on our living room floor next to the poinsettia someone had given us, our only Christmas decoration. The plant rested on the hearth next to the woodstove, which still held the logs Tom had laid in there three weeks ago. We stacked up Tom's gifts next to the poinsettia. The day hadn't been an especially poor one, in and of itself, but because it was Christmas and came with high expectations for good cheer, our day fell short. I think we were happy to see it end.

Tom gave us our Christmas gifts the following day. Pat held up her baby and he smiled. He reached for my hand. I asked him, "Tom, are you afraid?"

He shook his head – just a little.

The cloud analogy I wrote about in my journal applied to Tom as well as to me. Our clouds were mist; his were dense and oppressive and he dwelt among them. But every once in a while they separated and he was given a little glimpse of the real world before they closed in again, shutting him off from us. In those few open moments he tried to alter his environment. He tried by wagging his finger, by snorting air out of the corners of his mouth, by sending his eyes around the room. Yet, he was still very far away. Except for the one time, he was unable to signal an answer to our questions.

Paula told me, "You know, Tom seems to seek you out. He

looks like he's trying to respond to you. Maybe he feels more secure with you."

"I can't say," I replied, "I really don't know what I'm doing. I'm going on instinct alone." Instinct and my pesty little stimulation kits.

"It seems to be working," she said.

And it was true that he did seem more at peace, less confused when he opened his eyes. His repertoire of gestures now included the pointing finger, the outstretched flattened palm, and a "money" signal made by rubbing his thumb against the backs of his first two fingers. I don't know that I was of any special use to him, but because I didn't know what else to do, I kept repeating the explanation mantra ("You were in an accident...etc."), stuffing the swatches into his hand, and sticking the Q-Tips in his nose. And he *was* becoming more responsive.

He sent his left hand over to touch and explore the inert right one. We felt that was a very good sign. He repeated it several times. Was he curious about it? Did he realize it was not working? Would we ever know?

As we approached our moving date, I became somewhat apprehensive about Tom's pending experience at rehab. I began to think for the first time about the extent of his recovery and to wonder what might be ahead. Thus far, it had been one slow step in front of another, moving ahead with blinders on. Now I wanted to see more, to know more, but no one had a clear vista for me to see, or answers to my largely unspoken questions. The path was unclear. The only certain thing was uncertainty. And I do not do well with uncertainty.

On December 29th Tom was given the go-ahead by the trauma team. He would be discharged on the next day to the Rehabilitation Hospital. As if he understood his promotion, he put on a dazzling display of dexterity on the 29th. He held on to his keys, clutched his highlighter and various other familiar objects. Some of these he carefully set down, some he squirreled away under his right hand, and some he gave back to us. He was alert and awake all day in his chair, and went through an elaborate repertoire of hand and facial gestures. These were consistent, as if they had meaning for him. I hoped rehab would unlock the secret symbols.

CHAPTER 6

JANUARY 1994

"What is your name?" I asked.

"I can't reclep," he said.

The Guru had spoken. I wrote down every word. Throughout the day the words would be discussed, analyzed, and repeated among the pilgrims who gathered at his side, the eager disciples prepared to accept every syllable as evidence of an amazing revelation.

"What did he say?"

I would check my notes. He said, "No lengthaway is considered a utopian." Words fraught with meaning and mystery.

"Lengthaway, huh? Does he mean time? Length of time?"

"Maybe he means time goes away, but it's slow, it's a long time. A length of time. He's been here a long time and it's not a Utopia."

No matter that we couldn't understand him. If there were five people listening to him, there would be five interpretations. But *he* knew what he wanted to say and always seemed satisfied with his pronouncements. Let us worry about deciphering them!

In the spacious lobby of the Rehabilitation Hospital, groups of couches, upholstered chairs and little tables were scattered, much like an enormous living room. Paintings and flowers complemented the décor. A small snack bar provided a limited menu. Those of us who spent entire days at the hospital grabbed little meals there. A residential wing housed permanent patients, all of whom were tragic cases confined to wheelchairs or gurneys.

There were many sad stories among the residents. One was a young woman whose husband had abandoned her in the hospital once she became permanently disabled following an auto accident. She would greet us daily with a cheery "Hi, you look nice today," and then moments after we returned her greeting, she repeated it. "Hi, you look nice today." And on it went. I learned through the course of our stay that family abandonment was typical in the resident population.

The facility, which had been independent, was in the process of becoming a member of a large health care conglomerate. The impending merger also brought about a change in philosophy, which resulted in our increasing dissatisfaction. But on December 30, 1994 – my birthday and our twenty-first wedding anniversary – I was optimistic and expectant. It was going to happen here!

Tom was brought by ambulance and placed in a private acute-care room just behind the nurse's station in the hallway of the head trauma unit. A window into his room, as well as the generally open door, allowed constant monitoring. It also brought constant noise; I was very surprised at how noisy his corridor was. Admittedly, I was a novice insofar as head trauma treatment was concerned, but it seemed common sense that brain-injured patients would require a peaceful environment. And Tom, who was the most seriously injured person on the unit, was directly behind the noisiest area, the nurse's station. I assumed the hospital knew its own business, and I said nothing.

Helen, more experienced, assumed nothing. During our first hour of seeing him settled, a nurse came in to see him. "Tonight he'll have a shower, shave and shampoo," she told us.

"Do you have enough staff?" my mother-in-law asked. I think she was disappointed that her nursing services were not encouraged here as they had been by most of the staff at Jersey Shore. This did not stop her, or my mother, or myself, from making daily visits and checking up constantly on his care and therapies.

Andrea and I were prepared to swear that Tom tried to say a word: "sick."

"You're not sick," I explained to him. "You were injured in a car accident and now you are in a new hospital where you will continue to improve." The same old mantra. I worried he might not only be experiencing something beyond our comprehension, but also that he might be aware of his predicament, and confused or worse, afraid. I tried as gently and firmly as I could to allay what I perceived as his possible fear.

In reply, Tom pointed a finger and exhibited a tight, strained line of a smile. Now he added a new trick. He raised his eyebrows. He also began giving us little reassuring pats, as if to say everything would be all right.

No one in the family celebrated New Year's Eve. During the day Tom sat in a wheelchair out in the lobby, fully dressed in his own clothes for the first time in nearly a month. Because he still had no control over his right side, his right arm was propped up on a pillow and held in place with Velcro straps on the tabletop of the wheelchair. Throughout the day he would slip more and more to the right until the line of his shoulders formed a 45° angle with the tabletop. We'd straighten him out only to watch him gradually slip sideways again. He continued to point the index finger of his left hand and grimace, more as if he were trying to hold back words than attempting to form them. His eyes and general facial expression often conveyed fear...or madness.

It scared me. All the patients at the hospital, and especially the permanent residents, were at various stages of their own journeys, which forced us to consider where Tom was in his, and how far along he would go. Rather naively, I wrote in his journal:

> Of course, we all think it absolutely possible that you'll make a full and complete recovery. You won't accept anything less! And yet, it's so difficult when I see you all dressed and, in that chair, to see you not in a further stage of recovery, but rather as a parody of your former self. (Please forgive the raw honesty; I'm so scared. Your recovery can't happen too soon.)

My mother thought I should look for a little of the New Year's Eve excitement, so I rented two movies and she and Chuck came over to watch them with me. But our tiny television, which we hardly ever watched, was on a bookshelf up in our study, and I had a bad moment looking around at Tom's desk and all his books and file cabinets. I started to cry, the first big flood of tears since the accident. Maybe it was the New Year and the new hospital, or maybe the numbness that had sheltered me was beginning to erode.

"What is it?" my mother asked.

"It's all this," I said sweeping my arm to take in the desk, bookshelves, all of Tom's area of the study. "I wonder when or if he'll be back here at his desk."

Of course, no one had any answers and no one wished anyone else a Happy New Year. It was a low moment. They left before midnight and I went to bed.

Tom had company on New Year's Day, eight visitors. The hospital furnished a free buffet and we all tried to feel confident about the new start in the new year.

Our confidence was rewarded the next day.

Rich MacFarland and I were in Tom's room. I had just run through a series of the textures with Tom, rubbing the swatches against his arm and identifying each one. Then Rich said, in a very assertive tone, "Thomas!"

And Tom said, "Yes."

It was a whisper, but it was a word, his first word.

Rich and I screamed; we hugged each other; we hugged Tom. The nurses came running in to see what had happened.

"He spoke!" I said. He said, 'Yes.'"

Through the course of the day Tom said, "yeah" twice, "all right," "I don't know," and "well," which he repeated off and on many times. He also said, "It was implied" and "okay."

Once he said, "I'm sorry."

Taking him seriously, I told him, "You have nothing to be sorry about, Tom. You didn't do anything wrong" and I launched into the perpetual mantra of explanation. No doubt I over-estimated his intention, but I know it was dreadful to consider he might somehow feel responsible for what had happened to him.

None of his responses were direct replies to questions, but all of them were clear, though somewhat soft in tone and a little raspy. I had been so afraid his voice would be unintelligible or his speech slurred, but that did not appear to be the case. It did seem like speech required quite an effort on his part, as if he had to think out the words in advance and pronounce them carefully. But we had not seen evidence of thought, nor heard speech from Tom in a month, and to us it was wonderful.

To compound the miracle, Tom began exhibiting slight movements in his right hand. He lifted it with his left hand, poked it with a piece of paper, and then moved the fingertips ever so slightly – but definitely. We gave him a pencil and paper and he drew three parallel lines. He attempted to stand up by rapping his left foot on the floor, then pressing down on it and on his left arm and grimacing. It was more excitement than we'd had all month, and the first indication that the Tom who had gone out to the supermarket was finally trying to find his way back.

With these first words and a general appearance of normality he looked so "normal" that I half-expected him to speak up and ask what we were all doing there, sitting around staring at him. I brought him some new and handsome t-shirts to wear while he held court out in the reception room. I wanted Tom to look as put together as the other patients during what I imagined would be our few weeks at the facility.

We attended Tom's therapy bright and early as the work week began, setting a pattern that would eventually meet with some opposition from the staff. Maybe we were in the way, but this was our Tom and, as Helen expressed it, we wanted to be sure the therapists "do what they're supposed to do." At this stage in his rehabilitation, we were reluctant to free ourselves from the daily vigil we had become used to at Jersey Shore. And we desperately wanted to be present for any small sign that his cognition was returning.

We soon learned small, hope-inspiring signs of improvement were not consistent. They could not be commanded or even repeated. However, we insisted in viewing them as marvelous first steps toward the recovery we expected.

On Monday, the therapist said, "Touch your nose, Tom." Tom did nothing.

"Stick out your tongue, Tom," and she demonstrated. Tom did nothing.

"Pick out the red ring. The green one." Nothing.

This was difficult to watch. For the first time the distance we had yet to go dawned on me.

"Which is a ball and which is a glass, Tom?" In reply, Tom stared earnestly at the therapist, but nothing more.

Away from the therapists and back among friends in his room, however, we saw startling developments. Tom wrote carefully formed letters, all capitals, although they did not spell words. We asked him, "What is your name?"

"I don't know," he said. An answer. A genuine reply. Yet earlier he could not provide any answers to the therapist.

"Your name is Tom. What is your name?"

"I don't inquire."

"Can you tell me the name of anyone in this room?"

"I guess there's no room for me," he said. A sentence! A perfectly formed, completely appropriate sentence. For a few delirious moments I believed we were ready to be discharged.

He tried to carry his right arm over toward his left side, possibly to become more aware of it. We did not know it at the time, but he had lost nearly all his peripheral vision on the right side and was not yet turning his head to the right. I said, "Don't give up, Tom. Keep trying. Remember *The Little Engine That Could.*"

He laughed. A tiny, but a genuine laugh.

I felt we were finally on our way.

Bill and I spent January 6th at the rehab, watching Tom go through his paces. It was then that he pronounced the cryptic sentence, "I don't whether myself."

"Tom!" I shouted, "You've just given us the name for the book!"

Meanwhile, Bill needed attention. His checkbook was an adventure in creative accounting, and his return ticket to Idaho was snarled in red tape. Because he was such a support to me, I tended to forget that Bill was in many ways still a child who had to deal with his father's crisis, as well as the prospect of going off to a school three thousand miles away. With all my attention focused on Tom, I committed the unpardonable omission of not realizing how all of this confusion affected Bill. He appeared to take it in stride, but I could not be sure he wasn't putting on a brave face for me. However, there was no do-over in this game.

Very soon the reception desk at Rehab Hospital became as swamped with Tom's visitors as the one at Jersey Shore had been. Several visitors told us that before they could even ask, the person at the desk would look them over and immediately announce: "Sorrentino, Room 19."

I wondered what the receptionist saw in us . Did we all have that teacher look? It's said that anyone can spot an undercover policeman, but I'd always believed we teachers could go around incognito. Apparently not so.

One of the teachers who visited him told me, "You know, it takes a lot to subdue the high school, but Tom's accident did it!"

On weekends it was not unusual for him to have twenty

visitors a day. We broke all attendance records. He would hold court from his wheelchair out in the large lobby. Other families sat with their patients, two or three quiet visitors grouped around a loved one. Some patients, especially the residents, had no visitors at all. Then there was us, twenty chairs pulled up in a tight little knot, the wagons circled.

Some members of the family – my cousin Barbara and her partner, Tracy, for example – would drive three hours round trip to spend Sunday afternoons with Tom. Tom's brothers and sisters and their families were there. Our closest friends were regulars. People from both of our schools, and Bill's friends came frequently. And of course, Tom's mother, my mother, and I were with him every day.

Perhaps because we were there daily, we did not see his improvements as well as the visitors could, which had been our experience at Jersey Shore as well. Every weekend, they assured us of Tom's remarkable progress. We came to depend on their observations as the source of our hope.

Although I had many issues with the operation and management of the facility, and in retrospect realized we should have transferred Tom much sooner to the nursing home where he flourished, he made a great deal of progress in his speech development while there.

We learned that the police report was not released immediately after the accident because it was expected Tom would be a fatality. The policeman who had been at the scene called the trauma center to find out what had ultimately happened; he told the nurse he'd never known anyone to survive a crash as serious as Tom's. From this we took a great deal of hope.

Bill and I went up to Jersey Shore to dismantle the Christmas tree. We visited Clark, who would be going to Kessler for rehabilitation, and we found out that Mrs. Peterson was not expected to awaken from her coma. She was being moved to J.F.K. in Edison, a 75-mile drive one way for her family. "My mother really died in the accident," her son told me. But now they had to endure her living death. It broke my heart. We never saw the Petersons again, but heard from friends of ours who lived near them that the drive and expense got to be too much for the family, so she was brought down to their home where she eventually died. Clark was given extensive rehabilitation at Kessler but remained paraplegic. He and his girlfriend Robin were married on the *Regis and Kathy Lee Show* during a Valentine's Day wedding special. Aside from a few phone calls through the years, we lost touch. However, knowing the concern and interest his parents had in his recovery, I am certain Clark will benefit from whatever new treatments become available. I wish them well.

With us, little improvements continued daily. Tom filled pages of notebook paper with letters, numbers, and symbols although none of them made sense to us.

A few of Tom's friends, especially those who had known him when they were boys together, were afraid to see him. They had heard from the policeman on the scene that "things did not look good" for Tom. One of them however, plucked up his courage and showed up at the rehab. He said, "You know, Tom, even lying asleep here in this hospital bed, you'd be better at videotaping the basketball games than the guy they got to replace you!"

The first storm of the new year hit on the 7th. This was an ice storm, serious enough to close schools and pose a winter storm watch. To match the bitterness of the weather, we received the final accident report from the police, which presented the fellow who hit Tom as totally out of touch with reality: his legs froze,

his brakes failed, his girlfriend had "gone out" – a string of
nonsense. It did not help our mood. We decided the best we
could do was to ignore it, and take our encouragement
from Tom.

AND WE WERE, FREQUENTLY, ENCOURAGED. TOM, WHO HAD A
wonderful singing voice and nearly perfect pitch, actually
hummed briefly along with a song on one of his tapes. He
gradually increased the use of his right hand and once even raised
it to scratch his nose. It seemed as if he tried harder and harder
to communicate, but so far was unable to express himself clearly.
For example, two replies to the question, "What is your name?"
were "I can't initiate" and "I can't reclep." He created his own
vocabulary.

At other times, his responses seemed almost normal. I talked
to him about my adventures in straightening out Bill's checking
account. To be kind, the lad's check register demonstrated a
whimsical approach to accounting. But it was funny; it was
something to talk about.

Tom said, "Well, support is...intuitive." If he had been trying
to say that it is natural for a parent to want to help his child, then
he had expressed himself not only correctly, but also in a Zen-like
pattern of economy. I thought his comment was brilliant, lucid. I
began to think he would be home in a week.

"He's been very careless about addition and subtraction," I
said. "He will add the change and subtract the dollars on the
same line." I spoke as if I were talking to the old Tom, and for a
few glorious moments I believed I was.

"Oh, I understand that," Tom's reply came immediately.

I went on about Bill, telling Tom about Bill's girlfriend and his indecision about his future. Tom said, "It depends among William."

Never mind what "among" was supposed to mean – this was the first time he'd spoken anyone's name. How lovely that it was Bill's.

The first week of Tom's returning speech created a sense of euphoria. However, we learned very quickly that his ability to converse in such lucid terms was a short-lived phenomenon. As he progressed to more prolific speech, his meaning became less clear and his syntax more convoluted. We were beginning to sense that the road ahead was going to be long and rocky, and there would be many weeks before he came home. I was still thinking in terms of weeks.

We were having a wild winter. Every day brought a new adventure. Snow, ice, sleet, bitter cold, wind. There were many school closings and driving was always hazardous. It occurred to me we had better settle in, have a plan, and work within the rigors of the weather, the hospital and Tom's journey rather than take it day-by-day, as we had been doing. This was not going to be a short-term situation and we had to face the truth.

Joey and Andrea took Bill to Newark Airport. I was very concerned for Bill. He'd managed to resist "growing up" until now, preserving what I liked to think of as an intelligent, somewhat whimsical childhood. Now, suddenly, maturity was thrust upon him and it caught him unprepared. When he was finally able to call home after this trip, it turned out he'd been rerouted four times, his luggage was misdirected, and he missed registration for his classes. My heart ached for both my men, but at least Bill could assure me that he'd be all right, once his exhaustion dissipated.

He faced a daunting situation for the best of scholars, and Bill was not one at the time. In addition, he was far from home and worried about his father. Luckily, he had emotional support from friends on campus and family friends in Idaho, but he was very lost and adrift and not particularly successful in his course work.

The Blazer, a.k.a. the Demon Truck, tried to threaten me, but Tracy discovered all I needed was power steering fluid. It only cost $1.05, so I was pleased. Little did I suspect the vicious plans the devious vehicle had in store for me. Little did I suspect the $1.05 would only whet its appetite, not satisfy it.

I returned to school on January 7th. Both Bill and I were under the impression going back to school might bring a semblance of normality into our lives. That notion was dispelled quite quickly. Several of my students asked about my husband. "He's going to be fine," I told them, "He's in rehab now."

"Rehab? What drugs was he doing?"

After school each day, I headed down to the hospital, which forced me to drive Tom's Blazer in the dark and through the storms, both uncomfortable situations for me. My eyesight was not good enough for night driving and the truck was too big for me. In addition, there was a tremendous amount of shoveling required every time it snowed just to free the vehicle. We had 17 major storms that winter. We also had ice such as I'd never experienced, black ice on the roads. I learned after several spins that the Blazer did not perform well under these conditions. I also learned that power steering fluid can run out, and four-wheel drive did not necessarily mean I could barnstorm around our circular driveway to clear it without getting stuck. Nonetheless, I think I missed only two days at the hospital during the winter and both of those were because pipes had burst at home.

Bill was still trying to get a class schedule out in Idaho, and trying to make up exams from the first semester. Many years later (and yes, I am bragging) Bill would graduate "with honors" from an evening division college program. He will emerge with two majors and a teaching certificate, and accomplish all this while working full-time during the day, being a husband to Melissa and a father to three children. However, back in 1994, Bill was an indifferent college student, more interested in college life than college labor. Above and beyond all academic concerns was the apprehension about his father. This was not an ideal situation for Bill and I regret not being more aware of it at the time.

Back in New Jersey, I had to deal with the black ice, planning for my classes, and fighting hard to keep my spirits up. The irregular school schedule caused by many weather closings made the program difficult for our students, who relied upon consistency. This caused more than the usual amount of behavior problems. At home I had problems with the refrigerator, problems trying to replace light bulbs too high for me to reach in our open-plan dome, and problems with ice forming on the inside of the skylights. Nothing major under ordinary circumstances when Tom would have attended to all the little inconveniences. Major, though, for me. I needed him!

Despite the weather, Tom continued to have steady streams of visitors. In addition to both mothers, Rich and Susan MacFarland were there daily. Bernie and Roz Ressner came frequently; a good proportion of the Lakewood teaching staff stopped in. His little room was often crowded. Sometimes he slept right through his visiting hours and at other times he sparkled, showing us new tricks and giving us new hope.

I still carried my bag of goodies, the scent bottles and the box of textures, and performed my act several times daily. Professional reviews were mixed as they also were on the number of visitors he had. Some of his health-care professionals were afraid he was being over-stimulated and others felt he should have as much stimulation as possible. Since they couldn't make up their minds, I just did what I thought was right.

Generally one of the mothers or I sat in on his therapies. We were not always welcome, which created a tense situation. Away from the therapists, the two mothers tended to be critical (though quiet), usually offering me advice or requesting me to speak out about situations that troubled them, but I was reluctant to confront the therapists or the staff. I had to assume the professionals at the hospital were competent in their fields and would not welcome my comments. Moreover, entering into conflict with them when we were so early into the program seemed like a burden I was not yet ready to shoulder. Knowing very little about therapeutic techniques and procedures, I had to give the professionals the benefit of the doubt and place my trust in their abilities. I am not an aggressive person; I am, perhaps, too trusting and naïve. Gradually I learned that criticism, even if timidly and politely advanced, was not unwarranted in our situation. It took me a long time to learn the lesson. I only hope Tom's recovery was not affected by my reluctance.

In our defense, I want to say the main reason we sat in on the therapies was to watch Tom's progress, to take hope from every little advancement he made. We were still devastated by his condition and were desperate for signs of improvement. Our intention had never been to criticize or monitor the staff.

We had cause for complaint, but in my naïve assumption that the professionals knew what they were doing, I hesitated to voice them. Until we moved on to a sub-acute facility three months later and I had a basis of comparison, I was unaware of the shortcomings in the procedures at this facility.

For example, it was necessary to place Tom in a wheelchair to take him to the physical therapy room. At first, when he was dead weight, a Hoyer lift was needed to swing him in and out of bed. Later, when he could sit up alone, he had to be coaxed, pushed, and prodded to get into the chair. All of this took time and was often, if not usually, left undone until his half-hour of therapy began. The P.T. would find him in bed, and then have to wait until a nurse was called to transfer him. On one occasion when he was sitting on the bed, I said to the therapist, "Why don't you and I help him into the chair?" It was a simple procedure if he cooperated, and one our friends had done easily during afternoon visits.

"That's the nurse's job," was the reply. "They're supposed to have him ready. It's not my job."

We came to see that although the therapists and nurses co-existed in the same corridors of the hospital, there was little cooperation among them. As a result, we often wasted 10 minutes of Tom's therapy time waiting for him to be placed in the chair. At the other end of the therapy, it took about five minutes to swing him off the various exercise platforms and back into the wheelchair, but this the therapists did, the gym apparently being within their province. We generally lost 15 minutes of each half-hour in the simple machinations of delivering Tom to and from the room. I was disturbed by this, but it was not until we moved on to Jackson Health Care, where we saw a wonderful, common-sense approach to therapy, that I realized how poor this situation had been.

There were constant efforts to toilet train Tom, but they were doomed to failure. As much as it pains me to say it, I believe much of the blame here rests with the kind, but unfortunate assistance from Filipino aides. For one thing, they had heavy accents, and Tom was having trouble enough understanding familiar English. I thought accented English might be confusing to him. For another, they were short, and it was obvious he feared trusting his height – 6'2" – to little people who were trying to get him to stand. I saw fear in his eyes every time they tried to get him up for the bathroom. Attempts often had to be abandoned.

We again lost chunks of time because toileting efforts often ran into therapy slots.

One afternoon when I got to Tom's room after school the nurse informed me Tom was on a field trip. "What?" I was astounded. "Who took him? Where?"

"His T.R. (therapeutic recreation therapist) They went to the mall."

I was surprised. It seemed to me that the mall would be a very noisy and confusing place, especially for a person with head trauma. My surprise turned to anger when I saw him wheeled off the van an hour or so later. He looked gray, beaten, and weary. He was strapped into the chair, his feet dragging on the floor, and, to add insult to injury, on his lap was a pile of packages belonging to the therapist! It was as if Tom had been her personal shopping cart at the mall. I was appalled.

Tom slept for two straight days after the excursion.

If I endured, or rather, allowed Tom to endure shoddy procedures, it was only because overall he seemed to be making progress. I was not scared at the family meeting in early January, when we were told he'd been given four goals for the first month: To focus on a task for 10 minutes, to track horizontal and vertical movements with his eyes, to follow simple commands, and to orient his eyes to a speaker or designated object. His projected stay was three to four months. To my understanding, he would be home in April, recuperate through the summer, and be back at school in September.

His verbal expressions were expanding, accompanied by a little repertoire of facial and hand gestures. He was gradually learning to sit without support and once or twice stood up with assistance. During quiet afternoons with just the MacFarlands and me, he seemed to be most expressive. In their anxiety to find understanding and meaning – and thus hope – in each utterance, both mothers tended to finish sentences for him and offer explanations and interpretations. All the attention, no matter what form it took, stemmed from love. Tom's mother could not see progress fast enough; she was constantly prodding him to do more, move a leg, say a word, sit up. Whatever he did was never enough; he needed to move on. Her love and anxiety for him were prisoners of her inability to do anything beyond being present. We all understood his recovery would be a long process, but none of us were the type to wait patiently while the process unfolded. This was, after all, Tom, and Tom was no ordinary person!

My mother tended to discuss Tom in the third person although she was in the room with him. "Look at how he's pointing," she would say. "What do you think he wants?"

"Why don't you ask him?" I would invariably reply.

One day in speech therapy, Tom's therapist began asking him questions about the family members who were always with him.

"It would seem to come from our daddy," he replied, which sounded rather accurate. When asked the same set of questions later in the week, he answered, "They're in for the protective." Again, with prejudiced analysis, this remark could be interpreted as meaningful. We were there to protect him.

However, he followed up by explaining, "Well, I don't capture any frustons tree but I don't know if there's a separate place I look upon...But in whose horrorgraph...I can taste..."

To other questions he answered, "I mean...sure...I don't know how to react...I'm imodent."

We took great, but possibly undue encouragement from these brief snatches of conversation. On January 15th, I wrote in the journal:

> You can't imagine how bewildered we are! Everyone remarks about how well you look and how much you can do and how soon you are doing all these things. Why, then, do I worry when you can't match colors or pronounce names? It will come in time, it will.

Although we desperately wanted Tom to be "normal," we found it eerie in this abnormal situation when his remarks *did* sound normal! We could not account for what I came to call "crocus in the snow" moments: a perfectly formed statement would burst out like a crocus in the snow, as if it popped up through a layer of confusion. Sadly, rather than blooming, its moment was generally followed by a stream of incomprehensible and largely made-up words. The crocus wilted.

Toward the middle of January it definitely seemed as if Tom were making great strides. With the support of three physical therapists and an arrangement of belts and straps, he walked a few steps. But when I got excited and said, "Oh, Tom, that's wonderful!" he vehemently cried, "No!" and rolled his eyes. I got the impression he was expressing some sort of frustration at finding himself in this predicament.

My impression was furthered later in the same day when he was waiting for transport to therapy, sitting in the wheelchair in apparent distress. "Tom, how can I help you? What's wrong."

As naturally as could be, he answered, "Honey, I can't tell you."

I was jubilant at the normality of his reply, but at the same time sad that I could not help him. These kinds of bittersweet moments characterized so much of his early recovery. He seemed unhappy or annoyed with our little celebrations of his victories. But he was unaware of how far away he had been, and how far he'd come back. For him it had been a long sleep and was still a gradual awakening, and while this sleep had occurred we were up and alert, watching for every tiny sign. We celebrated each new achievement as if it were an event of enormous consequences.

At times I wondered, as Tom improved, whether his appearance of distress or frustration, or his inability to find joy in his achievements might not be indications that he somehow knew all was not as it should be, and felt helpless and out of control. He had always been a person in control of his own life, his own decisions, his own actions. And now, if he realized he was no longer able to make his body and mind work as they once had, he might be expected to demonstrate frustration or unhappiness.

Around mid-January, Tom spoke my name. When his therapist asked him something, he said, "Jo." Later, back in the room, he said, "Joanna." I was so astonished that I missed the rest of the sentence.

January 19th was an unusual day. When I arrived at the hospital, Tom was just finishing up P.T., sitting on the mat. The therapist said, "All right, Tom, we're going to help you back into the wheelchair."

Tom said, "No." It was not loud or emphatic, but it was a very certain "No."

The therapist asked him three times for his help in getting up, after which she moved in to start pulling him up.

He slapped her!

Three times, following three attempts to lift him.

I believe we were both shocked. Tom appeared unaffected. The therapist and I talked about getting help – a bouncer of some sort – and finally Tom relented and allowed us to help him into the chair.

They had been gentle slaps; the therapist admitted she'd been subjected to worse abuse from some of her patients. There was no talk of punishment or admonishment. I was surprised chiefly because Tom was not a physically abusive person; he preferred to settle arguments by discussion. This was one more reminder that this person in front of us was not yet Tom.

Later he remarked to another therapist, "Didn't you say that...be clever to repeat. No, that's why you would have in the closess...Well, that's what could have..."

"What is closess, Tom? she asked.

"I recrided that already," he replied.

When the speech therapist told him he was scheduled to go to the hospital for a barium swallow test to determine whether he could begin to eat solid food, he quite normally asked, "When is this?"

Yet, in the same conversation, he said, "I don't sight...I don't measure and then I don't know what the sammon – no, the sappens – keep using to go forward."

In these conversations Tom spoke carefully and clearly, but was generally unable to complete a thought and just drifted off to silence. I always sat close by and took down his words in a kind of shorthand, then transcribed my notes into the journal at night. We found his words, especially the invented ones, very interesting, but eventually learned not to interpret too deeply. Occasionally a clear idea came out, which was clearly understood.

We did not try to translate such words as "sammon" or "sappens." These words satisfied him, especially after he altered them to better suit the meaning he intended. There was no pattern.

There was no doubt about his words or his intention later when we were in the ambulance on our way to Jersey Shore for the barium test. I had been trying to orient him, telling him where we were, where we were going – merely doing what I thought was my job – when he cut me off.

"Jo, shut up!" he said.

Yes, I wanted reality – but not particularly that kind!

When we were traveling through a hallway at the Medical Center, Tom via wheelchair, we quite serendipitously met up with Tom's original trauma team, Doctors Sori, Becker, and Silverstein. I introduced Tom to the men who had last seen him leave on a gurney, comatose. Tom surprised and pleased us all by asking, "How are you?" when he was introduced. He obliged them with snippets of his conversation and they were quite impressed. They told me that when he'd left Jersey Shore three weeks earlier, they hadn't expected he would make this much of a recovery.

I interpreted their remark to mean that Tom had made, and would continue to make, remarkable progress. It boosted the optimism I already felt. I saw this Tom eventually becoming the Tom we had known before.

After two tries, Tom passed the barium swallow test. In fact, when the trauma team had heard him speak, they felt there was no need for the test. It was obvious to them that he could swallow without difficulty or obstruction. (Frankly, I felt the same way myself, but it was nice to have the team corroborate my diagnosis.) Passing the test meant he could be given food – pureed, but food nonetheless – and would soon have the stomach tube removed. I was anxious to see if use of the spoon returned to him as quickly as use of the pen had.

Torn between trying to be realistic about Tom's situation, as I understood the reality of it, and projecting a positive, up-beat attitude to avoid depressing him, I still expected a full recovery. I was also aware we were in uncharted waters. Here's my entry for the day:

I wish I could be more upbeat, more of a boop-de-doop for you because I know that's what you like. You always have a nice smile for the bouncy nurses and the guests who just bop on in. But it's hard to be boop-de-doop when I'm terrified, and I am - almost paralyzed with fear about this thing. Really, I am trying to be less stiff, to get in a little humor, but it seems that everything I say is wrong. I feel hopeless and scared.

Perhaps I was simply overreacting to his telling me to "shut up" in the ambulance.

The prospect of food turned out to be more exciting for us than for Tom. He got off to a slow start and had to be fed. The use of the spoon eluded him. He didn't like the meals, which were presented in the form of baby food. I had the feeling that given a dish of shrimp or macaroni or a sandwich, he would have eaten readily. However, the hospital had its methods and he had to progress from pureed to chopped and then to solid food, and this took a while. My mother spooned him a cup of coffee, which seemed to please them both. But mastery of a spoon was still a long way off.

He addressed Rich twice. Once, he said, "I'm pointing to Rich", and later, "You know what? I go from a hired head to...and I just...a buzzment, so, Rich..."

Another comment: "Why don't you make this slub definder and then to...hi!" This last word was spoken to a visitor who had just walked in. It was so natural! How could we not have hope?

He later explained himself in a rambling pronouncement: "There are methods that I live to be considered and... So I think that it's wild...Of greater would...Being attached to...Yeah...That's it."

And then bursting through all this verbal confusion, in another crocus-in-the-snow moment, he clearly stated, "I gotta get out of here!"

Although Tom showed little measurable success in his therapies and still could not say his name or point to objects on demand, his vocabulary and ability to express himself improved. His speech was always careful and slow. We had the impression he was trying with great concentration to explain things to us.

When I tried to take away his cereal bowl, from which he would neither eat nor part (the contents turned to cement), he told me, "I'm not centrified with your behavior."

When asked if he knew where he was, he replied, "Do you know what kind of foolishness exists?" In light of some of the practices there, this was not an imprecise statement.

Tom held court in the lobby on Sunday, January 22, from 11:30 AM to 6 PM. He sparkled with conversation and animation and even worked in a French accent! We grouped around his wheelchair and listened hour by hour as his awareness seemed to grow. It looked like he found pleasure in the attention he received and in the interest his guests took in his conversation. Tom always did love an audience.

When I walked in earlier in the morning, he said, "I think you'd like to love me extensively."

How many women would love to hear that from their undamaged husbands?

Later, I asked him the usual questions about whether he knew where he was and what was happening. His answer: "I don't know just what is happening. Listen, I'm only going toward what effects..." He paused and added, "Joanna, it wouldn't be slem to breathe you from...I wouldn't be likely to hear you from a carnation so, if anything, all we would do is get your tip from...That is the point...That would only get you to the point of either virtuous faith or virtuous technology, so in either way there's..."

Phew! Quite a long speech. Fortunately, Tom spoke slowly and carefully, so I was able to get everything down. But what an interesting opposition there of faith and technology. Each one, apparently, was virtuous, but you could not have them both. There may have been deep meaning there, but not for me, who was in some way paired with a carnation.

He was so sincere, so calm, and so intent on getting out his message. We, whoever was in his audience – and that day ten people visited – took everything he said seriously, neve questioning him about his meanings or explanations. They wer wrinkled-up enough as it was. Asking him to unravel t' statements was fruitless. I wrote down every word. And th words would tumble out in a stream, run for a bit, and then s suddenly. He modulated his voice, often dramatically conspiratorial whisper, an exaggerated cry, a drawn-out syl His hand gestures, left over from the old Tom, were appro dinner. When they walked into Tom's room, Tracy said, "Hi, Tom! You look great!"

"I feel great!" Tom said.

Another wow.

Can I possibly convey both the excitement and the pathos of such a simple exchange? It was seemingly so normal; it instantly raised our hopes. Tom definitely was getting better. Yet, we knew it was not evidence of a consistent upward progression, rather, it was a one-time natural response and we learned not to base our expectations on apparently normal replies. They seemed to come almost as an instinct, a deeply ingrained and well-practiced response as automatic as saying, "God bless you" when someone sneezed. Sadly, they were usually lost later.

When we returned from dinner, Tom entertained us by making faces at a gift someone had brought him, and framed out a sentence or two with a French accent. Then he tired of our company and said, "This is it. I'm going to bed."

We lingered over goodnights, reluctant to end this shining day, but Tom was insistent. "Get out! Get out!" he told us.

As we left, the Frenchman was back. We said goodbye, he said "'Allo, Allo..."

This was the most fun we'd had in two months!

We were nearly a month into our new location. I was beginning to feel quite scared about Tom and worried about his future. I was nearly paralyzed at the hospital. Despite my attempts to be strong for him and put on a good show, I was aware of being stiff and uncomfortable in actuality. I felt like I said all the wrong things. (What are the right things in this situation?) I was too frightened to relax. I wanted to be clever and helpful and to bring him things that would entertain him or help him improve his memory and vocabulary, but exhaustion or fear impeded my efforts. I couldn't be casual.

Bill called with dispiriting news about his class schedule, which still wasn't firm. He'd gone for a conference on his math and verbal tests. He was, in his own words, "phenomenal" on verbal and earned placement in an Advanced Composition class. In math, alas, his counselor remarked that when he was put together, the wires got crossed. He cannot do math. He was scheduled for a remedial class.

Every blizzard – and there were seventeen of them – meant I had to shovel the deck to get to the car, de-ice the Demon Blazer, and clear enough of the driveway to move the truck out. Eventually I learned to park it just near the street to save a good bit of shoveling. Of course, that was where the snowplows deposited the street snow. Why don't they lift the plow at driveways? Is that so unreasonable a thing to ask? I was trapped behind a three-foot high hill of hard-packed wet and heavy snow. Not that I am trying to evoke your pity, but you should know that I am only a little over five feet tall and was over fifty years old, all alone with that snow. (On second thought, I'll accept the pity. Pour it on.)

New Jersey is the most densely populated of the fifty states. This means more drivers are on the roads, and in our nasty winters, driving is treacherous. Black ice, poor visibility, spinouts, and towns out of salt are common here. There are enough jokes about Jersey drivers ("New Jersey, where the speed limit is only a suggestion"), so I do feel I should commend my fellow statesmen by noting that around Storm #14, we finally caught on, and many drivers began to exercise an un-Jerseyesque caution on the roads.

I enjoyed one particular spinout more than usual. There was a little red car with Idaho plates we'd spotted in our vicinity the previous fall. I'd hoped we might end up in a parking lot together one day, and make the acquaintance of a friend from our adopted state. As it happened, during my most spectacular spin-out, I was headed directly, if in a circular sort of way, into the opposite lane, and the little red Idaho car was leading the parade heading toward me. While wrestling to bring the Demon under control, all I thought of was, I'm going to meet those Idahoans after all... The truck yielded to my will, however, and our paths never did cross.

Occasionally there occurred a day out of *MacBeth* – driving wind and slashing rain. The snow washed away, to be replaced with freezing rain. School was dismissed. I will confess these times were few, but when they occurred, I skipped the hospital to go right home, feeling only a little guilty. The multiple tensions of Tom, school, our finances, the problems with the truck and the house, Bill's situation, and the weather all came together to convince me that an afternoon with a cup of tea and a good book was my due.

Don't think I got away with it. Oh, no. I'd get home and the house would be so cold that ice formed inside the windows, or the refrigerator made a funny noise, or the truck developed new delights of demonic disturbance. Each mishap was a calamity of epic proportions.

But January 26th marked the beginning of a spectacular set of circumstances, resplendent in their provision of Everything that Could Go Wrong. The weather cancelled school – the phone rang at 6 AM, and naturally I panicked because I thought it was the hospital or Bill. My legs cramped while I rushed to the phone, and my allergies set in from the change in temperature. The fridge started whining again. In my mind, the crazed appliance would burn or blow up, taking the house with it. Nothing was too horrendous for my imagination. When I decided the house and I would survive, I got busy shoveling the deck and clearing snow off the Blazer, and then set off for the hospital in dangerous driving conditions. I had to stop three times because there was a strange noise which I chose to believe was just pebbles iced into the tire treads. At a gas station a friendly fellow helped me shift into 4-wheel drive. I thought the problem was solved.

Until the next day.

The Vicious Vehicle rattled and flapped, making the kind of sound kids create when they clothespin a playing card onto the spokes of their bike wheels – you know what I mean. Three of the men at school looked under the hood and discovered the jug of windshield-wiper fluid, which Tom had stored inside the engine somewhere had worked its way over and under and through the engine parts and was wedged deep in the bowels of the motor. We got it out, had a good laugh, and I was safely on my way.

For about fifty yards.

The noise began again, not as frequently, but still there. In fear and trembling I reached rehab, where Tom walked better, fed himself a little applesauce, and was a bit brighter than he'd been. It was almost possible to forget everything else. Due to the road conditions, I could not stay long. I drove home very slowly (almost a sin in New Jersey) with no unusual accompaniment from the motor.

What is that movie with Ingrid Bergman and – Cary Grant is it? – the one in which he tries to convince her that she is losing her mind? That was precisely the relationship between the Demon Blazer and me. It worked overtime to convince me that I was imagining noises – or not. I was willing to bet its motor purred with satisfaction, knowing how close I was to the edge already. (This is the place for more pity. Send it over. I can handle it.) To offset my personal problems, we saw a little more progress. Tom walked with assistance, although at times he would stop and grip the handrail in the hallway and become fixed in place. At those times, the therapists would have to pry his fingers off the rail, not an easy task because of his firm, panicked grip, and push his feet to start him walking again.

He stared at a family group photo and was quite intrigued with his own image in the group, but unable to identify himself. He arranged the number cards from 1 to 4 successfully and put shapes into their correct places in a puzzle, all skills he attempted in the past but was unable to do them. These little triumphs gave me hope. I still expected he would be restored to full intellectual capacities, and told him so in his journal. I could imagine him laughing at his antics on that day in the future when he would read the journal.

On January 30th there were fifteen people in Tom's audience. We were beginning to suspect he would leave the hospital with a guru complex – such crowds of pilgrims to see him, hanging on every syllable, crowds who memorized, then discussed, analyzed every word, looking for depth of meaning and breadth of recovery.

"It only leaves my touch along with me, so it at first...Yeah, if at first you don't quantify, it's...it's just all conclusion along. So, for example, if it's medicine or greenhouse or any eventuality, just forget...forget...just have...in other words, if I get in line and you...yeah...undergo these...these...these...yeah...these are...yeah, but bunnyative."

"Bunnyative?" He could say "quantify" and "eventuality," yet finish up with "bunnyative." We were mystified.

To my mother, Tom said, "You have...I don't even know how

to say it...I know that you're a person who can, but...can but doesn't always...breeve. It leaves petty ways, so I have...I don't know what I can...what...I don't know."

To some of us, this cryptic message: "It's nothing against your head as what comes lipped cren in the way of...I don't even know what...don't...lip pack, you crazy. I don't even know what. You are some good [to my mother] and you are [to me] ...I can't even cunch a label...Well."

On this Sunday Tom was full of smiles, and very charming to his guests. However, he became a bit testy with me when I tried to convince him to eat. In his former life, Tom often tended to offer an analytic explanation when a simple answer would do. We sometimes saw traces of that tendency now. I asked him if he would like to have his apple juice. He might have merely said "no," but instead he gave us, "Wait a minute. If I'd rather had gotten one, I'd have gathered a position. Well, I'd rather have gathered...I rather would have gathered..."

Possible translation: "If I wanted it, I would have taken it." Maybe? Makes sense, doesn't it? In our new world, it did.

These situations were difficult. I wanted him to try to eat because I knew if he ate this pureed stuff, he would eventually get on to real food, and enjoy it. He wanted to explain his refusal. A sticky deal for both of us.

Once when Barbara and Tracy came into the room Tom greeted them with, "You people are relatives!" This was the first time he verbally expressed a connection among people; we were encouraged.

Two nurses who hadn't been on the Head Injury Unit for a month, who had last seen Tom when he was first admitted, found themselves checking the name on his door because they couldn't believe the charming, expressive, walking and talking Tom in this room was the same man who had been brought in nearly comatose a month ago.

How heartening that was to hear!

How could I help but be encouraged and optimistic? Unfortunately, there were storm clouds on the horizon, but I was totally unaware of their approach. January ended. Bill finally had a schedule, Tom was feeding himself an entire meal, and the Blazer, for now, was at peace.

CHAPTER 7

FEBRUARY 1994

We saw encouraging signs as Tom began his second month of rehabilitation. He was walking unassisted, and propelled his wheelchair by "walking" his feet. Although it was discouraging to watch him struggle and fail to recognize colors and shapes, it was at the same time heartening to see him achieve mobility, and to hear him put on accents for his guests, actions he made by himself, which I understood to be some form of cognition on its way to becoming complete recovery. What worried me most was whether his full intelligence would return.

Back in the early days of our adventure in the ICU at Jersey Shore, Dr. Becker explained to me that recovery from head injury would take a very long time; it would not be a straight-line process. Because the rehab had a Head Trauma Wing and was used to dealing with head injuries, I assumed they were aware of the recovery process and also expected a slow and staggered prognosis for Tom.

This was not the case.

Soon after our February 3rd family meeting, I was notified that Tom was not reaching the goals set for him by his therapy team. The insurance company had already indicated it would not support him at this facility unless he demonstrated measurable progress. His team doctor suggested I begin looking for a sub-acute facility for him.

"What is that?" I asked her. It never had occurred to me that I would need to find yet another hospital. He was supposed to be coming home after rehab. That was how it was supposed to work.

"It's a nursing home with rehabilitation services," I was told.

I heard only the first part and was aghast. "A nursing home? But he's only 47. Isn't he too young for a nursing home?"

"Not for a sub-acute facility." The doctor explained to me that nursing homes in New Jersey had undergone a metamorphosis of sorts. In the past, their function had been chiefly as a medically assisted residence for a geriatric population. More recently, they had added rehabilitation facilities as well, usually with a special wing for short-term clients.

"He's not making enough progress here to satisfy our therapy team, and the insurance company will not continue to pay if he doesn't make measurable progress."

"But he is making progress!" I protested. "He's walking, he's talking – he's showing wonderful improvement. I was told recovery would take a long time, and look how quickly he's made this much progress."

She just shook her head. "It's not enough," she said. "You have to expect that he may not improve much more, and if he's in a sub-acute facility, then he's already in the nursing home; he could stay there."

I was devastated. Here we were, amazed at Tom's progress

and fully prepared to wait out whatever time it took until he recovered, but his team was telling us he might be destined to live out his life in a nursing home. I simply would not accept it. I could not square their willingness to dismiss him with Dr. Becker's information, and, if Dr. Becker had been correct – and I was certain he was - I could not understand why this team seemed unaware that Tom's progress was to be long and staggered. Why were they making a judgment after only one month when the Jersey Shore trauma team told us brain injury recovery was measured in trimesters?

At the moment of my conversation with the team, these thoughts did not solidify in my mind. All I felt was overwhelming despair. I pictured the nursing homes I had known as a teenager when our Mariner Girl Scout choir used to visit and entertain in them: smelly, dark corridors with grizzled old men and whimpering old women drooling in wheelchairs. And Tom among them? Part of me was still clinging to the hope that Tom would be back in school in September, but now the doctors here were telling us recovery might take years, or not happen at all. It was very, very frightening not to know what to expect. But I was not even close to admitting they might be right. This was still our Tom and Tom was no ordinary person. Probably I cried. At any rate, my distress must have been evident because the doctor said, "We'll give him a little longer and see how he does."

February became a full-scale attack. It was Us against Them. While I was jubilant over his constantly improving language and mobility, they would point out that he could not yet point to his nose or name an object. That he was improving was not in doubt; showing measurable improvement was the problem. The insurance company was not interested in whether he could smile at his visitors and ask, "How are you?" They wanted to know how many rings he could stack according to size, how high he could count, or which letters of the alphabet he could identify. Objective, measurable progress. For the first time I began to see the enormity of our problem, and to understand that it was much more than watching for and rejoicing over Tom's little daily triumphs while awaiting his full recovery. There were huge forces out there somewhere – cloaked as the insurance company – controlling our destiny. We had to do all we could to assist Tom in his recovery; the threat of the nursing home loomed over us and I was determined to keep it from engulfing us.

By early February Tom had begun to experiment with the wheelchair, using his feet and his left arm to propel himself. He figured out how to turn the chair and with encouragement would wheel down the hall. At first, this was an exhausting effort, which even prevented him from eating supper in favor of sleeping, and then later, as he began to walk more, he lost interest in the chair.

He had definitely lost his zeal for the pureed food; we found it difficult ourselves to work up much enthusiasm for liquid zucchini. His uneaten meals were recorded as negative marks on his progress charts, but the afternoons he entertained us with a variety of accents were not noticed, officially. It was looking dismal for us.

The real world, still out there, added to my distress. But occasionally Coastal Learning Center provided me with a spot of relief. Two young ladies in the art room began what passed for serious conversation at our school. Each accused the other of lying about her weight. In actual fact, we had a size 20 (admitting to 16) and a size 24 (admitting to 20) facing off, with me (admitting nothing) in the middle. Girls' fights can be more vicious than boys' and are definitely funnier. And I needed funny.

The Sears repairman came on a Saturday to perform major

surgery on the fridge. He proposed two operations, but thought we could save her. The light in the kitchen blew out, but I could not reach to change it, even on a ladder. The morning left me a little depressed, but I cheered up when visiting Tom and his coterie of guests. I did not fool one of the nurses, though; she gave me a hug and told me not to get upset. In truth it was upsetting not to know what might be ahead for us. I listened to Tom ramble on, sincerely trying to express himself, and I worried he might never come back. Then I reminded myself that this was our Tom after all, and he will come back – all the way.

Bill called with discouraging news. He was unhappy, unsettled and restless. He admitted to escaping through too much of both sleep and TV. He was happy about his relationship with Kathea, his girlfriend he'd known since they were both eight years old and we'd begun spending our summers in Idaho. I cautioned him against placing too much reliance on Kathea because she and her family might represent security, something from the past to hold on to, and perhaps he is calling that "love." He understood. I suggested he try to be more involved with his artwork and creative writing and force himself to sleep less. The next day he called to tell me he was feeling less foul and had a brighter outlook.

Another blizzard struck on the 8th, resulting in the worst driving experience so far, made more so by the lack of salt on the roads; it had run out long ago. The local highway authorities should have paid more attention to the oak trees and the squirrels. Back in the fall there was a record number of acorns falling and they were huge – definite signs of a hard winter to come. The squirrels were unusually active in burying them. If the squirrels knew, you'd have thought the Roads and Bridges people might have grasped the concept.

Several times throughout the winter when the weather was spectacular and crisp, I realized that had things been otherwise, there would be lovely afternoons and evenings when Tom and I might go for a walk, enjoying the natural beauty. One night in particular I saw the sky red and glowing and our rural street as light as three o'clock on a winter day. It was remarkable and would have been fun to share. Winter can be very poetic on these nights in our semi-country setting, if by day it was quite a lot to handle.

February 10th was significant in several ways: it marked ten weeks since the accident and one year since I visited my family's home town in Italy – two events that affected my life. Last year's trip to Italy, like other visits I had made there, reinforced my love for the country of my ancestry, and rekindled my dreams to spend more time there. On the other hand, the accident demonstrated the power of reality over dreams. I was as far from Italy as it was emotionally possible to be, and the challenges of life right before us in Ocean County, New Jersey eclipsed the dream of returning to Italy.

On the mundane side, the Demon truck constantly reminded me that I was Here and Now. The windshield wiper fluid holes were iced over and I could not reach over the hood to get at them. (Five feet tall, remember. I could barely even see over the hood.) Consequently, as I drove I had to stop frequently to pour wiper fluid from the jug over the windshield. The other drivers, impervious to my situation, insisted upon spraying my vehicle with slush and salt. At school one of the teachers came to my rescue. He de-iced the holes and refilled the washer fluid. On the way down to the hospital the flutter noise began again. I knew the car had something against me.

Certain innuendos came drifting my way. It was suggested

that perhaps Tom had too many visitors, that his mother was too aggressive, that we were too much of a presence at his therapies. How could I explain our terror to them? Being there and watching for the smallest indication of progress was our primary source of hope. Tom was well-loved and respected and had generated a lot of interest. How could we ask people to stop coming to see him? Besides, those people were doing more than visiting Tom; they were and continued to be my support system. We shared the anguish and the triumph. Tom was developing a charm and sweetness and displaying it in the presence of friends and family, but he apparently kept it from the professional staff.

In fact, I learned that he was very uncooperative and difficult with the nurses when they tried to move him from bed to chair, or back again. He put up quite a fight and was not an easy person, physically, for them to manage. Moving six feet, two inches of resistance was an arduous task.

But we found such encouragement in our daily encounters.

"How are you doing?" I asked Tom one day.

"I said, wait a minute...Hello!" He raised his arm straight up in a salute. "And the guy went off but afterward I said, 'Hey, where was − were − you?' because he said, 'Well, I...I...I...'" and we both played on, well, at least...At least...16...Uh...Well, let me just say it's adverably 16 but we both... Wait a minute...No − and then he said, 'Wait a minute' and we both said, 'Wait a minute.' We were both impalsed by..."

And to think, some people might just have said, "Fine, thanks!"

Explanations like this had to have some basis in Tom's experience, but so far we had been unable to unlock the codes that would reveal his secrets. I was certain he was referring to an encounter on the unit. However, his memory deficits were so severe that questioning him about an event on a particular day was futile.

"Are you aware of your situation, Tom?" I asked. "Do you know where you are and why you're here?" Orientation was important to his therapists. I did my part.

"Yes, but the fifth of...I don't know what either to tend to make but if there's a...a... I don't even know what to say because I've already learned that there are one, two, three, four and all those kinds of things that I'm surely not aware to. Or is it?

"I don't know what it is but I do know that whatever... Uh...Whatever I'm coming through I'm always going to let's say make...with...with...

"I don't know what cape to fall through but I'll know what...Yeah, it's got to have 4/8 and appropriate city so that after...after...Gee, I'm kind of cobbling and imagining. So, apparently at least one, two, three but not so much blatant. Oh, sure!"

Didn't Gertrude Stein become famous writing this kind of stuff?

I continued. "So you do know where you are?"

"It's got one, two, three, four – one is the lithe of pay... yeah...when an overidge...He after all has device granting some super seque. Well...he...under...uh...and he's going villya – no, he's going *to* villya – that's what compares – so - I got a man alone – at a tegnancy. So that's number one."

"What is number two?"

"Well, number two is the...is...either the written or written and... uh...vinely termused...yeah...that the much...so, if it's going into the...but could it not be... then it would make a...so, my light...cause I would have to discuss – even if it's only 10 miniasands, but I have to discuss just what is, just what is...just what is."

Precision of language had been Tom's pride and joy before the accident. It was still obvious here as he searched carefully for his words, correcting himself if the words were not right, oblivious to whether they made sense to us. Whenever he finished a little explanation, he would sit up in his wheelchair and smile with satisfaction. Evidently, in his mind he had made his point. Was this not startling improvement?

But it was starting to become apparent that Tom had difficulty in finding nouns. This was anomial aphasia, and it became more obvious as his vocabulary and ability to express himself developed.

We learned if we made no fuss over Tom's meals and ignored him when his tray arrived, he was more likely to eat. He had finally mastered the spoon, but the food was still an unappetizing puree and his nutrition was still supplemented through the stomach tube.

Because he was giving the nurses trouble about staying in bed at night, he was harnessed in a "posey" − a kind of upper-body restraint. When I left him one evening as he fell asleep lying on his bed, I had the impression he looked like a fallen Roman soldier. The restraint vest was his shield, the short blue hospital gown the tunic, and the foot-drop boots with their fleece lining were the sandals. It was an arresting image.

During this time Tom made one interesting pronouncement that left itself open to interpretation: "I don't know if it's sanderin...Something...Something. I'm trying to find something − all right: I'm in some steady division that I can't and I can't...That I can't... Really. Oh, I can. I don't know what it is that is distributing..."

Was he trying to find his name, Sorrentino?

Toilet training was progressing, but Tom was still in diapers. Gradually, his food was upgraded to "ground" – only slightly more palatable than pureed. There was a good deal of discussion about apraxia; specifically, that Tom's apraxia was creating a situation requiring more long-term care than the insurance company was willing to pay for, at least at this hospital's rates. I looked the word up:

Apraxia: "A not acting" "Want of success" The loss of ability to carry out familiar purposeful movement in the absence of paralysis or other motor or sensory impairment, especially inability to make proper use of an object. Akinetic Apraxia: the loss of ability to carry out a movement on command as a result of inability to remember the command although ability to perform the movement is present.

IN LAYMAN'S TERMS, WE WERE DEALING WITH A SHORT-CIRCUIT problem in Tom's brain. As one nurse told me, "He thinks he's done it." Given a command, Tom nodded or even said, "Okay," thinking he had followed the instructions; he was completely unaware his fingers hadn't performed the task although it was registered in the brain as completed. At least that was a theory. What this meant for us was that recovery would be even longer, until he could become aware of a completed action.

On the plus side, his walking was much improved, although he was still assisted by therapists who held on to the strong gait belt he wore. A posse of aides was rounded up to get him into the shower. He would not change positions easily – once down on the plastic shower seat, he wanted to stay there; when up, it was difficult to get him down. This, too, was a result of the apraxia and its attendant confusion.

I was able to forget my problems for one evening when my friend Madli Monesson and I went to see Joan Baez – my personal hero – at Monmouth College. Joan was lovely. She hadn't lost her range, although her voice might have mellowed a bit. I had always wanted to be her. (Yes, I know, along with being an Olympic champion and a gypsy and a bunch of other forgotten dreams…) In this case, I was pretty close: I had the long, straight hair, the nose, and could manage a few chords on the guitar. But, alas, I have only a four-note singing range. I will never be Joan Baez, but I certainly appreciated the wonderful concert she gave us and the wonderful evening free from all other constraints.

As I knew it would have to, along came the day I decided was the perfect one on which to crack up completely. I gave it some serious thought until I realized that no one could easily come over to help me because of the weather, so the breakdown would be better postponed until May, if the snow ended by then. It wasn't Blizzard #12 that did it, or the shoveling, or having had to free up the Demon or the downpour of sleet and ice that followed the snow. No, it was the burst pipe in the laundry room.

I heard the water, ran into the room, saw the steam, and did what came naturally – I panicked. Finally realizing that was an empty gesture, I knew I had to do something else before I was scalded to death and the structural integrity of the house threatened. I shut off the pump and the electricity. Once the steam evaporated, I found that the problem seemed relatively simple and visible: the rubber hose was off the hot water faucet. I ran to the girl next door, who manipulated a flashlight while I did things with the hose and we got it under control. The rest of the day was spent in sopping up water from the rug with towels, and the hair dryer.

Since I was home for the day, I forced myself to search the yellow pages and at least make a list of local acute-care facilities. It was a depressing chore.

That afternoon I was supposed to attend a wake and had been undecided about going. Most of the people who would be there knew Tom. I felt that my presence, evoking concern for Tom, might be an unwelcome distraction to the family of the deceased, or perhaps add to the general gloom. The burst pipe decided the matter for me.

At long last I got mad at the man who hit Tom. While shoveling the deck for the third time that day, following the third little snowfall, I worked up a serious anger directed toward him. He could at least have been at the house shoveling for me and maintaining the truck!

Tom's conversation began to take on a new accuracy. He tried very hard to frame replies, although he still wandered far afield and invented words. However, more and more he caught himself and tried to correct a word or find a more appropriate one.

One Saturday I carried in his breakfast tray. "What are coming here?" he asked.

"Breakfast," I said. "Scrambled eggs."

"I don't want scrambled eggs."

"Why not? You always liked them. And they're real eggs, not chopped or liquified."

"I don't feel like myself," he said

A perfectly ordinary dialogue, but how happy it made me!

Later in the day, when the Monessons and the MacFarlands stopped in, Tom pointed to Mark, Rich, and himself and said,

"We...are...men." This was the first time he'd put items in a category, but there was no therapist present to record it.

He experienced a few spasms that afternoon, causing him to grimace tightly. "What's the matter, Tom?" I asked.

"I don't know what the hell is going on with me," he answered.

Words were now being used more appropriately, more often. At the same time, it was obvious we had a long way to go. I experienced moments of panic, wondering if we'd ever get any further. His visitors happily pointed out the great strides he had made, but I wanted more – more progress, faster! I wanted to pack his bag and head for home, together.

The chopped food did not interest Tom. We asked to have the tube feeding reduced, thinking perhaps if he felt less satisfied, he might eat more. Sometimes this was successful and he ate well; at other times he ignored the food completely. There was no pattern. From time to time he would pull out the G-tube and a doctor would have to be called to re-insert it. One morning I found him in bed, waving the tube in his hand. The nurse I summoned was downright annoyed and did not disguise her feeling. Her attitude contributed to our sense that we were no longer welcome at this hospital. (Had his feeding been up to me, I'd have eliminated the tube entirely and brought him a sub. I still see no reason why he couldn't have eaten one.)

Mark took the Blazer for a ride and determined it needed oil, more power steering fluid, and it was leaking antifreeze, so I brought the Demon to the place it always wanted to be – the shop. At home, the snow plows once again kept me out of my driveway and I learned too late that even four-wheel drive capability could not propel us through. Those TV ads where the Blazers go "like a rock" through mud and rivers have no relevance to a pile of wet, packed, icy New Jersey snow. Picture the Demon hung up on a miniature iceberg, its nose deep into a drift. The fellow next door (this family was getting used to being on hand to wrest me from the latest calamity) helped me and we shoveled the monster free.

Finally inside and warm, I watched the opening ceremony of the Olympics and mourned my misspent and very ordinary youth, as I do during every Olympics. I had always wanted to be an Olympic ice skater. Unfortunately, my skating experience as a child was limited to those few occasions when the artificially flooded "lake" in our local park froze hard enough to allow skating. My parents could never have afforded to support my ice career and I suppose I did not have the hunger. Ours was not the sort of family wherein a child might say, "I'd like to be an Olympic ice skater" and suddenly all the motions would be made – 5 AM practice sessions at a rink, trips around the country for tournaments, the sacrifice of everyone else's life for the potential champion's. No, mine was more the sort of family wherein should a child mention the Olympics, the family, when it stopped laughing, would remind that child of all the other things she wanted to be, and that she was, perhaps, a bit crazy. On this occasion, years and worlds away from being on Olympic ice, I wondered what these skaters would do with ice I'd been confronting.

But one lovely Sunday when I arrived home from the hospital, I found the entire driveway had been plowed. It was done by a neighbor down the street whom we hardly knew. He assured me that the whole street was concerned about Tom. Before this, we hadn't had much of a sense of "neighborhood". The houses were too far apart, set into the woods, and the people all busy with their own lives. What a pity it took a tragedy of this magnitude to draw us together.

Valentine's Day began with a good bit of shoveling to free the car. With each shovelful I yelled, "I hate you! I hate you!" to the hapless vehicle. But the Demon got back at me as soon as I drove away. It made the flutter noise, then a ping. Just as I reached the service station, the radiator hose emptied in a cloud of steam. It should not surprise you that I assumed the whole vehicle would explode at any second, taking major portions of Lakewood real estate with it. I interrupted the mechanic, apologized to the woman whose car he was repairing, and begged him to check out the possibility of explosion. This possibility was real to me, but apparently not to him, or else it was very brave of him to stick his head deep into the workings. Satisfied that all was secure, he returned to the other woman's vehicle. She was a stranger to me but for some reason I fell apart, telling her that I couldn't take any more, and I started to cry right there and then. Despite my plan to hold my breakdown in better weather, it felt very much on its way on this Valentine's Day.

Last year, at my cousin's insistence, I had called Tom from Italy for "San Valentino." This year there would be no call, card, candy, or flowers, and Tom would only be confused if I mentioned what day it was. Probably the expected sentimentality of the day and its empty reality were partially to blame for my meltdown. I now had to arrange rides for the next few days. As it turned out, the service station was owned by the husband of one of the teachers at the high school. The mechanic knew all about the accident and was very sympathetic. He promised to expedite the work. As for the woman who let me cry -literally – on her shoulder, she had my great thanks.

On a typical February Saturday we entertained seventee

visitors at the hospital, spread throughout the day, all of whom were entranced by Tom's increasing ability to respond, and intrigued by the long, rambling discourses he gave us, from which we tried to derive meaning. To relax in the evening I watched the Olympics, but I got really annoyed at the coverage. For an hour I kept track of the commercials; forty-one in an hour, taking a total of 25 minutes. This may sound like a trivial way to pass an hour, but I needed something to divert me because I was trying hard to ignore a series of scratches and scramblings from inside the wood stove. Obviously, there was a critter in there, but I had no idea what to do about it. I dared not open the door of the stove for fear of the varmint getting loose in the house, and it did not occur to me to go outside and open the hatch door set in the chimney through which we (Tom, that is) scraped out the ashes. Counting commercials provided a distraction.

My friends Madli and Marie met me on Sunday for breakfast at the Dover Diner ("Eat Here or We'll Both Starve"). It was a kind of intervention. Their purpose was to convince me that I needed to find a support group to help me through this stage of my life. I did not feel the need. I believed that I understood the is and was aware of the fragility of our prognosis. Besides, e wasn't enough time in my day to fit in anything else. And e remember, I was saving my personal crisis for May. I had it er control.

Tom was brightening a little, which was all the support I I brought in teaching aids and tried to work with him, again we were successful at times and at other times he rest.

20th was one of our bittersweet days. During the ad pulled out his G-tube again. In the morning he ing out of bed and walked rather poorly compared

their own lives. What a pity it took a tragedy of this magnitude to draw us together.

Valentine's Day began with a good bit of shoveling to free the car. With each shovelful I yelled, "I hate you! I hate you!" to the hapless vehicle. But the Demon got back at me as soon as I drove away. It made the flutter noise, then a ping. Just as I reached the service station, the radiator hose emptied in a cloud of steam. It should not surprise you that I assumed the whole vehicle would explode at any second, taking major portions of Lakewood real estate with it. I interrupted the mechanic, apologized to the woman whose car he was repairing, and begged him to check out the possibility of explosion. This possibility was real to me, but apparently not to him, or else it was very brave of him to stick his head deep into the workings. Satisfied that all was secure, he returned to the other woman's vehicle. She was a stranger to me but for some reason I fell apart, telling her that I couldn't take any more, and I started to cry right there and then. Despite my plan to hold my breakdown in better weather, it felt very much on its way on this Valentine's Day.

Last year, at my cousin's insistence, I had called Tom from Italy for "San Valentino." This year there would be no call, card, candy, or flowers, and Tom would only be confused if I mentioned what day it was. Probably the expected sentimentality of the day and its empty reality were partially to blame for my meltdown. I now had to arrange rides for the next few days. As it turned out, the service station was owned by the husband of one of the teachers at the high school. The mechanic knew all about the accident and was very sympathetic. He promised to expedite the work. As for the woman who let me cry -literally – on her shoulder, she had my great thanks.

On a typical February Saturday we entertained seventeen

visitors at the hospital, spread throughout the day, all of whom were entranced by Tom's increasing ability to respond, and intrigued by the long, rambling discourses he gave us, from which we tried to derive meaning. To relax in the evening I watched the Olympics, but I got really annoyed at the coverage. For an hour I kept track of the commercials; forty-one in an hour, taking a total of 25 minutes. This may sound like a trivial way to pass an hour, but I needed something to divert me because I was trying hard to ignore a series of scratches and scramblings from inside the wood stove. Obviously, there was a critter in there, but I had no idea what to do about it. I dared not open the door of the stove for fear of the varmint getting loose in the house, and it did not occur to me to go outside and open the hatch door set in the chimney through which we (Tom, that is) scraped out the ashes. Counting commercials provided a distraction.

My friends Madli and Marie met me on Sunday for breakfast at the Dover Diner ("Eat Here or We'll Both Starve"). It was a kind of intervention. Their purpose was to convince me that I needed to find a support group to help me through this stage of my life. I did not feel the need. I believed that I understood the crisis and was aware of the fragility of our prognosis. Besides, there wasn't enough time in my day to fit in anything else. And please remember, I was saving my personal crisis for May. I had it all under control.

And Tom was brightening a little, which was all the support I needed. I brought in teaching aids and tried to work with him, and here again we were successful at times and at other times he had no interest.

February 20th was one of our bittersweet days. During the night Tom had pulled out his G-tube again. In the morning he balked at getting out of bed and walked rather poorly compared

to his achievement the previous week. Resting on the chair-scale, he began to sweat profusely and was given medication. However, despite whatever bodily annoyances he was enduring, he was cordial to his visitors. He told us about a picture book he had glanced through.

"They never had whirlybirds but there were some people in the poets.

"They had...yeah... They had plowers and little fishes – they could have fingers. They said they could have fingers in the...yeah. They said they could have fingee, fingo – well they said they had extended like the fire...like the fire.

"But like the sentence that illustrates...like the sentence that illustrates the sentence that makes up in the fallows it can say what happens to ... to... yeah... yeah...It can say so. The fizzles are not all clonely deep. That means there's a symbol..."

One of his visitors claimed she understood the line about the fizzles. We thought about finding a bed in the unit for her.

When Barbara, Tracy, and I left, Tom called to me. "When are you coming back?" he asked.

I explained I would return tomorrow afternoon after school. It seemed as if he were trying to work out the concepts of school and home and Sunday/Monday. Suddenly, he reeled off the names of a string of months in proper succession: June, July, August. He was so happy that he looked at us with a big smile and said, "I just love this bag!"

Where are the therapists to write this down?

Occasionally we asked Tom to identify common objects. His replies were always sincere, always fascinating, but difficult to understand. Asked to identify a pen, we received this explanation "I can eklip to bringing this avense toward my fashion are unclean because they're... well... they're crinical but they're unforsaved..." Not very pen-like but the description satisfied him.

A year earlier I had left "my" town in Italy and returned here where I've never quite felt that I belonged. So much different was this year, yet I was still in a world where I didn't belong, this world of hospitals, blizzards, uncertainty and "malinconia" (as we say; "melancholy" as you say). Tom was sleepy that day and all my worlds, interior and exterior, were wrapped in a dense fog. A line occurred to me: Stormy weather.

And I wondered: *Stormy...whether?*

The critter in the wood stove was a squirrel. I finally remembered to open the hatch, but it was too late. I buried his body in the snow. More malinconia.

And more. I had to begin the dreary task off looking for a new placement for Tom, our team at the rehab making it increasingly clear that his days there were numbered. Despite what we saw as progress, he was not advancing to the degree that warranted the expense of that institution according to the insurance company. Bottom line: they were footing the bill. Rail against it as I might, they called the shots.

We often asked Tom to assess his own situation. I was always curious about what he thought about his condition, how he saw himself. "In circumstances of my life as well as my drestination, without any hircumstances for stale – you...okay?" he asked. That was his most recent assessment.

Sure, okay. Why not?

"It's not clearer than a noisy klingdon...It's not anywhere... Well, let's just say that in the...I know I can't neglect...there are so many states...I don't know which one I would choose."

It was tantalizing to find meaning here. The statement spoke so clearly (to me, at least): he recognized various levels in his present existence and that confused him.

In his former life, Tom was always careful and precise when speaking. What I found fascinating was his tendency in his new speech patterns to build the same precision, to correct his words until they satisfied him and apparently conveyed the meaning he intended.

"...and do you think that you could ever recapitulate the...I don't know...whatever closeness comes more recently to that circle bandis – no, not 'bandis' – bandiness. I mean, there's actually coal of regnancy. When we were, oh, about three weeks old, four weeks old – but no further – we actually lived in this and as I... I mean, I thought, 'Oh, my God, here's the deprition.' So, you see, I wanna recover this before I lakedly wanna –want to –resgain the...I mean, I could see that tegment. In fact, boy, I can deeply send all over the vail, so as you can think about my coming closer, I would like to regally."

As encouraged and excited as we were, it was painfully obvious Tom was not truly communicating. He was putting words together, but he invented many of them and did not convey meaning.

Winter storm #13 kept me away one more day. When I called the unit and asked the nurse to explain to Tom that I was unable to get in, she said, "Don't feel badly. You know, this is going to be a long recovery and you'll need a day for yourself once in a while."

Did you hear what she said? A long recovery, but a recovery! I appreciated hearing this; it reinforced my own belief that a full recovery *would* take place, in time. And we had time.

The gloom deepened the next day. The truck that hated me – and I know it did, so don't make excuses for it – made the fluttering playing-card-in-the-spokes noise all the way down to the hospital. At times I rolled the window down just to let the wind drown out the sound so I could pretend it wasn't happening. Tom was sleepy, sad and uncooperative.

Our case manager informed us Tom had reached a plateau and was not progressing fast enough to warrant the type of therapies provided. A family meeting was scheduled for the next day. This was the lowest point we'd hit so far.

I felt very depressed, very hollow. In its insolent perturbation, the truck was silent all the way home. Perhaps it knew more than I did; when I got home, I learned my cousin Philip had died. He was a man I wished I'd known better. The comparison between the Tom I knew so well, but who was morphing into someone else, and Philip, whom I wanted to know better but was now gone, was a sad and bitter one. Our cousin MaryAnn told me that in his last weeks, while at Sloan-Kettering, Philip realized I had worries enough and asked her not to add to them by informing me about his condition. What generosity! I wished our lives had not been so busy, so involved, so insular. You would have been a person to treasure, Philip, and I was deeply sorry we cheated each other of that experience. Life is not an easy thing to live through.

The family meeting was devastating. The team leader made it clear to us that Tom could not remain in the therapy program, and I would have to find a sub-acute facility suited to his needs. He was not optimistic about Tom's prognosis. The team offered the prospect of return "at some time in the future" if he prospered in the sub-acute. However, the team doctor also told me the apraxia, which was slowing his progress, could be a permanent condition. I cried at the meeting. I cried when I tried to speak. I cried when I tried to think. I did try to fight the tears because I knew they would not help our cause, but they came unbidden and unwanted. After having seen so many of Tom's little successes, I wanted to question this official prognosis, but as his apraxia impeded him, my tears impeded me. It took a great deal of talking to myself to get to where I could handle this.

Some of my private internal conversation did turn out to be profitable. I had borrowed my mother's car while Demon was, once again, in the shop. On the way home from that disastrous meeting, I talked myself into two courses of action. Number 1, the simplest, I will get a new (used) car. Number 2. I would not allow myself to tolerate the official pessimism about Tom. I knew he would make it, slowly, but definitely. There were too many little things, little success stories for him not to recover, eventually.

But the total effect of the day was to leave me exhausted, confused, and with sore, swollen eyes. I called MaryAnn to tell her I was unable to attend Philip's funeral. Madli stopped by for a while in the evening to keep me company. That helped me get through.

I also talked to other people, which was altogether more profitable than talking to myself. My colleague Denise offered an interesting scenario. "What's really happening at the rehab is that Tom is probably not meeting their statistical reputation for a success rate. These places pride themselves on success and they do have a very high success rate because they eliminate those patients who are not successful."

"But how can they do that?" I asked in protest. "It's unconscionable."

"Oh, they can do it. Especially now that all the nursing homes can take people – the unsuccessful people – on rehab."

Gradually, it seemed to me that Denise might be right. The big-name places did have a reputation for success, but only if their clients fit a particular pattern. Patients would come to the rehab directly from a medical hospital and stay for a few weeks for continued medical monitoring and a series of therapies. After discharge they would return for several months as out-patients and then – off they went, cured! The patient was functioning again and the hospital had another success story. But Tom did not fit this mold. Much later I learned the others at our rehab who also did not fit the pattern, the severely disabled residents, were going to be relocated as the facility became part of a larger corporation. I had come to know some of these people, and knew that for them, this was home. Now they were being evicted. It was a heartbreak.

Much later, after attending Brain Injury Association conferences and listening to talks given by brain trauma survivors, I understood that Tom truly did not fit the pattern of the usual brain damaged patients. His injury was more severe, his recovery more prolonged, and his future much more problematic than most. Patients who fit Dr. Becker's analysis – long and staggered recoveries – came through the Head Injury Unit at the rehab facility with shorter and less staggered patterns than Tom's, and were eventually discharged to lead fairly normal lives. Patients with Tom's degree of disability generally went to residential institutions where they lived out the rest of their days. Now, years later, I have a better understanding of why he was asked to leave. At the time, however, I was devastated.

To balance the depression created by the family meeting, I jotted down a few encouraging words and actions from Tom. He had begun to watch television and had laughed appropriately at *All in the Family*. He even shook his head in exasperation over Archie.

I had brought alphabet picture cards, and held up one of a chair. "What is this?" I asked.

"It looks like a little of sampson. Because it has samps," he said.

"And what is this?" It was the picture of a lamp.

"That's a usual trailing – yeah, trailing. It's oftentimes if not entirely based upon ...It's oftentimes based entirely upon...Well, I don't want to say any more."

During the afternoon my mother, Chuck, Tom, and I were tossing a ball to each other while we were sitting around the room. Once when Tom got the ball he actually feinted; he looked at my mother, smiled at her, saw her get ready to catch the ball, and then without shifting his eyes, he threw the ball to Chuck. Where was the therapy team to see this marvel?

As usual, we delighted in every achievement. In the journal, I tried to be as up-beat as possible:

I think it's going to be slow, but I refuse to think it's not going to happen.

But nothing occurred in the next week to dissolve the bleakness that had settled upon us after the last family meeting. Tom showed no interest in the alphabet picture cards, little interest in his food, and for the most part seemed restless and distressed. Both arms were being restrained at night against his pulling out the G-tube. He gave the nurses a fight when they tried to take his temperature. I had begged the administrative staff to give us a little more time. I felt so sure Tom could meet their standards, and I was so in dread of placing him in a nursing home. They agreed to a few extra weeks, but made up a chart upon which Tom would score +/- depending upon his success or failure at given tasks.

Since transfers to and from bed, eating, and cooperation with the staff were all on the list as well as therapy executions, the scores for the first week were dismal. I distinctly felt persona non grata among the hospital personnel. Only the horror of the nursing home helped me hold my position.

Tom was moved out of the observation room and into a regular semi-private room. Fortunately for us, his mother was at the hospital when the transfer occurred. He was scheduled for a room with another patient who was in a motor- operated bed which made a steady humming noise. Helen refused to have Tom put into such a noisy room. This probably did not help endear us, already in disgrace, to the staff, but we did obtain a quiet, empty room down the hall.

Later in the day, I tried to impress upon Tom the need to work hard and cooperate. "I'm very worried," I told him.

"You're spending a lot of affection," he said.

Normal? I thought so. Very normal and very nice.

He did a little act, performing both sides of a conversation, with exaggerated facial gestures and different voices. Part One said, "I don't know how many couples..."

"What?" This was Part Two in a different voice.

"Tom, c'mon, Tom." That was the first time he said his name!

"All along there's all kinds of things but each one is resonant."

A virtual play, but no audience except me to applaud.

As February drew to a close, I was more confused, scared and exhausted than ever. My attempts to work with Tom met with little success, but I would not allow myself or him to give up. Sometimes there was a rising panic when I thought about the situation we were in. I found I was almost floating above it, looking at us dispassionately. What I saw was a tiny island of two people fighting against a wicked sea that had the power to destroy us. Our little workbook pages of letters, numbers, colors, and shapes formed the fragile raft we might need to keep from being washed away. I was clinging to it and dragging Tom along with me. In retrospect I can sense the pathos and the desperation; at the time I was aware only of the need and the challenge.

There was a deep, hollow feeling of fright weighing me down.

The kids at school, inured by their own tough lives lived on raw edges, did not spare me: "Is your husband going to be a vegetable?" "Do you wish your husband died in the accident?" "I guess you don't have any sex life."

I was tired all the time, occasionally truly exhausted. Out in Idaho, Bill was trying to cope with everything, but having difficulties. It had been a raw month for us all.

CHAPTER 8

MARCH 1994

March began with a phone call at 12:30 AM, which jolted me out of bed. By now you know my susceptibility to panic. A call at such an hour could only be awful news. The long-distance operator at the other end informed me I had a collect call from − here she paused and I heard part of a name that sounded like "Frip" but was squeezed off. I was supposed to answer yes or no, letting her know whether or not I'd accept the call. In the provided pause, I told her, "I didn't catch the name. Can you repeat it?"

"I'm sorry," she said, not sounding a bit of it. "Your answer did not register."

You're right: it was a recording. Yet I pressed on and at the next opening asked to speak to a human being. Ha! There are no more human beings out there in the wires.

The tape lacked both understanding and mercy. I was instructed to hang up.

Of course, I worried all night long about who it might have

been. I never did find out. As you've figured out, this all happened before the era of caller ID, cell phones, and direct-dialing calling. At that time we just floundered in the backwash of these assaults on our well-being and were left to steep in the unresolved murk.

This was not a big or important issue. It was, though, typical of the kinds of small disturbances that occurred outside my customary existence, which centered chiefly around Tom. I was not yet able to either absorb these minor disturbances or immediately dismiss them. Instead, I carried them with me until I could resolve them at a later date. And so, the month of March began with this little, unsettling, unresolved phone call, almost a metaphor for the current condition of our lives.

The wildness of Winter Storm #15 matched the wild confusion I felt as we marked the beginning of the fourth month of our adventure. As soon as I arrived at school I realized I never should have gone in. I carried with me, under the oppressive cloud of the mysterious phone call, an overwhelming depression and fear about Tom, which was not a healthy way to start the day, especially at Coastal Learning Center. The kids are loud, abusive and volatile. I had no patience for them. Once the storm gathered intensity, we were sent home. I lost the courage I needed to drive the Demon to the hospital. Instead, I performed marathon shovelings of the deck to keep it clear for the next day, and settled for a little while with the news on TV. Lots of awful things were happening in the world but on the whole I had little interest in anything outside of Tom and our wakeful nightmare.

Perhaps I should defend myself here. Certainly, I am interested in world affairs. At that time, however, I had great difficulty absorbing and understanding anything not directly related to our situation. It was as if my mind was already filled to capacity and there was no room left over to fit anything else into it. Oddly, this was not a conscious decision. It just happened. From the moment I was told about the accident, and all the way through these early months, I was in robot mode. I went through whatever action seemed necessary or useful but with a kind of detachment. This was not me; this was not the life we had planned, and that poor man trying valiantly to figure out who he is, was certainly not Tom.

The Demon popped a windshield wiper when I tried to brush off the snow. I could not reach to pop it back without a stepladder and my feet were soaked through. I clomped along in Tom's size 11 space boots – a poignant reminder of how ill-suited I was to fill his shoes. But when I got to the hospital, I was rewarded: Tom sang! We played an oldies tape and he sang along with it in his regular, perfect-pitch voice. He did not have all the words, but had enough of them to cheer us up.

As we moved along through early March, all our energies were concentrated on proving to the therapy team that Tom was indeed making progress, and all of their energies were spent in chalking up minuses on his progress chart. We were in an adversarial relationship now, although I felt pretty certain my opponents were not awake most of the night worrying about their strategy, as I was.

My little boy turned 19 and was far away on his birthday, March 9th. He called and we talked. It was his first birthday away from us. Nature commiserated: rain poured all day. Tom was quiet. At home I watched a nostalgic program about old New York. It made me wish I'd grown up in Brooklyn in the 30s or 40s. (I have never forgiven the Dodgers for leaving.)

I looked at two sub-acute possibilities early in March. At one of them the woman heading Admissions asked, "What's a closed head injury?" That one was crossed off immediately. The director at the second place had at least heard of closed head injury but admitted Tom would be their first patient with one. They promised they would seek whatever medical or therapeutic help he needed. Theirs was a large therapy facility but with no special wing for the rehab, short-term patients, as opposed to their resident population. Also, it smelled like a nursing home. I didn't want Tom to be their experiment in closed head injury. I crossed it off as well.

Again, I sensed how alone we were in dealing with Tom's condition.

Survival itself among the severely head-injured was a new concept. Had Tom's accident occurred perhaps ten years earlier, he probably would not have lived. We were the beneficiaries of state-of-the-art medical methods, newer philosophies. Dealing with survivors, especially with those as severely damaged as Tom, was a relatively new and constantly changing concept.

The complexity of the brain also made a prognosis almost impossible. No two people, no matter how similar the injuries, will recover the same way. At some point in my research I learned that because Tom was left-handed, his speech centers were scattered throughout his brain, as opposed to those of a right-handed person, whose are more centrally located. Had Tom had the identical accident, but been right-handed, he would have lost most of his speech or possibly not have been able to form sounds at all.

Until recently, it was thought that brain cells do not regenerate. The belief was that once they were damaged or destroyed, they were gone forever. Newer evidence suggested that regeneration was possible, if limited. Certainly, this was wonderful news, but this theory had individual application depending upon the age of the victim, the areas of the brain that were injured, and how seriously they were damaged. It is yet to be proven that old learning returns with the regeneration of new cells, or that new pathways are formed to circumvent the damaged ones. In our case, Tom automatically picked up a pen and began to write, but had to be taught how to use a spoon. He could sing along with the oldies, recalling some of the words, but could not remember the names of his brothers and sisters. While the theory of regenerative brain tissue gave us hope, it had not this far brought about a restoration of the person he had once been.

Tom was severely damaged. If I may give a rather rough example, based upon his MRI, I would ask you to picture a walnut inside its shell. Obviously, the shell is the head and the nut meat the brain. Open the shell and there should be two nearly identical halves of the nut inside, corresponding to the right and left hemispheres of the brain. Now, picture most of the right half intact, except for a portion at the front (the frontal lobe), which is missing. But what remains of the left-hand side is deeply pitted. A huge section has been gouged out from the center, extending nearly the entire length of the nut. Very crudely, this approximates the damage Tom sustained. It was extensive.

We discovered a chief reason for the lack of literature about families dealing with cases like Tom's is that such people are not usually kept at home. Nearly all of them had been placed in group homes or other residential institutions where, without constant individual attention, they tend not to improve. Research shows an 80% divorce rate among couples in which one partner has a head injury. Why, then, did we decide we would keep Tom home when he completed his hospitalization? The main reason was that I still believed he would recover. Never did any professional, in the beginning, suggest that he would be profoundly and permanently disabled for the rest of his life. Even the depressing analysis offered by the rehab facility contained a couple of "ifs" – if he improved, he might return to their hospital to finish his therapy, if he was given more time in a less aggressive institution, he might be able to go home.

I discovered that I was a victim of my childhood reading. When I was a very young girl, the books I read all preached a similar theme: believe, work hard, and all will be well in the end. I loved *The Secret Garden, Heidi,* and a wonderful Swedish series about the triplets Flicka, Ricka and Dicka. The little girl heroines in all these books believed they could face adversity, help conquer it by working conscientiously, and eventually, because of that work and that belief, the crippled walked, the poor thrived, and so on. Variations, really, of *The Little Engine That Could.* That little girl reader still lived within me. It was she who urged me to join the Peace Corps, then to become a teacher, and now she told me that if I tried hard enough, if I believed Tom would recover, then he would. The system which I'd been taught by my little heroines allowed for no other outcome

Tom himself fooled us. He looked perfectly normal. He had no exterior injuries from the accident and no resultant scarification or disfigurement. Aside from a slow gait and the right-side neglect, he appeared to be fine. True, his right arm did not swing when he walked, and often when he stood and the arm rested at his side, the fingers of that hand fell into a limp closed-up position I referred to as a "rosebud." The palm of his hand turned toward the back, with the fingers pulled around the thumb, like a huge rosebud about to open. This was really the only noticeable physical effect of the accident. In his intellectual development, Tom surprised everyone. Much later in our journey, we would hear from professionals that he had exceeded all expectations regarding his cognitive development. From that we took great encouragement. However, that very progress also functioned as a red herring, deceiving us into believing that a continued pattern of improvement would eventually lead to his full recovery.

We also took heart from the only two cases of serious head injury with which we were familiar. One had occurred four years earlier. Eric, the fourteen-year-old son of friends of ours, was hurled through the back window of the car in which he was riding, and landed in a new world with which none of us was familiar. His family camped out by his hospital bedside and became the prototype for our vigilance at Tom's various hospitals. Eric's mother Linda maintained a positive attitude throughout their ordeal. Whenever asked about Eric's progress, she would say, "Fine. He's doing fine." It was the echo of Linda's voice that prompted me on the first night I was home after our accident to march around the house saying, "He's going to be fine." And Howie, Eric's father, appeared in the ICU after Tom's accident – a brave thing I thought, for him to do. Howie examined the machinery that supported Tom, equipment with which he was altogether too familiar, and remarked that only four years after Eric's hospitalization the technology already had improved.

Eric had been very seriously damaged. At times, his prognosis was not encouraging. But Linda and Howie were on top of it all, all the time. They would not allow Eric to languish for a minute. They became my mentors. As Tom moved through his first few months, Eric was gradually making remarkable progress. Although he had serious and permanent physical overtones to his accident, and must walk with braces, Eric became a fine young man who retained his off-beat sense of humor and who was able to attend a college where he studied at a pace suited to his abilities. In the journal, I told Tom he was the "middle-aged Eric."

The other head injury we met was perhaps more of a parallel to Tom because both men were approximately the same age when injured. John fell to the ground when the bottom of a faulty cherry-picker dropped out as he was in it on the job for a utility company. John's wife Rodney was a teacher. She left her work and was at his side constantly, as we were with Tom, and Howie and Linda had been with Eric. They taught us that we had to advocate for our patient, that we had to be a constant presence wherever our family member was housed, and that we had to educate ourselves about his therapies, his prognosis and his treatments. I learned a lot from them, and I thank them.

Not that it matters a great deal, but both of those families were able to realize generous financial settlements in their accident cases. In our case, the perpetrator was an unemployed man, oddly the same age as Tom, who was living with his mother in her small apartment after losing his house in a recent divorce. He had minimal automobile insurance, but nothing else. Naturally, money cannot restore a victim's brain, or buy a new one, but it could make the struggle a little more comfortable. For the longest time I had no patience with newspaper accounts of persons who were awarded large settlements for what I considered frivolous reasons, trivial compared to our situation. Another lesson in the unevenness of life.

The combined effect of Tom's progress, the two case studies we knew about, the fact that no one offered an entirely negative prognosis, and my own naïve assumption was to encourage us to keep Tom at home to await his full recovery. There was also a bit of Karma at play; I did for Tom what I think he would want, and what I would want done for me, were I in his place.

After this exposition, let's return to our chronology. It is still March. We were enduring the wrath of Nature and the more subtle, but still evident displeasure of the staff at the rehab.

Journal entry for March 2nd, 1994:

It's been three months today and more now than before I find myself thinking this is a nightmare from which we'll awaken, because it can't be real. Winter storm #15 kept me away today - I'm frightened of driving that truck in the snow and ice - but your two mothers were there and they told me you walked well today. Now there's a fierce gale blowing - it's unworldly - and snow and ice coat everything while sleet is hammering away at the windows. I wonder if you are aware of it, if the outer disturbance, wicked and wild as it is, isn't half of what your inner disturbance is like. I'm feeling scared and depressed. I can't reconcile sending you to those sub-acute places where their "young" population is in its 60s. And I truly still can't get past the fact that this happened to you - that you're there in that hospital room probably wondering what in the world is going on. This is the kind of fright I need you to help me withstand.

Although we saw small changes, which we took for vast improvements, the staff continued to let us know Tom could not be kept at the rehab much longer. Even Tom noticed how upset I was after a March 4th meeting with the doctors, and he commented on it. On good days he now began to sing with his oldies – a few words, but correct ones. He was starting to write his name, albeit with a few letters omitted, and his vocabulary and understanding seemed to increase. Despite the discouragement of the professionals, we were encouraged.

Unfortunately, Tom performed all his wonders away from the therapists. One particular day he walked well, put on an Italian accent, saying "si" for "yes" and sang along with *Whispering Bells*. But there was no one in an official capacity to take note. This happened time and time again.

I was asked by the new administration to take part in a "noise panel" at the hospital. Some of the patients, a resident or two and a few regular family visitors were asked to keep a four-day journal of noise levels for Quality Control. After the four days, we were given a little luncheon where we discussed our findings. It was quite interesting to hear the residents' view on this aspect of their lives. I was particularly touched by one of the residents, a young and articulate girl with obvious physical impairments that kept her confined to a wheelchair. She joined us late, explaining that she "just got home" from school. It was such a normal statement, in such an abnormal situation, very poignant. This was her home, yet the fact that all the residents were going to be moved to other facilities as part of the new philosophy added a dark depth to her report.

We continued to have little teasers of snow things. They tried hard to get serious but never lasted more than a few minutes before their meager energies wore out. I had hopes for an early and comfortable Spring until I woke up with a fierce migraine, this one prescient of Storm #16. I went to school but was sent home. Migraines and Coastal are not a happy mix. Only a little shoveling was required the next day. The snow was now slush, messy but not nearly as dangerous as it had been. Little by little optimism was creeping in. The weather was improving, Tom was improving, and when I wasn't scared to death, my attitude improved. I kept reminding myself of how far he'd come and assured myself that only continued success was ahead.

People tried hard to cheer me up when I became despondent over finding a new home for Tom. I looked at a facility that specialized in coma stimulation, but it was depressing beyond words. The common factor in all the places I searched out was the geriatric population. In spite of New Jersey's notion that these sub-acute facilities were expected to take on anyone over the age of eighteen as a short-term rehabilitation client, I saw no one who was young or even middle-aged. It became a depressing search.

The physical trainer from the high school and several of the phys. ed. teachers helped convince me that the sub-acute might not be so very awful. They felt it was entirely possible that Tom could succeed in that kind of placement, perhaps at a slower pace, but at least away from the pressure to show progress we were experiencing. A friend from the Science Department tried to bolster my mood by telling me how much improvement he saw in Tom since his last visit. His previous visit left me in tears after he had pointed out Tom's lack of nouns and relative difficulty in expressing himself. This time he wanted me to be sure I knew he saw progress.

Occasionally there were extremely lucid moments when Tom seemed perfectly normal. For example, once after Rich yawned,

Tom said "Why don't you go home and go to bed?" Rude, perhaps, under normal circumstances, but a chance to rejoice for us.

But these moments were rare. The usual commentary was the long, rambling, Jaberwockian explanation that resembled normality, but generally made little sense. In one of these rambles, the word "nemesis" appeared. Was it a sign of returning intelligence, or merely a variation of the old theme which suggests that enough monkeys, given enough time, will eventually type out *Hamlet*?

Tom's rebelliousness and distress were proportional to the degree of clarity he achieved. We wondered if, as he became more aware of his circumstances, he simultaneously became more confused and possibly even angry or frustrated. Maybe we were not complacent enough, or relaxed enough in his presence; we felt the need to keep pushing him, to keep him stimulated and to force him to achieve. We worked entirely out of love, and also out of fear, fear of what awaited us. But we knew that Tom, the old Tom, was a perfectionist and would have prodded himself had he been capable. This sustained us.

I continued to run the texture and odor stimulation exercises, and to supplement them with picture cards, letter cards, color matching, card games – anything I could think of to keep him moving along. My efforts were seldom rewarded, to be truthful, but that didn't stop me! My first thought of course was for his rapid recovery, but I would be less than honest if I didn't admit that in the back of my mind floated a scene in which the rehab team witnessed the startling results of my little program, admitted they were wrong and begged us to stay on.

Helen, an intense and serious person, conducted an instant learning program each time she saw Tom. She'd ask him a question and while he worked on his reply, she'd pop in two more, plus a direction to move his feet or touch his nose. She wouldn't give up for a second.

Were we wrong? I didn't think so, and in the absence of professional advice to the contrary, we sanctioned our own therapies. Occasionally a nurse would murmur about "over-stimulation" but we knew that Tom not only slept a great deal, which rested his brain, but also that he was completely capable of ignoring us if he chose to do so. If our program got to be too much for him, he could – and did – refuse to cooperate. As it turned out, we were vindicated several years later when a neurosurgeon who examined Tom's MRI told us, "I'm amazed that with this degree of damage, he isn't vegetative." I choose to believe we had been a tremendous help.

During one of his discursive rambles, Tom used a made-up word.

"Tom, I'm going to look that one up in the dictionary," his mother said.

"It makes the dictionary get nervous," he replied.

Another time, in a pique of rebellion, Tom wheeled away from his therapist. We all let him sit a while alone while we discussed what to do. Should we take him back to his room? Or into the lobby? Tom was listening. When we asked him what to do, he stated, "I don't know where I'm going but I know when I get there I'll be there."

How's that for an existential reply? And what hopes we pinned on such little words, such simple statements.

Barbara and I tried to interest Tom in singing with us. At one point in the conversation, Barbara said, "Well, Tom, you have two options – the TV or the tape."

"No, three," he said, and held up three fingers.

"What's the third?"

"Bye!" He waved us off.

I really needed the strength and optimism that arose from these little verbal encounters because another Family Meeting took place at the end of March.

At that meeting, the only progress the therapy team was willing to acknowledge was the gain Tom had made in feeding himself. In all other areas he had failed.

Fortunately, we knew better. We saw that Tom's native independence was slowly reasserting itself. For example, he would walk only if no one helped him or held him by the gait belt. He would eat if no one tried to feed him or indeed paid any attention at all to his tray. He spoke when he wanted to but not necessarily when it was best to, as in therapy. He could be charming and happy with visitors and surly with staff, and when he wanted to remove himself from whatever was going on, he could either drop off to sleep or fake it. This sort of progress was not measurable; it never got recorded on his charts. But it was what we needed to keep us believing. It was what we clung to when presented with the litany of failures that was his therapy report card.

When his sister Andrea visited, we tried to get him to say her name. Finally, after much encouragement on the part of Andrea and me, he said, "My baby sister is entitled with Andrea."

The G-tube was removed toward the end of the month. It was the last medical support system and with it went the wide support belt that had been put on him to discourage him from pulling on the tube. He was much more comfortable following this removal.

Tom was often recalcitrant or obstinate when his therapists came for him or when he was supposed to make a transfer from one position or seating to another. At times he was just left asleep on his bed and therapy was abandoned. It would have taken the entire half-hour allotted to the therapy to rouse him and transfer him to the chair. He was earning poor grades on his +/- chart, and was neither fooling nor impressing the team.

He spoke with foreign accents once in a while; because of his nearly perfect pitch he did a convincing job. Once, after he'd done a British accent, I asked him a question and he automatically replied, "I shan't." His speech was gradually forming itself into whole sentences, although they were Jaberwockian. Once, he enacted a little charade. After someone said something meant to evoke pity, Tom replied by miming a violin player (although his was more a cello) in a show of "no sympathy."

I continued to find great comfort in the support of family and friends. They were there to share the little triumphs and to help carry the burden of the disappointments. Seeing Tom's progress more objectively than I did, they were often able to point out little changes I had missed. Also, they functioned as an impromptu research team, always collecting bits of information about brain damage I might find useful. They tried to make my life as comfortable as possible and to help me keep it running smoothly. Madli took me to a Joan Baez concert. Barbara and Tracy continued to take me out for Sunday night dinner after their visits. Marie wrote up Tom's usual "March Madness" chart for the NCAA basketball tournament; the MacFarlands and the Ressners were at his bedside regularly. My employers at Coastal Learning Center were extremely supportive. Not only did they continue to send me a paycheck while I was out of school standing next to Tom's bed for six weeks, but they allowed me to adapt my schedule continually so I could leave when necessary for family meetings. As time and Tom's therapy changed, my teaching schedule evolved with them, and Coastal always helped me. This would have been a much more terrible time if I hadn't had such wonderful support.

But everything was not always great. There were several outright pests whose presence was a burden. As it turned out, these were the very same people to whom Tom in his former life would refuse to speak on the telephone and avoided in person. Why were they so annoying? As I see it now, the problem was that they were self-serving people who were of a generally negative nature and who made their visits into a truly depressing event.

Frank Hunter was a salesman of audio-visual equipment who had done business with Tom at the high school. He was an elderly gentleman who was genuinely fond of Tom, but he possessed no real conversational ability and, to make matters worse, had a habit of falling asleep when he visited. Tom was not so brain-damaged that he couldn't fake sleeping himself whenever this man visited, which left me sitting between two half-asleep men. We never got off to a great start anyway, because the old fellow invariably greeted me on every phone call or visit with the same words, spoken in a slow, sighing, monotone: "Well, how's our boy? "Do the doctors give you any hope?"

He had no qualms about pushing into Tom's room, even when the door was closed. The nurses tipped me off when he was spotted and I would hide until he left, or run to the supermarket and return when the coast was clear.

Another trial for me was Gladys, a school librarian and a woman Tom had avoided in his former life. She was an extremely fastidious person who had a habit of finding fault with nearly all the processes of her daily life at school. Furthermore, she was an incessant chatterer, entirely oblivious to the growing lethargy of her listeners. One Saturday, Tom slept away nearly all the day, and I am sure it was her fault. I had run into her in the parking lot the night before as I was leaving at 7PM and I told her Tom was already sleeping. She said, "Oh, that's all right. I'll just look in, leave a card, and go."

The next day the gentleman who was sharing Tom's room told me she'd stayed until after nine o'clock, chatting non-stop the entire time. I was angry with her, and furious with the night nursing staff for allowing someone to stay when visiting hours ended at eight! Of course I was sorry for Tom and his roommate, who'd had her presence inflicted upon them.

Like all of Tom's visitors, these two were well-intentioned and probably totally unaware of the problems they created. There were other people who had what they perceived to be useful information for me, people who no doubt believed I would be reassured by their remarks, yet ultimately I found their attitudes and what they had to say very discouraging.

They meant well, but had no idea of the gravity of our situation. "I know someone who had the exact same accident as Tom," these people would begin. "They had the coma, the hospital, the rehab – just like Tom."

Foolishly, I always asked, "And how is that person now?"

"Oh, he's back at work. Took him six months, though."

And to myself I had to say, "Then he didn't have the same accident as Tom."

People tried to cheer me up with these little anecdotes, but I had already been told we were to expect years of recovery, so I found little comfort in tales of other people's six-month bounce-back. This is not to say that I fully accepted the vague prognosis we were given; part of my consciousness always drowned out the voice of reason and reality by shouting, "This is Tom! It's different with Tom!" I began to understand his would not be a six-month recovery, but I never imagined, even at this point in his rehabilitation, he would not enjoy a full recovery.

GRADUALLY, I STARTED TO UNDERSTAND THAT ALL TOM needed was time. If recovery wasn't to be completed at his present location, it would happen elsewhere.

I had decided on Jackson Health Care as his next home. It was a pretty, clean place. Yes, it was a nursing home, but with a sensible rehabilitation program and a separate sub-acute wing for short-term clients. The staff had experience with head trauma patients and felt Tom was well-suited for their program. Before the transfer was made, representatives of various agencies flitted from place to place; the insurance companies had to be satisfied, the medical staff had to be satisfied, and of course we had to be satisfied.

Pat Smith, the rehab nurse sent by the car insurance company, was an intelligent and supportive person. She sat with me through several tearful episodes as we made the plans to transfer Tom to Jackson. Gradually, I was beginning to understand what a huge part the insurance companies, both private and Medicare, played in our little drama. Without their approval, Tom could receive no treatment. And when he failed to respond, as had happened, they were the ones to determine the next step. The rehab hospital had kept Tom beyond the recommendation made by the insurance company; it was an expensive facility and it would not fund his stay any longer. Jackson was one-tenth the cost and because, as Tom's team warned us, we might be looking for a lifetime care facility, the insurance company naturally found Jackson Health Care more acceptable.

March 23rd, Tom's 47th birthday, was a lovely day. The winter that had set records for horror was behind us. There was just a hint of spring, and we were on the threshold of a new adventure. I tried to be upbeat. We sat outside for a while and talked. Tom seemed alert and interested in the scenery and eager to show off his entirely independent walking. He had a good number of accurate responses when he spoke. He seemed happy.

He offered us such pronouncements as, "I never heard of anybody giving abstention off a razor can," and the curious, "No lengthaway is considered Utopian."

I liked this one: "It categorizes my dependy upon the notion that I would like to spend more time in the valley of this generation."

While we tried not to depend upon our interpretations, it was obvious Tom's speech, however convoluted, was very definitely forming itself into a proper syntax. He continued to correct a word and replace it with the form he preferred, even if neither term were an actual word. And always, now, he delivered his statements in an earnest and clear manner, careful in his pronunciation and his corrections. Never, at this stage, did he give any indication there might be confusion in his mind or in ours.

Tom was taken to the mall again, on another field trip. This time the leg rests were removed from the wheelchair, forcing him to "walk" the chair. He was exhausted from the effort. Had I been asked, I would have suggested a short excursion to the park across the street. However, since our time was almost up at this facility, and because Tom appeared to be in good spirits after napping away the rest of the afternoon, I let the matter go.

This new and optimistic attitude allowed me to concentrate on my own needs for a change. There was something acutely wrong with my left hand, but I had ignored it for months while my attention was focused on Tom. The hand was very painful, which I attributed to the fact that, as an art teacher in a school full of emotionally disturbed children, my hands found themselves in water a great deal. The kids were none too handy at clean-up, but very clever at mess-up. I had no idea what the relationship of water soakage to pain was, but I had decided to find a splint for the hand until it needed further attention. Ah, self-diagnosis is a wonderful thing. I'll never know how much my own "treatment' contributed to the major operation on the hand that awaited me down the road. I never suspected that surgery for basal arthritis was to be in store for me. I put the hand in a splint and that was that.

More troublesome was the fact that I had not received any mail for over two weeks. I asked my mother to mail a postcard to me, figuring that if it arrived, I would know I was not living in the Twilight Zone. Days passed: no postcard. A call to the Post Office revealed that our house was listed as "vacant" and all mail had been marked "Return to Sender." I never did find out how this happened.

Frank Hunter, the tiresome salesman, tottered in telling me he'd heard from Madli at the high school that Tom was being moved the next day. It wasn't true, but the announcement forced me to run around asking questions to check out the rumor. Like nearly everyone else at the school, Madli had left instructions with the secretary that she would always be "away from her desk" in the Guidance Office when Hunter dropped in, so he had not actually spoken to her at all. The man meant well, but he was intrusive and had a way of quelling even the highest degree of optimism and ours was not the highest.

In the ordinary scheme of things, these little matters would not have been so troublesome, but they typify the kinds of small inconveniences that loom larger than appropriate when so much else, of such greater importance, is asking for one's attention. It's not the journey of a thousand miles that makes the road difficult; it's the pebble in the shoe.

We got everything more or less in place for Tom's removal to Jackson Health Care. Helen was not too happy with the choice at first, preferring a newer facility that did look more impressive, but we'd had impressive at our last stop and I had not been impressed! Tom was medically and physically quite sound; therapy would do the rest, and I liked the therapy arrangement at Jackson.

ON OUR LAST SATURDAY AT THE REHAB WE WERE LOOKING AT the photos as I took them down from his wall. I presented Tom with the family picture from Andrea's wedding. "Where are you in this picture, Tom?" I asked.

He pointed immediately to himself.

"Wonderful!" I got all excited. "You know, this is the first time you've found yourself."

"It just didn't attract me before," he said.

"Who is this?" I pointed to his brother Joe.

"Let me give myself some time..." He didn't get it and I had to tell him. "That's....Joe?"

"Do you have a problem with that name?"

"Yeah – because I never conceived of naming him."

As I was about to take away the photo, he took it and studied it a few minutes longer. "Wait a minute," he said. "Just let me get these alter cultures."

Later I said, "Tom, today is Passover. You know, Pesach."

He immediately switched into a Yiddish accent and said, "Today is mein lieden beit."

I looked at my husband. He appeared so normal, so healthy, so confident. I tried to explain to him that we were moving to a new hospital, but I didn't know whether he understood. It would be so lovely if we were like the other patients, the ones who, when they packed up their rooms, went home. I wished we could be like that – normal, packing up and heading home.

On our last full day Tom made very easy transitions from chair to chair and even to the toilet. He tried to dress himself and he initiated conversation. He seemed a completely different person from the one who was pushed in on a gurney seven weeks earlier. I was truly grateful for this new burst of energy and new level of awareness. It took the edge off the melancholy inherent in the move to Jackson. In the journal, I thanked Tom for choosing this time to sparkle. We really needed it.

I said goodbye to the nurses and brought them a large box of cookies from a wonderful Italian bakery. I assumed I would never see that facility again, but the next day brought a monsoon, so I had to return to bring Tom warmer clothes and a raincoat for his removal by ambulance. The cookie recipients were weekend staff, which meant another gift was needed for Monday: they got a potted plant. No so exciting, but surely there were leftover cookies in the staff room; it was a huge box.

On the way down to the hospital the Demon and I hydroplaned and turned a half-circle on, then off the highway. Very scary. I told Tom about it.

"But you got here," he said.

How natural and wonderful!

I went ahead to ready his room at Jackson. It was really a very pleasant private room, which Helen and I had insisted upon, and the administration was pleased to accommodate us. Did the fact that one of the hospital administrators was a former student of ours at Lakewood High School have anything to do with their immediate compliance to our request? I chose to believe that we were not receiving preferential treatment but rather it was readily apparent that a youngster like Tom should not be forced to share a room with a much older, more needy, and possibly terminal patient. We also realized the number and frequency of Tom's visitors could well be disturbing to a roommate. In the end, we were very satisfied with the room, and its lovely view of deep woods, with even an occasional deer, from a large picture window. Tom deserved this.

The ambulance bringing Tom arrived in the afternoon. At first his new placement was a little confusing to him, but it was a measure of the progress he'd made that he was quickly able to accept it, especially after a good meal. There was no experimentation with food here. Tom was brought a plate of ravioli, which he devoured immediately. I asked for another plate, which disappeared as quickly. Good marks right from the beginning on his food chart!

I left him resting on his bed, listening to his tapes, and went out to buy some little tables for his room, and a TV stand. My expectations were still for continued rapid progress and the eventual restoration of the Tom we'd once had. A good feeling about Jackson assured me this would, finally, be the place where it would happen

We were immediately impressed with Jackson. By "we" I mean Helen, whose approval of the facility relieved me of one more source of stress. Arrangements were made with a friend to bring in a TV for Tom's room. That there was still a bit of smoothing-out to be done within the first few days was apparent when I had to leave Tom strapped in his wheelchair. He had been trying to walk out with me, but he was new to the facility and unfamiliar to the nurses; they sensed his disorientation and insisted a safety belt be put on him in the chair until they could better assess his capabilities. I had the feeling he blamed me for this restriction and was sullen, angry and resistant when I left.

As March ended, we felt apprehensive, but willing to give Jackson a chance. We really liked their program. Tom enjoyed their food and we felt that once he became familiar with his new routine, he would be content there for however long this new leg of the journey would take.

CHAPTER 9
APRIL 1994

Had we only known what wonderful progress Tom would make at Jackson Health Care, I would have demanded his removal from his previous hospital months earlier, rather than wasting so much time, energy and emotion begging the staff to retain him longer. We were very alone as a family dealing with serious traumatic brain injury, and learning there was a scarcity of literature on the subject – none, in fact, pertaining to the care of a patient like Tom who was not in a permanent residential institution. The dearth of materials not only forced us to grope about in the dark for solutions, but also prevented us from seeing an answer when it was presented to us. We had been so frightened of the nursing home with its aura of doom, so afraid it would be Tom's final residence, that it never occurred to us he might thrive in such a setting.

As we settled into Jackson Health Care we were frightened, apprehensive, and struggling to make the best of the situation. Tom's room was suitable, even if the furniture was not particularly attractive and the bed was very old-fashioned, very Jane Eyre. We brought in a table and lamp, some framed photos, and a television and soon the room took on a cozy and familiar look. He seemed content with it.

By some odd coincidence April Fool's Day and Good Friday were on the same day that year. An interesting religio-philosophical discussion could evolve from this, I was sure, but I only had time to remark upon it and get busy not with foolish or spiritual concerns but with serious and heathen activities – shopping and banking – before going to see Tom in his new setting. I dared myself to believe, as we began this phase of our adventure, that we just might have more cause to be optimistic than we'd been since our journey began four months ago.

Certain trends developed immediately. No dietary concerns were mentioned for Tom. After being given pureed and then chopped food at his prior hospital, he was delighted with his meals at Jackson. He ate every meal so heartily that we requested and were given double portions. From the first tray brought to his room on the first evening until his last day there, he enjoyed all his food. At Jackson there were no menu choices as there had been at his rehab, where I filled out his menu card. The nurses recorded the percentage of each meal eaten by each patient, as they had in the other hospital, where Tom racked up a string of zeros, rejecting the pulverized food. Now, in Jackson, they delivered the tray and automatically wrote 100% on his chart. The resultant nutrition improved his color, his energy level, and his attitude. I will always believe that had Tom been given ordinary, whole-food meals at his earlier hospital, he would have shown vast improvements there. I could appreciate that the staff preferred to err on the side of caution, yet, in my opinion, once he began to speak, prolonged caution was unwarranted. The Tom who ate regular meals at Jackson was the same fellow who only on the previous day had been given unappetizing chopped foodstuff. He did not miraculously improve overnight. We had arranged for Tom to receive his meals in his room rather than in the communal dining hall. I wanted to keep a little distance between him and the resident population, among which there was a good deal of crying and incoherent babbling as well as some unattractive eating habits. I thought he might find it more pleasant to eat in his room, where his visitors could join him and he would not be distracted or confused by his fellow patients. Certainly I found it more pleasant. My admission sounds harsh. To reiterate, I deliberately avoided medicine as a career. Perhaps I am not strong enough. At any rate, we were having difficulty enough facing our own reality, let alone the realities of a nursing home.

The important thing was that Tom was happy in his new setting and enjoyed the freedom of getting up and walking around. He was no longer restricted after an evaluation proved he could be independently mobile. In the evenings he sometimes had to be led back to his room. The wanderlust was not a problem; the confusion arose because all the corridors looked alike and opened out into identical hallways. It was easy to become lost. With time, he sorted out the problem.

Besides taking immediately to his food, Tom very much enjoyed his therapies and we found the program at Jackson to be sensible and effective. There was one large physical therapy room, administered by two or three therapists under the direction of Priscilla Miller, a marvelously sensible woman. Patients arrived for P.T. shortly after breakfast and Priscilla and her staff would apportion them out, placing each patient either at one of the therapy stations along the walls or at a rest stop, a chair between stations. From the center of the room where she worked individually with each patient, Priscilla could monitor all the others. Her assistant would travel from person to person around the room, moving each one on to the next station, or to rest. It was a sensible, quiet rotation and seemed to be very effective.

The clients enjoyed the company of others, the entire system could be managed by two people, and the therapeutic sessions could last as long as all day. There were no conflicts among the various branches of the staff and no prima donna attitudes on the part of the therapists. It was a balanced, harmonious, and friendly atmosphere and above all a very practical and sensible one.

Now don't laugh at me, but I also think Tom responded to therapy better at Jackson because the therapists wore white lab coats. His previous therapists had presented as a gaggle of young girls in jeans and sweatshirts, each announcing what to him must have been incomprehensible nonsense: "Hi! I'm _____. I'm your _____ therapist." Since he still had no idea where he was, or what therapy was, or why he needed it, it had to have been confusing for him. At Jackson, the quiet, professional manner and the white coats of the therapists immediately conveyed a sense of order, and he responded much more intelligently.

The white coat was a symbol of some sort of authority, something to which a person with a developing vocabulary and a disoriented sense of relationships could respond. Within the complicated confusion of Tom's returning consciousness, the white coat answered questions he might feel but was incapable of asking.

A separate kitchen and bathroom facility off the main therapy room was overseen by the occupational therapist, who worked on

ADLs with the patients. Here Tom learned to dress himself, to brush his teeth and to groom himself. He was taught how to operate major kitchen appliances and how to accomplish simple life skills. Like any lesson, the theme was constant repetition. Tom had not yet demonstrated any of his new learning consistently, but it was early days. We, neither the therapists nor the family, were not discouraged. In the evening, the speech therapist came to the patient's room. All of the therapists were professional and understanding, and within days we were beginning to feel much more optimistic about the sub-acute facility.

But our angel was Warren Strong, a man not inappropriately named. Warren was assigned as Tom's aide and within days they were buddies. Because he was same height as Tom, Warren could help him walk, pick him up when he fell, and assist him with toileting, dressing, washing, and shaving. It was only a few days before Warren had Tom out of diapers and nearly self-sufficient in the bathroom and shower. Warren was also the same age as Tom; they had some mutual knowledge and interests, not the least of which was sons the same age. Warren would talk about his boys and Tom was able to relate. I hold Warren responsible for a great deal of Tom's progress and more than that, for his well-being as a man.

If Tom developed a theme during his stay at Jackson, it was steady improvement, paralleled with a steadily increasing awareness of his situation and its incumbent difficulties and frustrations. His language gradually became clearer and his phraseology more nearly normal and with these developments there also developed a greater ability to express himself and to voice his own concerns.

The first few days showed promise, despite a little confusion and disorientation, which was to be expected. Tom exhibited a bit of resistance when asked to do some tasks; there was no pattern. Sometimes he would refuse to transfer from bed to chair, or vice versa, and sometimes he would be very stubborn in therapy. Gradually the problems subsided. One problem disappeared with the wheelchair within the first week. After an ambulatory therapist pronounced him able to walk, the wheelchair was simply taken away, thus eliminating one of the transfer problems. Tom had to learn his way to the elevator and down to therapy by himself. As he began to trust the therapists, his stubbornness dissolved. In a short time the entire setting became one quite conducive to learning and comfort.

Content with Tom's new placement and the therapeutic program, I dared to take time off during April vacation to attend to the house, read and relax. Of course, Demon caught wind of my plans and had to be shopped once again. I received a packet of mail that the Post Office had inexplicably sent out to our summer address in Idaho. It contained a lot of overdue bills. Daunting, but not overwhelming.

The possessed vehicle now required three or four days in the shop and over $500 to exorcise its devils. So, a total of over $1,000 in the past five months, plus the cost of rental cars, not to mention the great inconvenience to myself and to those who drove me around. Overwhelmed with the beast's machinations, I decided not to worry about the money if everything could be done once and for all to fix the vehicle. Ha! There ought to be a 12-step program for incurable optimists.

One of Tom's goals at his prior location had been the maintenance of a 10-minute attention span. He had failed. At Jackson I watched him stay on task for 30 minutes. What made the difference? In the rehab, therapy was held in the lobby or in small, open cubicles off a busy hall. The work areas were noisy and distracting; a great deal of outside activity transpired. At Jackson, patients went downstairs, away from the living quarters, and were given therapies in a quieter, calmer environment. All that busy-ness in the former location may have impressed visitors or prospective clients, but it did not work for Tom. His previous therapy units were a half-hour, much of which, you remember, was lost as nurses and therapists contended with each other to coax him into the wheelchair. At Jackson he walked to the elevator by himself and stayed in the therapy gym for the entire morning. The schedule was much more relaxed.

My mother, Helen and I attended the first team meeting at Jackson on March 31st. We were very impressed with the personality and caliber of the staff. We aired our concerns and they seemed willing to deal with them; they let us know their plans and expectations. There was an aura of confidence and professionalism, underlined with the usual, "Nobody knows with head trauma." We came away pleased and hopeful about the place itself and Tom's treatment, but we all agreed as the meeting closed that we were in the early stages yet. This meeting was more in keeping with the original prognosis given to us by the trauma team at Jersey Shore. This being Tom, I still expected the kind of rapid progress that would astound the professional staff. This also being real life, I understood I must accept the opinion of the staff, albeit reluctantly.

For all the talk there had been about aggressive therapy when we began this adventure at the other hospital, it seemed Tom received much more therapy and less aggression at Jackson. Admittedly, he was physically and intellectually more advanced than he had been, but because of the layout, there was no time wasted between or during sessions. He could remain downstairs for two or more hours, alternating between therapies and resting in a chair. Time on task was certainly longer and more productive than it had been.

I noticed Tom was beginning to exert a little bit of control over aspects of his environment. He would open and close the door to his room when he wanted to, straighten out items on his tables, throw things out. Tiny, seemingly trivial aspects of daily living, but significant. Perhaps this was a vestige of an ancient impulse in man to put his kingdom in order. Denied the ability to communicate in a meaningful manner, perhaps Tom was acting on innate instincts that pre-dated the development of communication itself. Or, perhaps I was romanticizing his small efforts to create peace within his little world. In any case, I saw progress, which is what we needed.

His cognitive learning did not develop as tidily. For example, one day I worked with him all afternoon on five speech exercises. He did so well that I tried to sneak in a sixth, but he stopped me, aware I had only asked him to do five. In the evening when the speech therapist arrived, he blanked out totally on the five exercises he'd done successfully earlier. In the same session, the therapist drilled him in naming common utensils; he repeated the words dozens of times, but the next day they were gone.

Tom made several heartbreaking attempts to go with me when I left at night. We finally worked out a plan with one of the night staff, who would follow us as Tom came to the door with me. If he tried to leave, she would come up and distract him with a trip to the vending machine or a TV show as I darted out and away. He took to wandering around at night and was given a wander-guard to wear like a wristwatch. It would trigger an alarm if he pushed open the outside door.

I spent most of my April vacation at Jackson watching Tom

go through his paces. He was quite active in physical therapy and seemed to enjoy the variety of equipment. He refused to work with some of the learning material I'd brought in. "They're second or third grade," he would say – upgrading the pre-reading workbooks . He was unable to do the work, simple as it was, and unwilling to try. He did, though, recognize that the work was too childish for the old Tom he may be remembering, the fellow who still resided deep within. There were occasional toilet mishaps but more and more he could initiate his own trips to the bathroom with no outside reminders.

By April 5th, in speech therapy, he was able to express his understanding of his situation quite clearly. "There's something here that I don't know about and until I know about it I can't be prepared."

And, "There's something amiss here, something amiss that I can't put my finger on."

Kathy, the speech therapist, said, "You're making great improvement, Tom."

"No, I really don't think so," he replied. "I want to say –there" and he pointed his finger ahead, "and I can't do that."

"Why do you think that is?"

"I don't know what the hell it is. Okay, I'll give it to you but I don't know that you'll understand it. I don't know that you want it but I don't think you will."

To us this was clear. Tom wanted to communicate, wanted words, and did not understand why they did not come.

Given two words to consider, Tom replied, "You know, both these words sound so familiar to me and I can't think of what they mean."

How could we help but be encouraged when we heard this kind of language?

Tom could have bursts of normal syntax, but if he were to be distracted, he would soon lose the thread. For example, his dinner tray was delivered while Kathy was in the room for therapy. Tom was clearly confused and uncertain whether to eat or have the lesson. Kathy said, "Why don't you go ahead and eat, Tom? We can still work while you are eating."

"Did you get to eat?" he asked but to and about himself, not her. And then he was off. "No. Did you get...This is so much...I don't know how far to conrast you. Conrast you? No! I don't know how far to – oy, this is so stupid. So, I can't play with you. I have had flavors from...I don't know how many weeks they have begun. Then, lately, I've had therapists – no – anyway, this was the first week I have had – I don't even know what to call them because one was a human being so she was a – I don't know what she was – but she came to me. Then we got on board and halfway through the lesson this came." He pointed to the tray. "So I said, 'What are we going to do?' She said, 'Don't worry about it.' So I said okay. But I really don't really know what the hell to do because – I don't know what the heck to do."

Obviously in this little narrative Tom was replaying the scene that had just occurred when the tray was delivered in the middle of his lesson. It was very interesting.

Later in the evening I presented him with a glass beer stein from one of his college proms. "Oh, I don't remember this," he said. "Oh, I'm probably sure that I encountered this somewhere. You're going to leave this with me? I can't believe that you did this. Okay. Thank you. I don't know where the hell this came from. Thanks. Thank you...It's incredible. You saved this? Why didn't you tell me this?"

His voice, in long narratives especially, had begun to take on expression, modulation, and color.

At the family meeting on April 8th, Stephanie, the occupational therapist, told us, "Tom told me things were going on in his head and he didn't know what they were. He made flashing signs by opening and closing his hands like this." She demonstrated by rapidly opening and closing both hands, fingers spread out when open and fisted when closed. To me, it was a definite characterization of mental confusion. Pretty well expressed, too.

I sat in on one of their sessions.

"Tell me about this, Tom." The O.T. held up a comb.

Tom pointed to each end of the comb. "There are two," he said.

"I don't understand. Tell me again," Stephanie asked.

Patiently, in his teacher voice, Tom again pointed. "There are two," he said again. "There are two."

Light was dawning on the therapist and me. We were a step behind Tom. Stephanie put down the comb and picked up a toothbrush. "Tell me about this," she said.

He looked at it for only a second and said, "It's eleven by four."

And yes, there were four rows by eleven rows of tufts on the toothbrush! Tom was seeing parts, not the whole. He understood the comb to have two sections, the thick prongs and the thin prongs, and he interpreted units along the toothbrush rather than perceiving it as an entity. And he did this instantaneously!

What did this mean? Did he automatically break a whole into its components, or did he understand only the individual units rather than the whole? No one seemed to know what this signified, but it was fascinating to behold.

Priscilla Miller told me, "A woman who is down in the gym

with him every day asked me about him. She said it appears his ego's been damaged as well as his brain."

We had to agree with the assessment. It was especially evident as Tom made progress and simultaneously learned to compensate when he did not know something, much the way an illiterate person can fool others into thinking he can read.

Pleased as we were with Jackson, it was not paradise. There was often extraneous confusion in the corridor, and not everything went smoothly, but little of it affected Tom. Once there was a very complicated mix-up concerning the substitute speech teacher, the general overseer of all therapies in the Meridian Health System, our case manager who was the liaison between Jackson Health Care and the insurance companies, and various therapists. It took most of a day and into the evening before it got straightened out, and I was exhausted in the effort, but he never knew.

I was often called out of his room to be an interpreter. Maria, an aged and somewhat demented Italian lady was in the room across from Tom. She shared the room with an extremely fastidious and selfish woman who would park her wheelchair in the doorway of their room and refuse Maria entrance, telling her she was "nasty" and "dirty." Maria would sit in her wheelchair, crying out in Italian. It was easy to interpret what she had to say because it was always a variation of a plea for her son Sam to come and get her, or an assertion that Sam had promised to do so. Her plight was a heartbreak in its own way and at times the staff asked me to spend a little time with her to calm her down. Tom was unaware of this, even though it took place right outside his own door. His world turned as smoothly and routinely as we could arrange it, and he was usually oblivious to outside altercations. Quite a refreshing change from his last location,

One day Tom suddenly got up and began tidying his room. He took all his Easter cards from the windowsill and dropped them into the wastebasket. He took his hospital ID bracelet, two packages of saltines, and an empty cassette case and dropped those in as well. His old school briefcase, which I'd brought in when the O.T. requested familiar objects, was standing on a table. He moved it to the doorway. He pushed a chair away from in front of his closet. Then he opened the closet door and began taking shirts off their hangers and folding them on the bed.

"Tom, what are you doing?" I asked. But I knew what he was doing and I was close to tears. He looked surprised at the question and replied as if the answer should have been obvious.

"Because I'm going..." he said, as he pointed his finger out the doorway, to the left, center, and right.

What a heartbreak. And I was the bad guy; I had to tell him he couldn't leave. He didn't pay any attention to me and continued to fold his clothes.

I looked at my husband, and I felt my heart fold in half. I saw a calm, quiet, but determined man setting out a course of action which could, under the right time and circumstance, be so normal, so natural, and so appealing to him. He wanted to go home; he was packing to go home. Alas, this was neither the right time nor the right circumstance. I looked at him and I hurt inside.

Fortunately, serendipitously, Warren appeared. "Hey, Tom," he said as soon as he saw what was happening and the helplessness in my face, "Let's give the bathroom a chance, okay?" While Warren kept him in the bathroom, I put the clothes back in the closet.

I felt so sad. There was Tom, so much back "in charge," putting his room in order and trying to exert some control over his life. And were it not for Warren's timely interruption, Tom and I would have had to deal with the distressing disappointment of reality: he had, in fact, no control at all. Disappointment such as this must have been what his fellow patient noticed as evidence of a hurt ego.

Tom would often get "stuck" in the bathroom and sit there for thirty or forty minutes. This time, after a reasonable interlude, I tried to lure him out by telling him about the figure skating program on TV. "Hurry up, Tom," I said. "There's a double Elvis on – Elvis Stojko skating to the music of Elvis Presley!"

He came out laughing, settled in comfortably, and seemed to have forgotten his attempt to move out.

In later conversation, he gave me this advice: "In case you don't understand, remember that whenever you want to get into the polling place – whenever you can – just do it." [Whenever I had to make a decision, I should just go ahead and make it.] He seemed to be quite pleased with himself for being able to help me with counsel. For me, another heartbreaker.

The speech therapist came in the afternoon. As part of her lesson she asked Tom for the opposite of push.

Kathy offered hints. She went to the door. "Look, Tom. I can push the door open or – what? Push or – what?"

Finally, he said, "I just can't....discern it."

Kathy and I laughed. "Anybody else would just have said, 'I don't know,'" I said. "But you said 'discern.'"

"As a matter of fact, the only time I used the word discern was right here," he said. "I never used that word."

We noticed a new trend developing in Tom's mode of expression. When he could not find the words he needed, he tended to dismiss the subject as something he didn't care to discuss. He could not allow himself to admit that he did not know, or couldn't express the rest of the thought. (The damaged ego, perhaps?) A typical example from conversation on that Saturday went as follows:

"I would like to reconcile the fact that over and over again teachers are just discreditly wintered in the – never mind. I don't want to get into it."

As his vocabulary skills improved, so did his compensatory "tricks." It was common, as time went on, for him to use such phrases as: "Oh, you don't know? Then I'm not going to tell you." Or, "I know; let's see if you know." These were obviously childish maneuvers to avoid having to admit his inability to answer a question. This problem never seemed to frustrate him at all, though. He did not wrestle with his thoughts, or ponder, or give any overt display of thought processes or his inability to marshal those processes into coherent speech. He was comfortable with dismissing it.

To my mind, these kinds of statements demonstrated a much higher intellectual process than his earlier attempts. He started out with an idea, stumbled over the words, became aware of the stumble, and saved himself from a complete fall by ending the discussion. (Aren't there times when we all wish we'd done the same?) I was always greatly heartened by these pronouncements and saw them as milestones on his road to recovery.

I noticed by early April Tom was finally reaching the goals set for him at the first rehab. They had expected him to attain those goals in two or three weeks. He apparently needed six weeks, because here in Jackson, in a quieter surrounding and at a slower pace, he was achieving. I saw a conundrum here. If the first hospital team expected these results in two or three weeks, they must have made an initial assessment of his abilities and decided he was capable of a certain level of improvement within a set time span. When he failed to reach the goals they'd set, rather than adjust their assessment, they set the motions into play that would eventuate in his removal from the facility. Did this mean the original evaluation was somewhat generic: i.e., all brain trauma patients will achieve these goals in a specific time? Because he was more severely damaged than most of their patients, the assessment was not really applicable to him. Wasn't that obvious? Did they not have a Head Injury Unit and were they not aware of the time needed to reach goals? At Jackson he was reaching the very same goals. Time had been needed, time his former rehab had not been willing to invest. I had to question whether the initial evaluation ever took Tom's individual needs into consideration or whether he was simply placed into a general category and then abandoned when he did not thrive.

To be fair, Tom had been much more confused and disoriented in his prior hospital, and was just emerging from his coma. I often wondered whether, had he been kept there, he would have eventually reached his goals. He had been offered the option of an eventual return to that facility once he'd reached a certain level of rehabilitation, but we were so satisfied with the approach taken at Jackson Health Care I would not consider returning.

Bathroom accidents continued to occur. They seemed to bother Tom. Once, after a stroll with the ambulation aide, he returned wet, and repeating "I don't understand what happened; I don't understand what happened." Warren came along to assist and once Tom was clean and comfortable, we assured him he was all right and making progress. "I'm just annoyed," he said. Happily for him, like so much else, the incident was soon forgotten.

If anyone thinks toilet training a child is difficult, let me

assure you that training a 47-year-old, brain-injured man is no romp on the beach either!

Tom's colleague, Bob Bonardi, had been making a running videotape of Tom, a process we'd begun in the Step-Down Unit. On April 10th, as soon as Bob aimed the camera at him, Tom was "on." He played to the camera, eating applesauce as if it were an exercise for drama school or an audition for a commercial. We watched the tape from the beginning, although most of us watched Tom watching himself. He was fascinated. He remarked, "I know that's me, but I don't remember it."

I found the tape both revealing and upsetting. I'd forgotten how somber and serious and sick Tom had looked at the onset of the journey. Also, as the tape unfolded, I realized all the little triumphs we'd celebrated so wistfully earlier in his progression were frightfully crude and primitive compared to his present persona. All the little triumphs that had caused us to rejoice seemed so trivial, and the confusion in his eyes was manifest. He was now a different person altogether.

A friend of Bill's brought up a significant event from the past. "Mr. Sorrentino," he asked, "do you remember when Bill and I spraypainted the neighbor's house?"

"I can't say I remember the episode, but I do remember the idea of it," he replied. How clear; how lovely.

Later, he and I talked about teaching. Tom said, "I want to read," in a tone of voice that implied he could read and wanted to, not as if he wanted to learn to read. Denial of his inability to read was thematic throughout Tom's eight-year recovery.

"I have a study plan," he announced. "I want to achieve the two-to-three unit course and then go off to do some unit work and then focus the last section on whatever thrills in my behavior. I want to locus...locus? No...focus...focus on some ballyhook."

Does this sound a little like teacher talk? But it hurt me to hear it, to hear the sincerity in his voice and the plaintive ache from somewhere deep within his being to continue the studies that had always been a part of his life. I definitely looked forward to the day when he could focus on some ballyhook, whatever that was.

This was so wistful and sad, like his trying to pack up his clothes on the previous day. He was a little boy playing "grown-ups" very sincerely, very earnestly, and completely unaware of his inability to carry out the activity. My heart broke for him at these times.

Poor fellow. He was trying so hard to make sense of his situation and so bravely trying to control it.

I arrived after school one day to find him and a P.T. aide nearly at the front door, having a "discussion." Tom's discussions usually took the form of long, rambling unfinished thoughts, but he was always sincere and serious and careful with his words. And the staff respected his earnestness. I suspected this time, once again, he wanted to leave the facility.

"Look, Tom. Clean clothes!" I said, holding up the bag of his laundry. "Let's go put them away, okay?" We got him back to the room but he seemed unhappy. When the aide left and we were alone he said, "There are two who lied to me."

"What do you mean?"

"They told untruths," he said. Interesting. He could explain what the word "lie" meant, but could not explain the statement.

"Can you tell me about it?" I asked.

"You come in on a custom that doesn't confuse you, but I, on the other hand, come in on a custom that confuses me."

"I think I understand. You're not sure what's going on here," I said. It did seem clear; he was expressing himself quite well.

"I'm confused," he began, "about the same kinds of interruptions that generated – all I know is, I'm confused and I'm not confused."

"Do you know where you are, Tom? And why you are here?" Not that I hadn't told him a million times, hoping to prevent just this kind of confusion.

"I've got all kinds of events to take advantage of," he replied. It was not an answer, but an implication of the answer. This is the same kind of thought process that produces haiku poetry!

He never was able to explain who lied to him, and about what. I suspected it was a simple misunderstanding between Tom and a staff member.

More than once, and more and more often, I had the feeling Tom was speaking as if in translation. He had words to choose from and sometimes selected one that was close to, but a little off from the meaning he intended. At other times he invented words that sounded close to what he needed, but this was happening less frequently now.

It had been a bittersweet weekend – sweet and sad. He was fighting a ghost – probably many ghosts – and it was so difficult for us to help him because we couldn't see them.

Two ladies on Tom's hall stopped me one afternoon before I went into his room. "Tom had a bad time today," one of them said.

"We all did," the other added, and both of them nodded their heads at each other.

"What happened?" I asked.

They told me there was a new and very aggressive P.T. assistant who worked with them today. She made an unfavorable impression on these ladies, but Tom froze when she was telling him what to do – and then he walked out. As I later learned from

Warren, Tom came back to his room, but he did not get to the bathroom in time and was very wet. Warren said it took quite a while for him, with the help of another aide, to get Tom into the bathroom and Tom was very upset.

I found him looking dejected. "What's wrong?" I asked.

"There's nothing I can do," he told me.

We talked a while and I tried to get him to understand that a few short weeks ago he hadn't been able to go to the bathroom at all, much less discuss it. He simply could not understand how much progress he'd made because he had no recollection of the accident, the coma, or his early rehabilitation. But he knew his body wasn't working right and he felt his own helplessness and lack of control, all of which was impeded by his difficulty in communicating.

Sometimes, perversely, the easiest and happiest part of Tom's situation was, in fact, the loss of memory. At the time of the above incident, after our talk, a short nap, and a good supper, he was fine and had a sparkling session in the evening with the speech therapist. The distress of the day had been forgotten.

Incidentally, the new P.T. Therapist was not hired. Her initial impression on all the clients was unfavorable.

Tom made several attempts after that to try to explain his situation. His speech was still rambling and incomplete and open to interpretation, but the ideas were there. It was a constant "awakening." He told me he was going through "mental phases" and was confused by so many people asking him questions in the past "three months." That was quite clear. Also, he was obviously annoyed by the presence of a nurse or aide when he needed the bathroom. I explained that as soon as he could manage it on his own, he would be left alone. A little while later he did go to the bathroom alone, but was not sure how to flush the toilet. Once I demonstrated, he was fascinated watching the water go down. Just like the Joad kids in *Grapes of Wrath.*

He began a pattern that was to continue, wherein he interpreted all appropriate gatherings or situations in scholastic terms. His therapies were "classes," his therapists "teachers." Even months later, after an afternoon of playing pool, he would report his success in terms of a grade. "I got A+ on all four games," he once said. Or, "I only got 75% today. I lost one game." A true example, I suppose, of taking the teacher out of the school but never taking school out of the teacher.

The first time this occurred was on April 13th, nineteen weeks after the accident. He couldn't understand why his language "class" was held in his room.

One night the nurses' station called me. Tom was found sitting on the floor, unable to get up. He seemed to be unhurt and there was no explanation he could give for landing in that predicament. Did he miss the chair? Or try to tidy the room and fall? At the time, we didn't know.

One Saturday Tom held court, as usual, with his visitors. He had many guests but they were spread out through the day so he was not overstimulated. All of them came away impressed by his lucidity and new abilities.

"How do you like it here?" my sister Paula asked.

"I've never even projected a place like this because it's senior citizens," he said.

"But are you happy here?"

"I'm having a ball!" he said, and immediately acted out a little scene with changed voices. "I'm in the name front of everything that happens. 'Oh, good evening, Mr. S. Good evening, Mr. S.'"

I think he was telling us that everyone made a fuss over him and he loved it.

A bizarre incident occurred one afternoon. Tom had had afternoon therapy – he now went downstairs twice a day – and was in his room managing polite society with the MacFarlands, but he looked tired. "You might like a little nap, Tom," Rich suggested. Tom headed directly for his bed and fell immediately into a sound, solid sleep.

Forty minutes later, after Rich, Susan, and I had had a cup of coffee, we tried to rouse Tom and could not. We called for an aide but she had no success, either. Rich raised the head of the bed, thinking it might be easier for Tom to step off, but even in a slouched and semi-sitting position he slumbered on. I was getting scared; he simply would not awaken. I put a cold, wet towel on his face, I poked and prodded, but got no response.

Then, suddenly, he woke up and looked around, a very wild look in his eyes. "What the hell is this?" he said. He seemed upset and disoriented.

His tray was brought in and he began to eat, standing at his table. With the help of the aide we got him into his chair and as he ate he seemed to calm down a little.

When he was calm, I asked him what had happened.

"It was frightening!" he said. "It was terrible!"

"Can you tell us about it?"

"I don't want to think about it," he replied.

We believed he must have had a nightmare and its frightening aftermath still sat on him, but he lacked the words to express himself. Instead, he changed the subject. "I never wore clothes like this..."

Later, I asked him if he could tell us about his dream.

"There were all kinds of little things... Little things... All by unit."

This was as far as we could get.

Bernie and Roz Ressner visited, which dispelled the angst over his dream. When they left, as I always did with visitors, I reviewed with Tom who they were. "They are going to Italy this week," I told him.

Immediately he brightened; I could see the light bulb go on. "Now I know who they are!" he exclaimed. "And I know where they live!" There was pride in his voice. The old Tom loved to know things, and this new incarnation also derived pleasure from the bits of "knowledge" he could demonstrate to us.

The following afternoon Tom tried to be polite but was obviously tired after his therapies. He said to my mother and me, "Would you and you like me to use that?" and pointed to the bed. Moments after we said yes, he was asleep. But he initiated the question – a big step!

He told the speech therapist that evening, "I was expecting you to get serious and then break off and you did get serious but you didn't break off."

Now, he was able to express himself when asked to name the objects she held up. Although he still couldn't name them, he could and did offer excuses for that failing.

"I don't even know the word but I could make it up"

"I can sure take a guess."

"I don't know because I never saw such a thing."

"I just don't know what they are – if I could just have ten, eleven minutes."

After the therapist left, Tom spoke for nearly a half hour about his experience the day before, the probable nightmare. He called it, "what happened last Monday", and, in fact, the day had been a Monday. He told me he was scared and glad I had been there to help him.

"Because I saw something there that wasn't there," he said.

The experience was still very much in his mind and he was remembering it, which was a long time for him to hold onto a memory. It must have made quite a disturbing impression.

Tom continued to take delight in his meals, although he still needed help unwrapping the various containers. He insisted upon "drinking" anything that came in a small cup-shaped container. This included salad and ice cream. Warren told me Tom was taking good care of himself and washing well, which he knew because he placed tiny ink dots on his patients' bodies and then checked to see if they had been washed off. The nurses told me Tom would often wander out to the nursing station at night and sit there, listening and even occasionally laughing. I hoped he wasn't lonely.

Despite all the progress, I still worried about Tom reaching another plateau and being asked to leave, as had already happened to us. The team assured me that Jackson was not so strict, not as pressured by the insurance companies. At least, I told myself, if he did level out, it would be on a much higher plateau than the one that got us ejected at the end of March.

In language class Kathy asked, "What is this?" and held up a shoelace. The last time she'd presented it Tom had no idea what it was. This time he said, "It's one of two pieces that I was considerably unearthed by."

"And this?" A lock.

"Well, I won't be able to tell you anything more than the last time I looked at it. I don't know anything more about it."

"And this?" She pointed to the bed.

"Well. it's a two-infested, three-infested, four-infested...What? It's a one, two, three, four..." He pointed to the legs, but could not finish. He seemed to make a strong start in these exercises but faltered as they continued. That was evident in the last item Kathy held up, an apple.

"It's a havrigon. H...A...V...R...I...G... Well, you pronounce it differently."

At home that night I looked through some old photo albums, and thought what a crime it is to rob a man of his memories.

The Blazer from hell broke down for the last time. I called my friend Madli from the shop. She picked me up and took me to a car rental agency where I learned, to my chagrin, that I could not rent a car because I didn't have a credit card. Frustrated, I started to cry. It's amazing how tears disarm the people around the crier. The attendant immediately called out someone from the back office and that wonderful person recognized Madli as a teacher in the high school, and also knew Tom's story. She allowed me to rent the car using Tom's credit card. The next time a credit card offer arrived in the mail, I took advantage of it and got my own.

Madli had contacted a school friend of hers and Tom's, who now worked at Pine Belt Chevrolet. He was the Finance Manager, not a salesman, but he arranged to have a number of used cars ready for Madli and me to test drive. I told her what I was looking for and between her and Scotty Howell at Pine Belt, I would be able to forget about driving the Blazer forever, although I planned to keep it for Bill when he returned in the summer.

On the day of the test drive, I explained to Tom that I had to leave early. This was four days after his nightmare and I had assumed he'd forgotten about it. However, before I left I asked him if he felt well. A shadow passed over his face and he shrugged his shoulders and said, "Well, you remember..." and I knew the effect of the dream was still with him.

A refreshingly diverting event at school: one of our young ladies managed to commandeer a school bus. She drove it a short distance, with other kids aboard, before the police thwarted her ambition. The boys at Coastal were loud and threw things (like desks and bookcases) but the girls took misbehavior to a higher level. I had to admire this one. After all my trials with the devilish vehicle we owned, I would still not have had the expertise or the raw courage to start up a school bus, never mind trying to drive it. There might have been a lesson here for me, but if so it was too complicated to be of use.

I bought a new (used) car. Scotty lined up five choices for me. Madli and I took each one for a spin and I made my choice. We proceeded to the mechanic's to pick up the truck and put down another $600. Madli drove the new car to my house while I followed behind, driving Demon, taunting it and forcing it to look at its replacement. I also threatened the vehicle: "No more mechanics," I told it. "Next time, a witch doctor, a rattle and a dead chicken." I believe it was properly chagrined.

Tom exhibited a good deal of agitation after he asked Helen where his father was. She explained that he died the previous September. Tom had no memory of that and the knowledge affected his afternoon at therapy. Once again, I was stuck in the middle when the therapists suggested that I ask Helen to limit her lunchtime visits with Tom. Why didn't they ask her? Not that it was a helpful rationale, but they explained they were mothers, too, and they knew what being there meant to Helen. Here was a woman whose husband had died the previous September after a long battle with cancer, and whose son was severely injured the following December. She was strong, but had to be near the breaking point. And I was supposed to ask her not to be there? What was I to say? Were it not for my work at school, I would have been there all day as well. And once again, Tom's continued progress certainly seemed to be evidence that whatever we were doing either helped him or at worst had no effect on him.

He initiated a nap at 3:30 every day, and was taking himself to the bathroom. His sporadic attempts to leave with me at night continued. It always broke my heart to explain that he could not come along.

Some of his clothing disappeared from his room. Through the winter I had made several emergency runs to buy new underwear because he'd gone through the supply I left at the hospital. Accidents were still frequent, although less so. This time his good L.L.Bean and Eddie Bauer sweat suits were gone. Since he was a tall man and most of the residents were small women, his clothes would have been of little use to most of the other residents. We suspected that wandering patients with dementia had taken his things. I did not think real theft or malice was involved. Warren found a few of the missing items in other rooms and I replaced the rest with cheaper things. Tom's mother brought him some – to be generous – "unstylish" clothing which even in his confusion he rejected. "I don't think so," he said. "Give them to Bill."

One Saturday morning toward the end of April, at about 10:30, he pointed to the TV and told Warren and me, "I want to go there."

"Go, then," I said. We wanted to see what he meant.

To our surprise he eased himself slowly and carefully to the floor, leaning against the bed for support. Then he scooted over to the TV, which was on a turntable, and turned it around to the back. Carefully, he unplugged the wires and cable, coiling them neatly and placing them on top of or behind the television. Then he swiveled the TV around to face the wall.

"Why are you doing that?" I asked.

"I'm ejecting it," he replied.

For the next hour or more he propelled himself around on the floor, refusing all help. He could not get up alone. I tried it myself and found it very difficult to do with no sense of my right arm and leg, as was Tom's situation with the right-side neglect. When the supper trays came, Warren simply lifted him under the arms and sat him in his chair. Tom laughed and thanked him.

This little episode might have explained the recent mysteries: the night the nurses found him sitting on the floor, the afternoon when I found the TV unplugged. Since Tom enjoyed TV in the hospital as he never had before the accident, I can only surmise that each attempt to unplug it was another manifestation of his desire to pack up and go home.

But he had a new explanation for his situation: "I'm pouring through time," he said.

I told Tom that Kathy, the speech therapist, would be coming.

"Is that Kathy? K...A...T...H...Y..?"

Wow!

Kathy asked him for the opposite of "empty."

"Sequestered" was his immediate reply.

True, it wasn't the correct answer, but – sequestered? Where did that come from?

Again Kathy asked him for the names of various objects and again Tom, while not able to produce those words, was aware of his inability and able to express that:

"I know what it is but I can't identify it."

"I know that we're both talking about the same thing, but I can't..."

"I do know but I don't know."

"I know what it is but I can't think of what it is."

There were wonderful highlights in Tom's recovery, but April left him still bereft of nouns, valiantly trying to be part of the conversations in his room, and not completely sure where he was or why he had to remain there. I was having a bit of trouble with the situation myself because I had hoped for more dramatic, faster improvement and that was still elusive. More than once while driving my new car, I wished I could just drive on and on and away from it all.

CHAPTER 10
MAY 1994

May 1st saw a real revolution for Tom. He suddenly began talking about his placement at Jackson with such clarity and lucidity that his sister Pat, her husband Dennis and I were stunned. We heard a wonderful sequence of explanation and discussion. It was not, mind you, a full restoration of his ability by any stretch of the imagination, but it was far ahead off any conversation he'd had so far.

Before the accident, Tom had been a thoroughly organized person. He kept small notebooks of things he had to do, made out financial charts, kept neat and orderly files in his desk, and ran his life on a smooth schedule. This propensity and his valiant attempts to restore it brought a poignancy to his recovery. He was also very proud of our son, and pleased with the plans for his education at the University of Idaho in Moscow, Idaho, and our eventual move to Idaho.

On Sunday, May 5th, Tom was happily watching basketball on TV. He had always loved basketball and even now was able to comment when some plays were executed. I was answering Pat's question about Bill and must have mentioned that he was still in school in Moscow.

Tom looked over at us, visibly confused. Then he said, "Are there courses in the English language?"

"He must be thinking about the other Moscow," Pat said, once we finally understood the confusion. I did not immediately reach that conclusion because I never would have imagined Tom was capable of that kind of thinking at this stage.

"He's in Moscow, Idaho, Tom," I said.

"Oh, that's all right, then." He returned to his basketball, the confusion having left his face.

But a moment later, he turned to us and said, "I know I'm only an extra here, but I'd like to help if I can."

Do you see what I mean? I had to leave the room to cry.

During the game, Tom watched a commercial featuring basketball players. "I really dislike these rec -no- these basketball players."

"Why?" someone asked. It was not me; I was recovering from the crying spell.

"They're too bright."

"Too bright? What does that mean?"

"Not in the way it's usually meant. They're too slick." Slick: as fitting a word as any to describe someone in a commercial.

Later, we asked Tom if he would like to walk outside."

"No."

Never one to let things pass, I persisted. "How about just once around the building?"

"Well, that's outside."

Our visitors asked Tom about his stay at Jackson and about his therapies. His response was indicative of the latest trend in his speech development. He could manage short, almost automatic answers much more handily than longer explanations, where he began to flounder.

"It's something that's not in school as much as it is the way school is run. For example, there are people who... I can't do it... I don't want to get into the physical property of the one important service that I know exists, but I can't excel that, even though it's very possible and does so much. There's nobody there who would say, 'Yes, this is the reason for your impression.'

"Right now I'm not good at whatever it is that I'm doing. This is terrible. I'm ready to go home."

It was all very exciting. The next day, though, was a messy one. We had given Warren a lovely new nylon sweatsuit for Tom to wear for his first visit to the doctor who would be supervising his discharge and further stages of recovery. Tom promptly had diarrhea. Warren washed and dried the outfit and Tom seemed quite pleased with his appearance when his mother and I arrived to take him out. Unfortunately, this did not last long; he vomited in the car both on the way over and on the return.

The doctor's visit was more of a success on two counts; first, she agreed to a discharge in six to eight weeks. I saw nothing but a straight ascendency from there – on to a full recovery. My childhood reading was vindicated. Heidi and the Swedish triplets were right behind me, cheering me on.

The second aspect of his success amazed all three of us. Over the doctor's desk was a poster of four hot-air balloons, which caught Tom's attention. Noticing this, the doctor asked, "How many balloons are on the poster, Tom?"

"There are sixty," he replied immediately.

"Will you count them for me, please?"

"Fifteen... thirty... forty-five... sixty..."

We gasped. Tom was absolutely correct – in base fifteen! Tom counted the balloons using an advanced mathematical concept. I wanted to scream with joy.

Despite his fatigue and the confusion of the day, Tom sparkled during his evening speech therapy.

"Touch your nose, Tom."

"It's on my body but I don't know where it is." He did not touch his nose.

"Touch your legs."

"Well, I had an impression of where they were, but outside of that, no."

He did not touch his legs.

"Can you close your eyes?"

"So, if you close your eyes.... you don't have any...any sight." He did not close his eyes but this statement was the closest he had come yet to demonstrating an understanding of the question. A little moment to rejoice.

"Will you open up your mouth, wide? Very wide?"

"'You're serious about my opening my mouth? Okay...here it comes...Maybe I won't. I decided against it."

There was a pattern. Tom was either unwilling or unable to obey simple commands. He became an expert at talking around them, asking questions about them, laughing at their seeming insignificance. Was the apraxia still with him, preventing him from obeying the simplest command?

Kathy would sometimes try to trick him by framing the same question in different words. "What do you walk with?" instead of "Touch your legs," for example.

He caught on immediately. "What's the matter with you tonight? I know – you're teasing me!" The understanding was

there, but not the corresponding action. Where was the disconnect?

The best measure of Tom's improvement was through the rapid growth of his speaking abilities. Naturally, I was concerned about and pleased with the progress he was making in physical and occupational therapies, but those skills were not the measure of the man – not of this man at any rate. If he did not master them, many of those skills could be accomplished for him by someone else. It certainly would make life easier for both of us once he learned to dress himself, to attend to his personal grooming, to feed himself, but we could compensate for those losses. The speech damage and its resultant losses were significant. We constantly looked for progress in those areas, progress destined to re-create the Tom we once had.

Language, per se, was not our only interest. His ability to express himself reflected his intellect; we had no other yardstick against which to measure his intellectual progress. Probably we would never know whether his language and his intellect developed together, or if the inability to use language prevented expression of intelligence. We were looking for both, of course. And it was there in bits and pieces, but so far there had not been any consistency. Plenty of clear statements, an abundance of crocus-in-the-snow breakthroughs, but no evidence that he retained the information or could build upon it.

Tuesday, May 10th, was a good day – for me. Tom made terrific strides in expressing himself through speech. I was so encouraged. Bill called. He claimed he was on top of all the little procedures he needed to accomplish in Idaho, but was anxious to come home. He wondered how Tom would react to him. For the first time, Bill told me, "It hurt" to see his father so helpless. This had been so difficult for Bill, so I was pleased to assure him he would definitely take heart when he was able to see his father's progress. He hoped Tom would recognize and remember him.

To prepare for the first meeting, I showed Tom a photograph of Bill and asked who he was. Tom said, "I like this guy and it annoys me to have to think about this...He's terrific. He's such a great guy...It just doesn't finish. I know what to say but it just doesn't come."

He was unable to pronounce Bill's name, but it was evident he recognized him. "I can give you a lot of information, but only if I spend some time." Sadly, this was not true, but he didn't know that.

Kathy showed him a comb and a pencil and asked how they were different.

"The comb? I don't know what the hell I'm doing. And I *know* what both of them are. Well, I've got 50%..."

He counted to 19 and asked, "What is the language for petuating all of the remaining...What is the nature of the x+5?"

This prompted Kathy to write out a few simple arithmetic problems. He looked at a page of simple addition and then subtracted the numbers, but correctly. Once we pointed out the error, he was able to go back and add them. Kathy was so pleased that she gave him homework to do over the weekend. Tom, ever the teacher, knew this was work beyond his daily requirements. He said, "Well, give me extra credit."

To offset the frequent joy we found in Tom's steady improvement was a growing sensation that things were moving along quickly – almost too quickly. I was starting to spin a little out of control. The winter behind us had slogged along through its terrible weather, mirroring our uncertain situation, but we had built up a rhythm, slogging by as well. Now spring was running like a thawing river, too swiftly and carrying us along with it. I was dealing with lawyers, bills, and insurance claims. The team at Jackson was already talking about the next step: Discharge! School, with all its attendant stress, was almost a side-effect. At least there I was in control and knew what I was doing. Not so in the outside world. Kathea's mother, my dear friend Cassie, wrote to me expressing her ambivalence about the "engagement" of our two kids, which became one more situation needing a sort-out. I developed daily migraines. But at the same time, Tom was increasingly lucid, giving us a great deal of hope. It was a strange, seesaw kind of situation.

The pebble-in-the-shoe, Frank Hunter, continued to show up. Tom would close his door for his afternoon nap and Frank would open it and walk in. The presence of this caring, but tedious and pessimistic man, or the threat of his imminent presence created an unwelcome tension almost daily.

At school, one of our lusty lasses, a girl named Tracey, came in to show off her baby. The poor infant, a girl, had birth defects that would require extensive equipment and medical attention. Tracey tenderly described the father, whom she was no longer seeing, as a "scumbag." This baby was eight months old and Tracey's Baby #2 was due in August. A different, already departed young man (presumably another scumbag) was responsible for #2. Tracey related that when she learned the new baby was to be a boy, she cried for three days because "boys are punks." What a tragedy, an all-around tragedy for mother and children. Such were and such would be the population of Coastal Learning Center.

And I thought we had trouble!

Bill was on his way home. Earlier on the day he was to return, we explained everything to Tom, who struggled to find words to express his comprehension. "I know that it's one thing and I know that in my mind it's something else and it's frustrating, very frustrating and I don't understand...This is pathetic."

We needn't have worried. Tom knew Bill immediately and the two of them settled into an intense conversation for a few minutes. Then Barbara complained, "Hey! No one's paying any attention to *me*!" Tom got up, went right over to her, kissed her forehead, took her hand, and made a fuss over her. It was delightful!

Barbara and Tracey took us out for dinner at a local diner where Bill hugged girls, then to a friend's house where he hugged more girls. (I assumed he knew all these young ladies.) It was good to have him and his youthful spirit back home again.

The next day Bill spent more time with Tom. He saw the progress, but was still upset by the whole presentation. It was difficult for him to understand the very small, but almost daily improvement Tom had made, and to appreciate how much more room for hope there was. He must have expected more.

Tom had been fitted with a WanderGuard bracelet because of his nocturnal ramblings. He questioned it and then ignored it, except for the times he managed to pull it off and throw it in the wastebasket. A resurgence of his native independence, perhaps? A manifestation of his desire to go home?

As Tom progressed, it wearied me to be the recipient of his distress, as I often was. For example, if I tried to help him by offering him a spoon when he was attempting to "drink" his ice cream, he would get annoyed with me. Whenever I tried to help him with his homework, or even suggested that he do it, I was rebuffed. And still, when something finally clicked after I'd repeated it dozens of times, he would become upset I didn't tell him sooner. It was a lose-lose situation for me!

In retrospect, I suppose I was so eager to push along the

progress in any helpful way that I probably became a bit over-bearing at times. It might or might not have done him any good, but I thought it was the right thing to do despite the way it wore us both down. And I didn't know what else to do.

Remember, we were playing without a rule book, making it up as we went along. There is precious little information available on dealing with Tom's sort of injury, because, until recently, Tom's sort of injury led to death. There was no game at all, thus no rules.

If you'd have asked me at the time, however, I am sure I would have told you my little efforts were discreet and subtle.

"What are those things on the bed there?" Tom asked. He was pointing to me. I was sitting on the bed.

"Do you want to lie down?" I asked.

"What else is a bed for?" he replied.

Such a seemingly trite conversation, and yet it was a landmark. Most of his nouns had been lost in the crumpled Toyota; whenever one surfaced, especially an unprompted one, we took it as a sign of returning memory. Alas, we hadn't yet accepted the ephemeral nature of these moments.

But *there was* perceptible growth. In reply to being given a sheet of homework by Kathy, he remarked, "I don't understand. I did this for you last week..."

"Perhaps you're not in the mood to do it, Tom?"

"No, it's not that I'm not in the mood; it's that getting into the mood is more difficult than when previously attempted."

How's that for normality?

In the same session with that burst of perfectly acceptable words was the following exchange:

"What's the opposite of front?" Kathy asked.

"I have questions about this. It can mean different things…Of what angular appreciation is that front?"

When Kathy explained how she meant it, pointing to the front of her body, he immediately said, "Rear."

My dictionary listed seven different meanings for the word "front." Was this what Tom was trying to tell us when he asked, "What angular appreciation is that front?" Was he wondering which use of the word Kathy intended? I chose to think so.

He continued. "I'm feeling that people can express a lot of different things – that two people here might of course be accepted in ultimate circles but they could be unaccepted there, too." Was he telling us that he realized different people might have different interpretations of the same word? It certainly sounded like it.

Even though Tom was now able to admit his difficulty in finding words consistently – "I have yet to do it with constance" – he rarely made up words any longer and nearly always spoke in complete sentences. He was more and more aware of his word search problem and, though frustrated, dealt with his difficulty with good humor.

"I do understand your question," he said, "but I don't know how to relate it to my circumstances."

Bill was a day or two into his home life, which meant he drove the Demon all over Lakewood to see everyone he knew. He visited the boys of his youthful escapades and ex-girlfriends, while also spending time with his father and consoling a good friend whose brother had just died of a drug overdose. Through it all, his good nature was constantly at the fore; he was a great comfort to me. I was very impressed with Bill's ability to handle Tom's conversations. He was able to cut right through the confusion, then simplify and explain. It's a gift. I was equally impressed with his ability to manage Demon – or was that pernicious vehicle just taunting me by getting along so well with Bill?

Tom was now slowly moving toward discharge, although the steps were erratic. On good days he would wait for me, and for the coffee and cookies I brought him. "What have you got?" On bad days he used me to vent his confusion. He could be charming and gracious to others then stubborn, defiant and cutting to me, challenging what I said and denying its validity. If he asked where dinner was and I told him he'd already eaten it, he would deny it. My intention was to be as frank, simple and honest as I could be, but even then I got in trouble with him. He was beginning to wear me down. With all the running around I had to do, and the stressful school day, I went to bed exhausted and woke up tired.

I researched a facility for his outpatient cognitive therapy. One hundred percent of the Head Injury cases that I knew of – that would be Eric and John – had selected a particular facility, so I settled on it as well.

The Demon began to give Bill trouble. At last it was an Equal Opportunity Devil. Back to the shop again. That meant more transportation adjustment, for two of us now. Out of this circumstance we saw that Bill's brand of humor, though clever and witty, was somewhat exhausting.

"You are not to consider the Blazer your personal recreation vehicle," I told him.

"Why don't you make a cheeseburger of resentment and serve it on a platter of hatred," he replied. He intended to be witty and sophisticated, not mean. I knew that. Yet now both my men offered me screwball conversation.

Came the day when I was concerned that aliens had landed and left us a changeling in place of Bill. First of all, he went out and got a job at Great Adventure. After that he (or his robot clone) did a hefty day's work inside and outside the house, all without being asked. He was also driving me to and from school in my new car, and running errands for me while the Blazer languished in the shop.

I was now becoming quite discouraged about all the time, money and effort that had gone into our mobile scrap heap – not to mention the inconvenience it imposed upon us. However, a silly, sentimental part of my being kept reminding me that Tom loved his Blazer, and I knew we were keeping it alive because we wanted it available for him when he'd be ready to drive again. For another few days Bill and I had to dance around each other's plans to manage our responsibilities with the use of only one car.

As May moved along, Tom became patently aware of his circumstances and of the role I played in making decisions. He said, "You're my closest person. You can't do what another person tells you to do. You have to do what *you* want. Because if you don't, who fails? Me!"

And: "I can't tell you what to do. I can't make your personality for you. You are closer to the first, second date of my – what? – my substance here. So you've got to come up with either a deciding vote to do something or not to do something. So these are your two choices – that's it. At the end of the function you have to make a decision."

Statements like these convinced me that he understood – and possibly appreciated – my role in making decisions for him. It helped me a great deal to live with that understanding, even though I recognized it might be ephemeral and would be forgotten moments later. But the statement was there, clearly expressed, and I was happy to accept it for what it was at the moment without giving it any further or deeper significance.

Tom amazed a group of visitors one day when he indicated

the other residents at Jackson were "sixty to eighty." When we asked him if he'd found anyone at all in his age group, he held up his hand over his eyes as if peering into the distance and said, "Hello? Hello?"

Also, he informed us he only planned to stay "two more days."

His speech and ability to express himself were definitely improving. When his speech therapist asked for the opposite of real, Tom replied, "Something that has no existence at all."

We'd be thrilled, until the next question illustrated the hit-or-miss nature of his answers. When asked for the opposite of straight, he replied, "I can see it going all these ways [making hand motions for a straight line and then for a circle]. It goes off. It goes around and you know it's very interesting for me to talk of the first thing [making a straight line in the air] first because you know you've got to get to the point and now you've got to…[hand motion indicating crooked, zig-zag path]."

What did we have? Evidence of understanding, but inability to express it. Everything was in there; our challenge was to extricate it.

Tom's school planted a tree in his honor on its grounds. The children gave a series of little performances dedicated to him including a parade of signs, each bearing a letter of his name with a personal attribute beginning with that letter: "S" for "sincere," for example. Helen and I attended the ceremony while Bob Bonardi videotaped it. It was very moving. I thanked the children and I'm sure the microphone picked up the catch in my voice as I told them that with care and support such as they had demonstrated, I was positive he would recover and return to them soon.

Later, in therapy, Kathy asked, "Does a dog laugh?"

"I think it can make sounds," Tom answered, "but I don't think it can make that kind of sound."

Because we had no game book, and because even Tom's teams of professionals had no consistent rules for us to follow, I often found myself caught in the middle of situations similar to the controversies back at the first rehab over the number of his guests or the possibility of overstimulation. What was I to do? All of us were acting out of love and concern and, to be truthful, sheer panic. We did what we thought was useful or helpful, and we hung around the edges to watch and assure ourselves that progress was happening. Who was right? Who was wrong? Was there even a right or a wrong? If the game analogy held, what we were playing was Blindman's Bluff.

Besides, we had amazing progress on our side. Whether our antics were positive or negative, the results were startling and many among the professionals who treated him were pleasantly surprised at the advancement he'd made.

At any rate, I mentioned something to Tom about his occasional lack of cooperation in therapy.

"I kind of decided that this is all bullshit," he replied.

His tray appeared and with it, a Yiddish accent: "Look at this – oy, here they come again. Oy, oy. Oh, my God, let's go to woik here..."

With his improving speech and increasing independence, it now became apparent that memory loss was the most debilitating result of the accident. His speech, convoluted as it was, indicated he knew – and knew that he knew – a great deal more information than he was able to express because he'd forgotten the words. One of his doctors wondered whether anoxia might have occurred at the accident while he was pinned, unconscious, in the car. No one to date had mentioned the possibility, probably because until his speech developed, we were not able to assess his memory.

It was obvious that both long and short-term memories were lost. We could see noun retrieval was a problem, but in addition he was unable to recall any past event in his life or, indeed, even what he'd eaten for breakfast on any given day. His abilities to read and to do simple arithmetic were all gone. He could write letters of the alphabet, but not words. The biggest obstacle to the full recovery I still expected was this profound loss of memory. And yes, even in the face of an overwhelming negative prognosis, I still expected a full recovery. I was realistic enough to push the date farther away; returning to school in September did not look like it was going to happen, but there would be other Septembers out there.

Tom was truly aware of the losses. In the early days, when his speech was still emerging, he would grimace and shiver in his effort to recall a word. As time went by, he began instead to say, "Here we go again" – if he were in a good mood, or "Jesus Christ!" if he were upset – as he tried to find his words. The awareness and its attendant frustration were so evident at the moment, but usually forgotten minutes later. In one way this was fortunate, as he was not prolonging his frustration, but in another way, this immediate forgetfulness may have impeded his ability to learn from mistakes and seek improvement.

When praised for his achievements, Tom, demonstrating his awareness of his failures, said, "Well, that's an awfully nice thing to say but it's not valid."

How could we not be encouraged? Still, we saw so much physical improvement that, by contrast, the slow intellectual recovery seemed frightening to us. I had to resort to my journal frequently to remind myself of how far he had already come.

Tom could expend tomes of verbiage in his frustration, telling us, basically, that he *knew* the concept but could not recall the word. At one session he was trying to find the names of Kathy and me. "I want to get the word in first and if I can't, I don't know how to function. And that's the same in both cases [pointing with two outstretched fingers to each of us]. They're like so current to one another that I can't make a difference – that's how similar they are. I can do this time and time again and when I get to it, it's...ugh! It's not you and you – and when I get to this, there's something that I have to - I can't even say it because I know what I have to do, and I know it's not good...I know I love my wife."

To us, in translation, it was obvious he did not want to hurt our feelings by admitting he couldn't say our names, yet he knew he knew them. Also, he wanted to make it clear that although we, and our names, were "similar," he made a distinction between us and he loved me, not the therapist! I remembered an earlier convoluted speech in which I was somewhat compared to a carnation. We've come a long way!

For the first time he seemed to understand what we were saying when we told him, for the thousandth time, what had happened to him.

"I can live with that because it doesn't make sense to me. I can't help it – it's what I feel and I know that I'm doing this and I don't like it. I don't like it!

"I don't know if I agree with it. But I don't know a lot of things – a lot of things that go along with this conception...I said I don't know if I agree with these explanations.

"I didn't enter a lot of things and think that's the reason for my behavior. I didn't do that because I'm more inclined to – to what? – oh, come on – to give the reason a... So, instead of accepting something I'll give it one, two, three, four – however many tasks there are and so decide to – what?

"I don't want to relate what I feel to all this experience. I don't want to relate these feelings that I have because they won't essentially work for it.

"Yes, but you need to understand me. I understand a lot of things that I usually don't give my portion to...I'm ejecting a communication.

"When I first came into this program – let me think of this – God damn, I can't think of it – Oh, I didn't...I didn't understand what the hell was going on, but I went along with it. But the first, second, third, fourth, fifth time I didn't know what the hell was going on. When you gave the questions I thought you were crazy.

"But that phase is over with.

"How should I improve?"

A heartbreaker. Crystal clear. Clear as a bell. But a heartbreaker, nonetheless.

Yes, there was a dawning awareness. Tom was certainly much more aware of his situation, with its triumphs and failures. Yet, hearing him speak, we knew what he did not, that the knowledge, the circumstances giving rise to such long and impassioned speech would soon be forgotten. He could now give voice to his frustrations, but he could not remember the circumstances leading to those frustrations well enough to amend them. Each day was a new puzzle.

"I'm making so many mistakes. If I did this [copying words] for me, personally, I would not make these errors."

He could not understand that he was really making progress; he had no idea how far he'd come. And when we told him, he replied, "See, I don't believe that, I really don't believe that...If I don't believe that, will it defer whatever progress I'm making? So, in effect, I can make all kinds of progress...You can't make a promise more cautious than my expectations...I don't disavow what you're saying. I don't want to challenge it one way or another. I want to see it!"

He was concerned about whether this disbelief would hinder further improvement. (Goodness! Had he read *The Secret Garden*, too?) To me, this indicated a sophistication he had not shown to date. Of course, he had an explanation for the success of his therapies: "It's also a very systematic environment." Exactly what we'd been saying about Jackson! Had he figured out the differences between the two hospitals? And please notice the beautiful sentences: "You can't make a promise more cautious than my expectations" and "I don't disavow what you're saying."

We began to talk, in a vague sense, about discharge to home. I explained that Priscilla Miller, the chief therapist, would make the final decision. Tom asked, "She didn't express a thought about here and now?" And with those last words he made circles in the air indicating his room. He was ready to go!

By mid-May Tom began to get tired of some of his therapies, although he tried to be polite. I believe he understood the work was too simple, yet the vestiges of pride he retained would not allow him to admit he could not do even such simple work. When Kathy tried once again to give him homework, he rejected it. "Not homework...No, no, no...I don't accept it."

We were becoming so used to Tom's sentences now that, although they still amazed us in terms of how far he'd developed, we were able to look past them to the more serious problem, which was the memory loss. This is not to say that we did not appreciate the increasingly more comprehensible speech. His sentences were now nearly always complete, he seldom made up words and, although noun retrieval was still a problem, he was increasingly able to express himself in a comprehensible manner.

When Kathy missed a therapy appointment, Tom told Bill, "Kathy said she would make a reception for us at 6 or 6:15 but guess what – she didn't make it."

One day as I was getting ready to leave, we discussed whether or not to leave the TV on. Tom said he didn't want it. "Can you turn it on later if you change your mind?" I asked. "And change the channels?"

He looked at me in surprise and answered, "You don't know that your husband knows how to operate that?"

Here was a man who was once able – over the phone! – to help a friend extricate a snarled videotape from his cassette player. Owing to the "adult subject matter" of the tape, the friend was embarrassed to take the player to a repairman. Tom had been able to talk him through the problem in a clear and successful manner. So, yes, I did know he certainly could "operate that."

I left chastened, but energized.

In the few, rare times when just Tom, Bill, and I were together, watching television and laughing, I experienced a kind of dream-like sensation. This was just like when the three of us traveled west each summer, only a little askew. The room was just a bit too small for a motel room, but arranged like one. We were not in quite the right clothes, but close enough. The background noise from the hallway was not subdued as in a motel, but it added to the slightly "off" effect. So close, but not quite there – yet.

The discussion of clocks and time was a concept still too abstract for Tom, despite the daily schedule he followed. He understood the day was divided by mealtimes. "They're periods when I usually look toward gaining a – what? Time! A time, that's it. I want to tell you there are one, two, three; there are three segments.

"This is not a problem for me. When I can agreeably make time – whenever I can do that, I do it. But sometimes I can't do it. I don't know why. I don't even know why.

"I know because it's going to happen and it's going to happen a lot more often than I can ignore.

"This is something different than what we look about earlier today... What I want to temper is something that occurred to us earlier in the day...It was closer to this time. But it was a schedule...I don't know how to explain this."

Did he understand that the noon meal is "different than what we look about earlier today," which would be breakfast? Does he appreciate the schedule of his meal times? I thought this was what he was telling us, and pretty clearly – for the Tom we had at the present time.

Once again he was asked to name us. "I know what I want and I know what to do and I can't do it. It's a tragedy."

After a few moments' thought, he added, "That's what I'm talking about right now but I'm not getting anything in response...I'm sorry, honey."

Was he "talking" to himself, thinking, trying to remember our names and getting no answer? If so, what a predicament for the poor fellow, who was once so very articulate, whose speech was so carefully thought out and whose vocabulary was so extensive. These moments had to have been agony for him. How ironic. We were able to accept his agony only because we understood that the greater loss, the memory loss, would quickly allow him to forget his struggles.

The old Tom surfaced amazingly when discussions about money came up. I told him about the disability compensation we'd be receiving and he was pleased with the amount. Without taking any time at all to do the math, he said, "Eleven hundred dollars a month? That's three hundred dollars a week!"

We had a conversation following an earlier discussion about the lawsuit against the driver who hit him. I said, "Such a sad thing that happened to you."

"Well, yes and no," he replied.

"I don't know how it could be no."

"Well, we could make a billion...Maybe half a billion."

Besides having some sort of grasp of money matters, he was suddenly interested in his career. "I want to know whether or not I will be employed once I get to September."

Of course, we marveled at all these statements, but we would have rejoiced much more had they only been consistent, had they been remembered and repeated from day to day, had they formed a basis for new learning to be carried along as a foundation and built upon. But sadly, they were simply more sophisticated forms of the old crocus-in-the-snow moments: a sudden, lucid burst, bright and colorful, but fleeting.

When I told him I had only three weeks of school left, he said, "That's 7-14-21?"

You have seen the seesaws of emotion we experienced. What I found most depressing was my inability to help. He was trying so very hard and so very earnestly to understand, but there were barriers in his brain none of us could see, so we could not help him jump over them.

On the upside were several little vignettes enacted in his room. One time he became quite protective of a latex glove Bill had blown up like a balloon and had drawn a face on it as well as its name: "Happy the Glove." I was playing with it, just idly tossing it around, when Tom admonished me. "It means a lot to the kid,"

He took it and stroked it, saying, "This is all he's got," several times.

I told him he had more. He replied, "This is all he has in my house," and with that remark swept his hand around the little hospital room, his "house."

Those kinds of moments usually brought me to tears. You know that.

On the very same day I had a fierce headache and was feeling depressed – or melancholic – enough to cry. Tom assured me he was there to look after me. He was so confident, so natural, so sincere. All I could do was cry a little more.

With discharge approaching, I experienced a kind of ambivalence. The Tom we would bring home was not the man I expected would leave the hospital. Increasingly worried about the future, I was losing the shine on my optimism. Tom, I knew, had totally forgotten all our hopes and plans from life before the accident, but I hadn't. He was content. I was the one who would have to knowingly abandon that former life and those plans for the future. I also knew this wasn't supposed to be about me, but I was part of it, was I not?

It would have been rather saintly of me to simply surrender all my hopes and dreams – all our pre-accident hopes and dreams – and give myself over completely to Tom's care, to tell myself that this was to be my life from now on. I was not, alas, a saint, merely a human. For that reason I did not then and do not now reproach myself for feeling, at times, a tad bitter.

A plumber had to be called when the laundry room floor flooded again. It was the iron filter this time. Providence had it in for me. For all of us, actually. Demon was in the shop again;

Helen and my mother shuttled Bill and me. Tom's progress lacked its earlier drama. We were given a discharge date of June 11th, and suddenly there wasn't enough time.

As May ended, Tom was showing increased independence, increased lucidity, and increased expression. He began to initiate conversation; he could take himself to the bathroom. We began to think of him as nearly normal – a regular guy with some memory problems and a quirky way of expressing himself. I was still optimistic-ish about his future. This was the old Tom beginning to fight his way out of the clouds. I placed my hopes on the possibility that the move home would jolt Tom as the move to Jackson did. But where would we move him after that?

CHAPTER 11
JUNE 1994

The six-month mark was a milestone, the first landmark on the six-to-eighteen month road we were told would be important in determining the potential for Tom's recovery .

In many ways it had been, for me, a swift half year. I could still remember quite vividly the awful Thursday night and the policeman at the door. Then, in the intervening weeks were the long hours standing by Tom's bed, and the tension of getting to the hospitals through 17 of the worst winter storms New Jersey had in years. There was the back-and-forth of dealing with Tom's demon Blazer, and all the machinations involved in getting Bill home, then back to Idaho. There was the daily parade of visitors, the fights and pleading with the first team of therapists, the remarkable progress at Jackson, and of course my teaching, where I dealt with highly charged, emotionally disturbed youngsters in my art room. It had been an invigorating, tiring, hopeful, sad six months but in retrospect it had gone quickly.

To prepare for what awaited us in just a few days when Tom came home, I held a little talk with myself. It occurred to me that I needed to shift my thinking about Tom. He was now so much aware of all that went on around him, and so anxious to be a part of it that we could not treat him as anything less than the man he presented as. We had never patronized him through the course of this recovery, and now the only right and fair way to act was to accept that he was a normal man, but one having a bit of difficulty with some mental processes. This was a subtle, but important thought transition for me. Rather than orient ourselves constantly to what he might become, we must take him as he was in the present moment. The Tom he was now, not the Tom he once was, and not the Tom he might become. He was normal for now.

Yet, when I read my journal of only the previous month, it was apparent that the pace of the progress had slowed considerably. As dazzling as Tom's speech was, as normal as he appeared to be, there were admittedly only tiny increments made since early May. I had hoped for more dramatic improvement.

The month of June provided us with drama but it was tragicomedy, and as his discharge date approached, I was very apprehensive about our ability to take charge of his life.

Incidentally, you should know I was still writing the journal in the second person. I imagined Tom reading it one day, and enjoying the flow of "You did this, you did that..."

He had adapted quite well to his schedule at Jackson, but increasingly it seemed he wanted more, almost like a baby who'd figured out the lay of the land while crawling and now wanted to stand up and move around to see more of it. For example, one night as I was about to leave, he was quite confused. He felt he was supposed to go somewhere, and wanted to know his "schedule". Pointing to the clock, he said, "There is eight, nine, ten, eleven" – the evening hours – and he did not know what to do. The confusion may have stemmed from the fact that his customary evening speech therapy had been moved, weeks ago, to the afternoon. But the change had happened quite a while before this evening. With the help of nurses and aides, to whom he was very cordial, we got him to understand there was nothing more to do during the day. We helped him back to his room, but he was still a bit uneasy.

This was disheartening, yet the next day he was able to tell the hairdresser he wanted his hair "not like it is but like it once was."

Part of Tom's confusion may also have been derived from Warren's absence. Warren had been in a car accident and was gone for three days, which changed Tom's routine slightly. One of the aides discovered him one morning, very confused, with toothpaste on his face instead of shaving cream. Thankfully, Warren returned, but I began to wonder if we would need to move the Strong family into our house to keep Tom organized.

He'd taken to wandering at night, walking around the unit. Sometimes the nurses would seat him near their desk where a TV kept several roamers occupied. Eventually he'd get to his room, but often the confusion lingered. I chose to think this increased confusion was merely the result of increased activity. Each new level of achievement carried along with it an attendant confusion, until he mastered the new circumstance and moved on. None of the staff seemed unduly concerned about these temporary bouts of disorientation. We all took them to be, in actuality, the evidence of progress.

Now we were able to take him out in the car for short visits – we went to his mother's house, to see Madli and Mark, and to

Burger King. These were all short, local trips and he did well. Although he enjoyed the trips, Tom could not tell us that anything looked familiar, and he always seemed a little confused when he returned to the nursing home. This disheartened us, especially as the discharge date drew nearer. Madli and I took him out for a ride one afternoon past our house, his mother's house, and the schools. He did not recognize anything. We were only gone an hour, yet he wasn't even sure of the hospital when we returned. He looked very puzzled as we walked through the corridors, but brightened up as he entered his room. "No wonder it looks the same!" he announced, happily unaware of his memory loss.

Bill had been invited to the Senior Farewell at the high school and I wanted him to use my car, so I took the recently ransomed Demon. About a half mile along, it froze. I just abandoned it, walked home and left it for Bill to handle. He did, then followed me in my car to be sure the truck behaved.

On the other hand, there were encouraging bright spots. Back in our old life, we used to have a running joke. I'd say I had been "gently bred" and he would counter with, "And heavily buttered." So I said it now and he automatically replied, "Too bad you're so intensely buttered." An insult, perhaps, but a memory! Also, he wanted to change his clothes to "look better" when we were going to spend an hour with friends. He was able to undress, but experienced some confusion getting re-dressed. Could we ever manage without Warren?

D-Day, June 6th. I asked around but no one knew what the "D" stood for. Tom would have known. There was a great to-do about it on television, but to my mind, rather than only celebrating the event and remembering the fallen, the news commentators should have underlined the horror and ugliness of war and tried to figure out why people still couldn't get along. I had a brilliant idea – let the insurance companies finance war rather than governments. They would set limits, as we had learned in our adversarial experience, and once the money and time limits were gone, the war would be over and everybody would be sent home!

Tom had two more outings in preparation for discharge. One was to his mother's house in the afternoon for coffee, just like a hundred other afternoons when we stopped there after school and grouped around the kitchen table. After supper on another day we went to the Monessons' house. I definitely heard conversational growth as we sat out on the patio with Mark and Madli. He participated, asked questions, told us when he didn't have the words, and seemed very content. However, he was confused again upon returning to the hospital.

I needed to buy a few things for the house to ready it for Tom's return. He could not climb the stairs to the loft safely, so we relocated the TV to our bedroom on the first floor and I bought two little chairs for viewing. He needed bathroom safety aids, grips and mats and a shower stool. Just little things. He would find the house essentially as he left it.

And so the balancing act of triumphs and failures continued, yet the discharge date remained fixed at June 11th, with out-patient cognitive and speech therapies prescribed.

June 10th, my last day of school. I thought I had it all figured out when I learned that the students were going to be dismissed at 12:00 and the teachers were to have a meeting at 1:30. I felt positive the intervening time would be perfectly suited for a little surprise farewell luncheon for me, with perhaps a small, but tasteful parting gift. I even assumed the 1:30 meeting was just a ruse to put me off suspicion. All morning I tried to act normal, as if it were not completely obvious to me that "An Event" was about to happen.

Who knows what might have been? At precisely 12:30 the hospital called me to tell me that Tom was still in bed and not responding to any attempts to awaken him. All his vital signs were normal, but the staff was concerned. Both Bill and I rushed over. Helen, already there, simply demanded that Tom wake up. We all talked to him and he did finally wake up, rather astounded to find us all there. I suspected he was just exhausted from the outings of the past few days.

By the way, at the time I left school there appeared to be not the merest hint of a luncheon or a small, but tasteful parting gift. In fact, two of the teachers had gone out and had just come back in with their own sandwiches and sodas. Ah, well...

From the moment Tom awoke on June 11th, he told the nurses and aides it was his last day. When I arrived to take him home, he was visibly very happy, and made a victory march to the exit, waving as people called out, "Goodbye, Tom," "Goodbye, Mr. S!" I could not know what he was feeling other than what the grand happiness stretched out all over his face told me. I was still cocooned in the belief he was going to improve constantly, if slowly. Why would he have been discharged had that not been the case? His family and friends would be his support team, and I had an array of brain-enhancing supplements from the health food store to shove at him every day: grape seed, pycnogenol, COQ10, vitamins. I was prepared to, and expected to, see a miracle. Heidi, the Swedish triplets, and I would settle for nothing less.

PART III

*In all things it is better
to hope than to despair.*

– Goethe

CHAPTER 12
MORE OF JUNE 1994

"Oh, no, Tom! Not again!"

I bolted out of bed and ran to the kitchen as soon as I heard the splashing, but I was too late.

"I will be so happy when you learn the difference between the kitchen and the bathroom," I said.

Tom looked at me benignly as if I had been the transgressor, not he.

"Where should I go?" he asked calmly.

"Come. Let me show you. Again." I took his hand, making sure both of us stepped around the puddle on the floor, and led him to the bathroom. "This is where you should go," I said. "This is the bathroom. Please, please, please try to remember that."

"Oh," he said, and laughed.

Let me tell you about his laugh because it made all the difference. It was sweet, gentle, and innocent and its purity sustained me after I'd got him back to bed and while I was cleaning up the kitchen floor yet another time.

We'd been home for a few days and matters of hygiene were still hit-or-miss. Generally, Tom got to the bathroom on time but occasionally Bill or I would have to intervene (quickly) because Tom was in the bedroom taking down his pants. I could deal with a spill on the tiled kitchen floor, but the bedroom was carpeted.

It was taking the combined efforts of Bill and me to get Tom into the shower. The big step up over the edge of the bathtub scared him because he had to balance on one leg. The right-side neglect made him somewhat unaware of his right leg, and in the short space of time needed to raise the leg, he felt his equilibrium threatened. The transfer to the shower seat was awkward, requiring a half-turn once he was in the tub, and then a repositioning to sit. Mostly, he stood there, pointing to the seat and repeating, "You want me to sit there?"

"Yes, Tom. On the shower seat. Please."

"Oh, okay," and a little laugh.

No movement, however.

"Please, Tom, sit down."

"Oh. Where should I sit down?"

And so it went. It was a struggle that went on for weeks and I confess, at times when I hadn't slept well, had a severe headache, and was dealing with allergy problems (all of which usually occurred simultaneously), I wasn't up to the time and effort involved and we skipped the shower.

But there were sweet, bright spots in those early days. Tom and his father had built our little geodesic dome house and at times his words seemed to reflect a distant memory of the work.

"You know, a lot of time goes into an environment and sometimes people who are not used to that environment don't see how it...collapses on you."

Also: "You know, a little house like this plays at you, but not while you go through it. With me, it's a little different. It's a little different and I can't subject you to that, but for each of these walls there's a little bit different encounter and I can't sell that to you...The whole thing has to make a passion, so I'm doing that. It's not just one thing or another, it's the whole thing – the whole thing, honey – and I'm trying to encounter that. That's what I'm trying to do.

"I'm not in this attempt like you or like – what's his name? – Bill. I'm in a different class."

You know I was brought to tears, don't you? How carefully and how clearly, given the circumstances, he was expressing his affection for the house and for the work he'd put into it. And how sweetly sad.

A bit of routine settled around us in the first weeks. Tom had an out-patient therapy schedule involving physical, speech, and cognitive exercises. The goal of physical therapy was to help him proceed from his shuffling gait to a regular walk. This included home exercises geared to make him aware of his right side, and for the most part he was successful. Although his right arm remained motionless at his side when he walked, his feet eventually figured out what to do, and his stride appeared quite normal, especially if viewed from the left. This was not a big worry and P.T. was phased out much sooner than the other therapies, as it was apparent he needed work on speech and cognition more desperately.

Tom clashed immediately with his cognitive therapist. He characterized the fellow as "the dullest man I've ever met," "stupid," "dupey [dopey]," and "a bird." A week or so later he told us, "He creates the illusion that there's something going on, but there's nothing." A most astute evaluation! I believe he found the man somewhat haphazard, disorganized, and indefinite in contrast to the therapies he'd had which were more efficient and quite specific. Tom probably could not understand the more abstract nature of cognition as opposed to the very subjective physical and occupational programs. As an intrinsically organized person, Tom no doubt was uncomfortable with the laid-back approach of this fellow's treatment scheme. We asked that he be assigned to a different cognitive therapist and soon he was much more successful with the woman who replaced "the bird."

He continued to refer to all of his therapies in scholastic terms: the therapists were the "instructors" and he was "taking a course." Sometimes he would be puzzled: "I'm the only one in the class."

Based on the erratic nature of his recollections, I realized Tom's memory returned in waves: it swept up, left a little deposit on the shoreline of his mind, and then flowed away to return later with another sweep and another deposit. With enough deposits, he created a sandbar – a memory! For example, after several visits to his mother's house, the house he had lived in for 18 years, he finally looked at it in amazement one evening as we drove up and said, "That's my house!" He walked through it in wide-eyed wonder and it all seemed familiar as he nodded his head, smiled, and made little affirming comments: "Yes," "Okay," "Uh-huh." However, after dinner he needed to be shown how to get to the bathroom. The tide had gone out.

Sometimes the old Tom who used to insist Bill not use the phone after 10 PM on school nights surfaced; he once asked Bill to "get off the phone" when he received a call at 10:15. Then the present Tom came forward and told him he could only have calls from "licensed vehicle owners." We think he recognized that Bill's friends were now older and did not have to do school work or get to bed by 10.

At other times, Tom's meaning was clear, even if the words and an occasional letter got confused. I continually tried to persuade him to sit outside on the deck to get some fresh air, but it was often a futile act on my part. He asked, "What is this lingering you feel for this extraterreferal?" Well, lots of normal people have trouble saying "extraterrestrial."

These moments sometimes made me feel like I was in a second marriage to a man I didn't know very well.

The heat and humidity were oppressive. As the winter had set records for cold, ice, and snow, so the spring followed suit in the opposite direction. Tom seemed to be unaffected by the weather while I was laid low. In normal circumstances I do not do well in the heat and this summer was shaping up to be mighty abnormal. Headaches, allergies, and sheer exhaustion dogged me, but those problems were offset by what looked like major breakthroughs in Tom's general awareness. I had to keep reminding myself this wasn't all about me, was it?

I showed him a photo of our home in Idaho and he immediately said, "It is for the quiet time." [Summer? Or the peaceful quiet we find there?] He made a sweeping motion with his arm [distance?]. Then he said, "It's Idaho!" He spoke very matter-of-factly but I was excited. A living memory!

Next I showed him a picture of his father. He could not name him but called him, "the most treasured receiver of my heart."

We developed a parlor trick. He could not identify letters. If I wrote B-I-R-D, he might say "J-L-D-M." However, if I said the letters aloud, he would reply, "Yeah, bird." Amazing. People were fascinated whenever we showed off our magic and Tom never complained about performing it, although I doubted he understood exactly what about it was so interesting.

Not all the returning vocabulary was clear. One night he

wandered around the house looking for the "silver mystique" and the "universal land," both of which turned out to be the bathroom! Later, he explained those phrases were "feelings." We never could figure out what he wanted once when he went in search of a definite something, explaining, "I use it as a thing which ordinarily has use but in this case doesn't have use."

Tom was more and more simply a foreigner slowly getting a grasp on his new language. He placed his words carefully, trying to find the correct term, and reworked his sentences until he could say what he meant and be understood. At times he was a foreigner with a thesaurus in his head, pulling out the longest or most abstruse synonyms he could find, but he was certainly moving closer towards completely understandable speech and, following the same allusion, he was a foreigner becoming more familiar everyday with his new environment and the customs, language, and expectations of its people.

Sometimes I felt like I was sloughing uphill in the mud, but Tom finished the month of June content, in good humor, and amenable to attending his "classes." The first team meeting held at the Therapeutic Center was positive. He was diagnosed as severely impaired but his progress during just the first two weeks of attendance at all sessions showed signs of improvement and a cautious prognosis was offered of continued success.

In the progress summary from the Center for the end of June, it was noted that Tom presented...

"With moderate-severe deficits in all aspects of communication abilities including auditory comprehension, verbal expression, graphic abilities and reading comprehension. In addition, cognitive abilities are compromised which include orientation, awareness to deficits, memory, reasoning and judgment. Speech characteristics include fluent spontaneous speech with appropriate grammatical markers and social gestures but void of comprehension and awareness to irrelevancies. He demonstrates an unusual preservation of memorized materials and repetition abilities are intact for even long complex utterances without com-prehension. Naming is impaired. Graphic abilities and reading comprehension are nonfunctional except for the most basic word-to-picture matching."

A sobering report, but we were not yet a year post-accident and we continued to pin our hopes on the evidence we had at hand. I made a personal diagnosis: Tom had a problem with conservation, meaning in this case the ability to carry over one idea to another context. For example, I was sorting laundry in the living room while Tom sat uneasily nearby. I had placed the bedding on one of the living room chairs, but sensing his restlessness, I suggested he take a little nap.

"The clothes are gone," he said, pointing to the stripped bed in the adjoining room.

"Here they are," I showed him. "I'll do up the bed."

He looked very surprised but then laughed when I started to make the bed. He'd had no real understanding of the relationship between the sheets in the living room and the unmade bed. This kind of reaction spoke to me of a conservation problem.

Food loomed large, as always, in Tom's environment. One afternoon he expressed a desire for "egg drop soup", then added, "and more than egg drop soup." Bill immediately ran out for an order of Chinese food.

More than telling us about his culinary desires, Tom was telling us we now had, in many respects, a normal family life. For Bill and me, that tasted better than the egg drop soup ever could.

CHAPTER 13

JULY – OCTOBER 1994

The rest of the summer organized itself around certain themes. Tom's continuing improvement was the major motif; his increasing mobility and independence, his rapidly expanding vocabulary, and his contentment with the circumstances of his life were the notes. There were leitmotifs playing against the stronger theme. These included the record-setting heat, which was relentless, an oppressive background beat to every other aspect of the summer. There was the continuing flow of visitors, to which was added the irritant of the Frank Hunter Experience, an off-key note that beset us with atonal misalliance. There were increased forays into the outside world, grace notes of visits to other people's homes and to restaurants. And there was the minor-key undercurrent of my own existence, marked by tones of exhaustion, pain, depression, and anxiety with an occasional ornament.

His constantly improving speech was the only yardstick we had against which to measure Tom's intellectual progress. In ou excitement over each better expressed sentence he put together, we neglected to notice that memory did not seem to be returning to the same degree as the vocabulary. He was building new patterns and learning new routines, but he still could not recall very much of either the distant or the immediate past. By now we only partially convinced ourselves a full recovery was ahead. Of course, it was what we wanted, but we seldom spoke about it as enthusiastically as we had done previously. We were, almost by a tacit agreement, satisfied to let each day unfold with his own surprises, to let it carry us along as it evolved. Possibly the reality of Tom's situation was tingeing the outside edges of our optimism.

Tom began to initiate little routines around the house. Each night, on his own, he prepared the bed by neatly folding the quilt and placing it on the floor at the foot of the bed in a sensible, methodical way that hadn't occurred to me in twenty years, and in a manner reminiscent of the old, careful systematic Tom. He began to set the table for meals and he became a fan of the 10 o'clock news, which he learned to access via the remote. At first, he could only turn on the television but could not adjust for volume or channel. Still, I got all excited about it. He looked at me in surprise and said, "I am a Media Specialist, you know." And 'e had been, in his former life.

He described his physical therapist as "ultra-felicitous" [very 'oy] and said of himself, "I'm looking to tempt reality." [Trying ' what's there.]

sked him if he liked the new car. He hesitated, then "It's two inches too thick...For a six-footer, it's okay." He was two inches too small for a six-foot-two person like

' a delight for him. As he set the table a bit early one

evening, clueing me into his hunger, he said, "I have a..." No word came.

"A request?" I asked.

"Yes! I want 1-2-3-4-5-6-7-8-9-10 little lumps." He made a "C" out of his thumb and forefinger and moved it in a circle around the perimeter of the plate.

"Ravioli?" I asked.

He shook his head.

"I know! Shrimp!" Right. We had eaten shrimp, one of his favorite meals, the night before. He could have come out of this trauma satisfied with egg salad, but oh, no. He forgot nearly everything else but he somehow remembered shrimp and lobster. I was happy to prepare it for him, realizing one advantage of short-term memory loss: I could serve the same meal night after night!

On the other hand, Bill asked if he'd like to watch a particular movie on TV. "No," Tom said. "I saw that years ago." And he was right. Yet ask him what he'd had for breakfast, or where he went to grade school, and he couldn't say.

At times he spouted nouns that had eluded him in the past. Where he once said, "What about that?" when he wanted a lamp turned on or off, he now said "Turn on the light." These wonderful breakthroughs were sadly not consistent, but they occurred more often than they had in the past and we clung to them.

When Barbara was with us in the living room and Tracy was out in the kitchen, he said, "Where is the husband?" Good words, a good perceived relationship.

For reasons we could not explain, some memories persisted. For example:

"I don't like this commercial!"

"Why not, Tom?"

"It's the twentieth time I've seen it."

The number might have been off, but the memory was there and probably accurate to some degree.

WE CONTINUED TO HAVE SPORADIC BATHROOM PROBLEMS. Toilet paper was a mystery to him in the early months of the summer. Our house was round; one night he was making circular tours of it, confusion on his face. "Are you looking for something?" I asked.

"I know what I want but I don't know what I want."

On impulse, I ran ahead of him while he was still at the kitchen leg of his tour, and I turned on the light in the bathroom and opened the door. Sure enough, that was it.

Impulse often became the motivating force behind any action I took, especially if it might possibly concern the bathroom. When he pointed to his groin and said, "How thick should all this be?...I mean the outage..." I got him straight to the toilet.

Helen said, "Decision, decisions, decisions," when she was talking about having to make some choices.

"Sometimes the best decision is no decision," replied Tom the Philosopher.

On TV someone said something about wanting to get together "to dialogue" with someone else. Tom immediately caught it: "To dialogue? What kind of verb is that?"

ALL THESE WERE WONDROUS, BUT NOT CONSISTENT.

The shower continued to be a problem, especially after Bill left for school and I had to deal with Tom by myself. He always tested the stability of the shower seat by reaching out to it and rocking his hand on it. I mentioned that it was perfectly safe, and his father had used it.

"And look what happened to him!" Tom said.

As the summer progressed, the bathroom issues gradually resolved themselves, although there were occasional accidents. It was new learning, and as I have mentioned, new learning was an evolutionary process for him, a two-steps-forward, one-step-backward kind of thing.

"I like this course that I'm taking last on Thursday." All correct.

But, "A bit of an hour to the north" meant "make it later."

We spotted a walking-stick — the insect, not a cane — on our deck. "It's old," Tom said. "They're rare around here." Right and right.

He perceived I was agonizing over our insurance. One fund was about to run out. Another had to be initiated, but I wasn't finding anyone at the various offices I called to help straighten it out. Tom had a flash of brilliance: "Why don't you make an appointment with the right person and tell them, 'You are a service. This is not a service.'"

I came out of the bathroom after a shower and could not find Tom. He was not in the house; his television was turned off. Naturally, I panicked. (You've known me a while now — did you think I would not?) I ran outside and circled the house. No Tom. I ran to the street and looked up and down. It had been a quick shower and when I began it I settled him in front of the TV, so he couldn't have had time to go far. But he was not in sight.

It seemed like the best idea would be to get in the car and ride around looking for him. When I got to the car, there was

Tom, sitting in the driver's seat. I slid into the passenger's seat beside him. "What are you doing, Tom?" I asked.

"I want to ...," He moved the steering wheel with his hands.

"You want to drive the car?" My heart started to hurt for him.

"Yes!"

"You can't drive just yet, Tom."

"I know how."

What could I say? How could I tell him in a way that wouldn't hurt? It took me a minute but something gelled in my mind. "You know you were in an accident, right? A serious accident? Well, in that accident your right leg got hurt and now it doesn't move as quickly as it should."

He didn't look at his leg but continued to play with the wheel. I had no idea whether he understood me, but I continued anyway. "You need to be able to move that leg very quickly in order to step on the brake. Suppose a little kid runs out in front of you and you can't move your leg fast enough to stop the car?"

"I can move it." Aha! He had understood.

"Yes, but not fast enough. Not yet. Once you can move that leg fast enough, then you can drive." Knowing that it might never happen, and that he would probably forget this conversation anyway, I was comfortable with the lie. "Now how about we make some lunch?"

He laughed and the drama was over for the moment.

However, a few days later the situation arose once again.

"Why can't I push this vehicle?" Tom asked as we drove home from therapy.

"You don't know your address, Tom. You need to know your address before you can drive a car." Yes, I knew my answer sounded curt and cruel and probably wasn't even true. But sometimes in the course of this adventure I just didn't know what to do or say, so I made it up on the spot.

Later on that same day Tom took an envelope addressed to me and carefully copied the address onto a piece of paper, putting his name, such as he was able to write it, in place of mine.

"What are you going to do with that?" I asked him.

"I'm going to memorize it and then use it."

Crying time again.

Despite these little impasses we were all pleased with the continual progress Tom was making in his various therapies. His speech therapist called him a "speech pathologist's dream" because he was so articulate and intelligent and because he carried around in his head what she referred to as his "personal thesaurus."

He was comfortable in the therapeutic setting, perfectly at ease and not the least bit shy of interacting with others at the offices. Perhaps this was the result of his academic career. He was familiar with an educational environment, and he viewed his therapies as academic classes.

Tom's brother Richard arrived from Chicago and sat in on some of the therapy sessions. Based upon what he witnessed, he was very hopeful and talked about successful recovery. However, after he spent a few more days observing Tom, his prediction was less optimistic.

The summer moved along. Most of our friends who were teachers and thus free during the day, stopped by for visits in Tom's off-hours from therapy. Barbara and Tracy continued to visit, as did the mothers, Chuck, Bill's friends, and the family members who had been with us all along. I realize now what an undertaking it was for them as we did not have air conditioning (we had spent all our previous summers either camping or in

Idaho), and the heat was intense. From time to time as our schedule permitted, we'd escape to Helen's to enjoy her AC or to my sister's to plop in her pool.

Tom was very hesitant to step into the pool. I think he felt unsure of his footing. However, Paula's partner Dominick always got him involved in a card game, which he enjoyed very much, and which kept him occupied so I had time to cool off.

A word must be said here about Dominick. He had met my sister shortly before the accident, and never knew the "old Tom." However, he plunged right in, took Tom as he was, and they became buddies. Dominick played cards with him, gifted him with autographed photos of himself, gave him baseball caps, and developed a secret handshake for the two of them. More importantly, he always greeted Tom with a big hello and involved him in some sort of shenanigans right away. Dominick immediately sensed Tom's level of comprehension and performance and worked with it.

This is not to say that Paula didn't have a suspicion or two. When Dom and Tom would watch some silly movie on TV, they would both laugh heartily at the antics. "Tom has an excuse," Paula would say, "but what's Dominick's?"

But he was a good friend to Tom and the only person who was not motivated to offer friendship out of respect for the person Tom had been, or out of interest in seeing what he would become, and I very much appreciated his attention to my husband.

Apart from our invaluable friends who genuinely cared about Tom, there were others he'd known since boyhood who could not bring themselves to meet him after the accident. I'd like to be able to say I respected their attitude; however, I believe if they had taken the time to make a visit, they might have felt less afraid of him and more optimistic about his situation, and he would have very much appreciated their visit. My lack of respect for their decision stemmed from the deprivation it cost Tom.

While I am on the subject, it might be important to state that a crisis such as we experienced is a wonderful catalyst for bringing out the best and the worst in those who are tangential to it. Some friends and family members will exert themselves, will participate, will show true concern for the brain-injured person, who, admittedly, is not the same person they once knew, while others will shy away from him. The general excuse for avoidance is that they want "to remember him as he was."

Would they have felt the same if he'd had a physical injury – an amputated leg, or serious burns? And which of us, unless we are completely stagnant personalities, is always the person he once was? Life is an evolution, a period of growth and change. Remembering Tom "as he was" did not preclude accepting him "as he now is."

And then there's too much attention, the continuing saga of the Frank Hunter Experience. On July 7th he called our house to tell Bill he would stop by at eleven. Bill explained we were at therapy and he was heading out to work, so no one would be at home. Nonetheless, Frank showed up and left a note and a bag of blueberries. His note promised a return call. We had visitors in the afternoon whom I could not enjoy for fear the poor old bore would show up at any moment. As soon as our guests left at 4:30, we scurried over to Helen's to enjoy air conditioning and supper. When we returned at 9:00, there was another note. Had he had his way, each of his visits would have coincided with a meal. What a pest! The heat was enough to endure, but I knew I would become ugly if I had to balance both the heat and the Hunter.

The following week I was close to falling apart. Getting Tom in the shower had been an ordeal and I got plenty wet in the process. Then I went food shopping while Bill was home to look after Tom, who napped after the exertion of his shower. I decided I was too wiped out to go over to my mother's as planned. I just wanted to be home, to do some art work, maybe watch a movie. I decided I was, somewhere in all of this, entitled to a life. But as soon as I got home, Bill told me Frank Hunter had been to the house. Bill had friends over, told him Tom was sleeping, whereupon he promised to return at 2:00. I knew if he came at two, he would be likely to drone on and on. Tom would feign sleep (he wasn't so brain-damaged in this regard) and I would be left with the tiresome man and his depressing questions. Feeling defeated, as if I had to flee from my own house, right in front of Bill and the groceries, I started to cry.

I packed lunches, roused Tom, and off we went to my mother's as originally planned. As it happened, She had some friends over who enjoyed seeing Tom, so the day turned out halfway nice despite my deep desire to collapse and sleep for a week.

That wouldn't have done any good because a week later, the Hunter called again, stalking his prey. I told him we'd be in therapy from nine until noon, he said he'd stop by at 11:30! Do you see why he drove me crazy? Even on the phone, the depressing questions continued: "Was Tom reading yet?" "Writing?" "How much longer do we have to go?" And my favorite – "Do the doctors give you any hope?" I chose to believe I could tolerate his presence, were it not for those disheartening questions.

Well, I may be a coward when it comes to confrontational tactics, but I am not above lying when necessary. The temperature was in the high 90s with humidity to match, so I told him we were busy and off we went to Helen's.

Finally, we couldn't avoid him. I was out of lies, plagued by guilt, and caught off guard. But – I had A Plan. On the appointed day, we told Frank Tom had therapy until 1:30, so he could visit at 2:00. I ran around doing errands while Tom was at his "classes," then got home around 11 to drop off my bundles. Guess who was there? He said he'd be back later, and we parted. By the time he came back, Barbara and Tracy were at the house and The Plan was put into action. They readily saw that Frank Hunter, though he was concerned and meant well, brought my spirits down below sea level, so, when he finally got up to leave, Tracy walked out with him and explained, ol' pal style, that I was becoming too stressed, too exhausted with the general situation plus all the company, and went on to tell him I'd rather not "entertain" during the week. A good Plan. I was anxious to see if it would work.

My willingness to help Tom, I must admit, was often severely strained as I sat with him to watch the totally classless TV shows that made up the bulk of his at-home hours. Because I believed that asking him questions about the shows would be a form of mental exercise for him, I forced myself to attend to programs with absolutely no redeeming value whatsoever, and worse than that, to think up questions and comments about the shows in an attempt to keep his brain working. Thus, we endured such horrors as *The Richard Bey Show*, *Rikki Lake*, and *Married With Children*. We watched -heaven help us – obese people sitting in chocolate pudding and then imprinting their rear ends on art paper. We saw pathetic young couples holding a baby and expressing tears of anger or frustration – generally not joy - as Rikki produced the results of DNA tests that did or did not prove paternity of their baby. We followed the stupidity of Al

Bundy and his dysfunctional family. Greater love hath no woman than to watch daytime TV with her man.

This last statement gives me pause. Did I take care of Tom out of love, or duty, or because it was a responsibility thrust upon me? Certainly, I loved him and certainly I wanted the best for him. But the Tom I had loved and married and lived with for 22 years was not the gentle stranger with whom I now shared my life. The belief that the original Tom, the man I married, would one day emerge from within this new incarnation was definitely what propelled my earliest efforts to aid his recovery. But as it gradually became clear that full restoration of the former Tom was not going to be granted to us, I had to admit that the attention he now received was derived from both loyalty to the old Tom and a sense of duty for the care of the new Tom, a responsibility I had agreed to undertake by marrying him. (Not from our marriage vows, however. We did not say the "in sickness and health" speech, opting instead for a more modern promise we had written ourselves.)

Don't get me wrong: It was impossible not to love the new Tom. He was sweet, gentle, innocent, easy to please and undemanding in his needs. Yet, I would be deceiving you, and myself, if I said this was the same kind of love that had once existed between us. All appearances to the contrary, he was not an adult male. We usually characterized him as a happy eight-year-old. The conversations we'd once delighted in, the long and profound discussions we'd once had were all gone now. The companionship, the shared life, the goals and the solutions of everyday problems were all gone as well. What we most admired about each other, our intellectual strength, was a commodity that had all but disappeared in him and was now destined to go unrecognized in me. This, the most difficult thing for me to accept, often led me to bouts of depression.

I loved him as he currently was because he was the shadow and the promise of old Tom. Everyone loved him as he was now for that reason and also because he was consummately lovable. But, there's love and there's love – you know what I mean – and you will understand if I tell you that given these circumstances, love morphs into another form of itself. It happened gradually, as a natural occurrence, and it happened without any effort or even recognition on my part. It simply was.

This was not as desperate and depressing as it sounds. We often had moments of shared joy. Tom existed in a world that had been geared for his comfort, pleasure and safety. He seemed to be quite happy in that world. At times, like a Venn diagram, our two worlds did overlap and a mutual understanding occurred.

The Chinese poet Lin Yutang wrote: "Happiness is moments." Tom and I definitely had moments of happiness as life moved along, but they stemmed from different origins. Tom's happiness was a constant, it existed for the moment, stimulated by an external source such as television or food, and each moment, though short-lived, was immediately replaced by another. My source of happiness stemmed from the new connections I heard him make, from the more and more articulate conversation of which he was increasingly capable and of course from the eternal hope that each of these tiny moments might eventually lead to greater recovery. This is the sort of happiness parents feel as they watch their child grow and develop new skills, and recognize that the child is always in a state of becoming. So it was with Tom – he was always becoming.

Tom was often quite capable of speaking single lines of wisdom that indicated he fully comprehended the situation under discussion. For example, when Bill wanted to change from being a waiter at his summer job to being a dishwasher, Tom knew intuitively that Bill was a "people person" and advised him to stay with the waiter's position. "You have an orientation with people that you don't have with that ["that" meant washing dishes]. That's what I want him to have." Bill remained a waiter.

We still did not have consistency, but we did have these brilliant flashes of comprehension. Taken superficially, it appeared that Tom was able to make himself understood, if in a somewhat roundabout fashion, even able to understand some complex and abstract ideas. But the ephemeral nature of his comments remained. If asked for the same information at a later time than when he had first given it, he would not be able to comply.

We were watching the movie *Private Benjamin*. I asked him why, if the character is so unhappy in the army, did she join in the first place?

"It's the only place that gave her an identity... That's why she joins this." Tom was absolutely and amazingly correct. Private Benjamin joined the army and did discover her own personal worth there. This rationale is implied, but never stated in the film. Tom, however, grasped it.

I learned not to be fooled, though, when he appeared to have understood a concept in depth such as Benjamin's motives for joining the army. While he could voice his reaction, he could not expound upon it. He could neither explain why she had not found her happiness in her former life, nor why the army satisfied her. We could have question and answer, but no analysis.

We saw an action movie starring Sylvester Stallone. Tom probably followed the plot better than I did; after a few too many fights, car chases and explosions, my mind just drifts away. The interesting thing about this was that ever since the accident Tom tended to equate height with superiority. He himself was tall, therefore –perhaps—the relationship of height to superiority was for him an immediately perceivable concept, especially in the absence of any other markers by which he could evaluate his status. During the movie, Tom constantly shouted out, "Watch him! Watch him! He's the best! He's the best!"

"Tom," I said, "Stallone is not a tall man and you admire him, so it's not only tall people who are the best, right?"

"But he is a tall man," Tom replied. "He wins all the episodes. He's bigger than his height."

He's bigger than his height. How's that for insight?

Thank you, Lin Yutang, for helping me to understand and grasp these moments of happiness, and for so subtlety suggesting that this was enough to expect.

Bill returned to the University of Idaho in August. He called home frequently but his tone of voice did not transfer his usual confidence and optimism. He had not yet told us that studying and concentrating on his academic pursuits were difficult for him at this time.

Tom and I discussed Bill's rather cavalier attitude toward studying. Tom understood and even had a plan to help. "He's really scared," he said.

"Why do you say that?" I asked.

"Because he always bucks it off. I'm afraid for him. I've never admitted it before, but I'm admitting it now. I figure two semesters, maybe three. We might have to pick him up."

Perfectly clear. And prescient, as it turned out.

As September loomed, Coastal was willing to hire me as a part-time art teacher, and to adjust my school schedule to Tom's therapy schedule. I was quite willing to work, and thus afford the school another opportunity to provide a little luncheon and a small, but tasteful gift when I eventually had to resign again.

The progress we noted so happily continued by tiny increments into September at which time I thought I should begin to make some serious decisions regarding the house, cars, Tom's retirement, my job, and our future. I asked the therapy team for a report and it was blunt. They felt that barring a miracle, Tom would never return to work and could never drive again. They saw a continuation of small gains over a long period of time, but did not expect he would ever again be the person he once was. On the positive side, the report cited his social awareness, cheerfulness, friendliness, and his pleasant personality. A realistic assessment, if not the one I wanted to hear.

I was left to deal with the vacuum of intellectual solitude – that I would never have the companionship of Tom as an adult. But this was my own problem to solve and I needed to set about creating my own life within the vacuum.

Spurred on by the excitement of Andrea and Joey moving to a new townhouse, I decided to sell our dome. As much as we loved the house, it was an open plan and did not offer privacy except as we respected each other's needs. Prior to the accident, Bill generally played or did homework in his room, I had a little study in the laundry room and art space in the kitchen, and Tom had his desk upstairs in the loft. We had one small TV, also upstairs, which we seldom watched. After the accident, the TV was moved into the downstairs bedroom. It was on nearly all the time when Tom was up and awake, and its sound permeated throughout the house and made reading or concentration of any sort difficult for me.

Contrary to just about all the people I know, I love to move. I love the excitement, the challenge of sorting through and discarding some of our possessions, decorating new rooms and exploring new neighborhoods. Yes, it was a wrench to think about leaving the house Tom had built and the place our son was raised, but I had good reasons for the move beyond simply keeping me occupied. Twenty years into the life of the dome, pipes had begun to burst. Appliances were aging. The rough winter of last year had entailed so much shoveling and I couldn't face the thought of doing all that again. I had no quiet place to read or do art work. But most significant of all, the contrast between the Tom who built the house and the Tom who now ambled through it disturbed me. Together we had planned and worked on every inch of our home, and now he could not find the bathroom. A heartbreaking situation and one I thought best remedied by leaving it behind us.

I told Tom I thought we needed to move, that we needed a different sort of house. "I'm not like the person who plans and then executes his plans like you do," he said. I took his comments as agreement.

Helen asked him how he felt about moving. "Well, there's nothing for me to do at our house," he said. "I'd like to help."

This led me to ask if he were satisfied with the way things were going, and he replied, "Nothing went."

This may sound like fairly normal, even somewhat sophisticated conversation, but I doubted Tom truly understood what the concept of moving entailed. He was much more precise about concrete things. For example, we were eating what he thought was a too-early supper and he stated, "I don't understand why this is so young."

His dining room chair had some stains on it, which he never mentioned. I cleaned the seat. At the next meal he stared for a minute at the chair and said, "This one isn't disgusted anymore."

I took heart from every little statement, never completely discounting the possibility of the miracle the therapists thought we'd need. In fact, he played Scrabble with his speech therapist and was able to form and place letters correctly. With no clear evidence of an ability to read or even to name letters, he was still able to fashion words in Scrabble. How could this *not* be encouraging?

In thinking the move might be a jolt to Tom's recovery, as the move to Jackson had been, as the return home had been, it was possible I was simply justifying an action I had determined to take, knowing it was for my benefit and not necessarily for Tom's benefit. When I called Bill to inform him about my decision, he questioned it in his own style: "Who are you and what have you done with my mother?" Bill does not like change; I thrive on it.

Packing occupied me. I treated myself to thoughts of what I would do in the new house, even as life around me continued.

"That's not what I'm paradoxing about," Tom said once, meaning he was puzzled. A great word, paradox, not an everyday for anybody. Spoken only the one time, we never heard "paradox" from Tom again, and yet there it hid among the synapses in his brain, just waiting to be released. This in itself was truly a paradox. Imagine a balloon seller, the old-fashioned kind in the park, with a bright and beautiful array of balloons for children to buy. But once a child lost his grip on the balloon, he could only watch it float away into the sky, never to return. Tom's words were like that – they were released, floated about us for a brief moment, and then they disappeared. Of course, the balloon seller and the child could always get more balloons, which kind of weakened my analogy. There are no brain stores.

For all the little highs, there were equal servings of little lows. I felt so depressed going through his desk while looking for the deed to the house. He had so many plans, and was so organized. All the details he put into lessons! What a shame it was that students would be deprived of him.

Heart-break time: I found a typed sheet he'd created titled, "What We Need to be Happy in Idaho" with a detailed and cost-estimated list of items stretched out to several years in the future.

Yes, tears.

I asked him if he felt unhappy about all this work he had done and would not use. He replied, "I'm never unhappy anymore...that word is not in my vocabulary." I desperately wanted to believe that was true, and I wanted to believe that this well-expressed attitude was the best kind of gift he could give us.

Meantime, I began to ready the house for sale, found a realtor, and looked at a little house in Pt. Pleasant Beach that "spoke to me." I was back at Coastal, working three mornings a week while Tom was in therapy. My life was filling up and heading into the sunshine with a new form of optimism. This was a more settled, perhaps more mature form of optimism. It accepted the reality of our circumstances, while still storing away in some secret part of my heart the hope for greater recovery. It accepted the present, but looked ahead to the challenges of the future, especially those of the new location. It was, at long last, a feeling that we would make it, one way or another.

In keeping with the spirit of this new optimism, one Saturday I noticed a different cast to Tom's face – a new intelligence and alertness – a shadow of the old Tom. This occurred at the same period in which his sentence structure was improving and he was initiating conversations, often even in the form of questions. ("What do we have for outerwear?" when he wanted a jacket.) No doubt this "sudden" emergence had been months in the making, but it erupted on that Saturday and made him seem more in focus, "clearer," and less faraway.

To keep him updated on the move, so it would not come as a surprise if he'd forgotten it, I tried to talk about it often. "The kitchen will have to be remodeled in the new house," I said.

"We don't want to do that," he replied.

"We don't? Why not?"

"What do we want to do – make ourselves an empire?"

We talked about some of Tom's old, boyhood friends who were afraid to come see him. He offered an astute assessment: "I think they're phonies. Because if you really want to know something, you go and find out."

As wonderful as these statements were, I could never be certain that he remembered the specific people we were talking about. He may have understood the concept of his abandonment by some friends, but I doubt he could name or even recognize the people until they showed up. That he did grasp the content was evident after I told him some of those men were nervous about approaching the "new Tom," a stranger to them.

"You have to convince them that their way of looking at things is not reality," he said. He balanced "reality" and "phony".

Although I took heart from sentences like these, there was still no evidence of returning memory and no indication he was capable of reading or writing. And on any day when he made a great sentence, he was still not able to tell you what he had for breakfast. I would have a desperate moment now and again – a little bit of fear for the future, a little pity for our present plight, a little bit of mourning for Tom's lost past, and a great loneliness. I missed the old Tom, who was wonderful to talk with and who made me feel secure.

We watched the movie, *Superman*. I asked Tom to tell me what the story was about.

"It took place in this world... It was 1938, just three years before the war... it was about a young man who was the last of his own people to survive. He had to hide. He had to protect himself... He lived with a couple. He was the last of his world."

Entirely accurate, wouldn't you say? But he could not go further.

Rich MacFarland sent me a copy of someone's doctoral dissertation: *Coping Strategies for Spouses of Individuals with Traumatic Brain Injury*. Some of the spouses in the study were speaking from as many as 20 years post-TBI and were still looking for recovery. I felt much less alone after reading it and I could see we were not so terribly badly off in some ways. In general, I learned once again the TBI victims being discussed were more highly functional than Tom, or were doing so poorly that they were in residential placement.

Bill called in early October. "Are you sitting down? I'm in trouble."

Of course, a hundred horrible possibilities flashed through my mind, but at least he was alive and able to speak, so I controlled my panic. It turned out he was out of money. Since he and even simple arithmetic are often at odds, he thought he had three hundred something dollars left in his checking account but in actuality all he had was 36 cents! He was stricken. I told him I'd wire it the next day. One crisis averted.

I offered Tom a sweatshirt to wear in the house to keep warm. Instead, he opened up his arms, spread them out, and said, "I'd like to think about getting an environmental request." He wanted the heat turned up.

His pleasant demeanor was something for which we were

grateful. He was calm, complacent, and affable. He was careful and congenial. He was also beginning to spot my frenzies and he often tried to ease my worries to reassure me I should not worry so much. Believe me, I would *not* have worried at all if I knew a normal life was waiting somewhere ahead – conversation, discussion, shared information, and pleasures. Even if I could convince myself that there would be no improvement at all, and we'd better just adapt to what we had – it would have made things easier. But his constant improvement always teased us with hope and to settle for what we had would mean the abandonment of all the hard work we still needed to do. I was not yet ready to settle. I had to accept the not-knowing, and the not -knowing made daily life difficult.

You have probably noticed a seesaw of determination among my thoughts. At times I was saddled up and ready to ride, and at other times I lacked the energy to even get the horse out of the stable. Although I am no fan of hers, I thought Emily Dickinson expressed this restless uncertainty quite perfectly in her poem *If You Were Coming in the Fall*. In this poem, she relates how she can tolerate any degree of waiting, if only she had a definite date when her lover would come back to her. The amount of time she must wait does not matter; only the certainty that the date will eventually arrive sustains her. But she has no certainty, therefore no hope. Very similar to our position.

Leaving a restaurant with his mother and me, Tom allowed us to precede him. "Always be the beginners; we are the enders." [Ladies first, men after.]

"Tell me one good thing about this morning's class," I asked.

"It ended."

He began to increase the little chores he performed at home. He had been setting and clearing the table and taking down the bed; now he swept the deck of leaves each day. Extended exercise tired him; after even a short walk, he needed a nap. I appreciated and applauded his willingness to be useful.

I told him the realtors were going to bring over a contract for the sale of the house. He said, "Tell them you've got to talk it over with your husband." When I repeated the comment to the realtor, I began to cry.

Sometimes I wondered whether this pretense of normality was worth the effort. It was, on the one hand, difficult *not* to perceive him as normal because he *looked* perfectly fine. Then we'd begin a little conversation and I'd watch him grope for a word or struggle to explain an idea and I'd become shaky, wobbly inside, and think, *I can't stand this; this can't be real.*

Were he not content with his life, we would naturally move heaven and earth to make him happy, to help him find contentment despite his deficits. But he *was* happy; we were the ones facing the great dark fear.

It is not entirely true, though, to say that Tom was unaware of his problems and limitations. He did, from time to time, refer to them. But the comments he made, like all of his conversations, were short, pithy and soon forgotten – by him, anyway. He never dwelt on his situation.

"Look at this – it doesn't work!" This was in reference to his right arm. He had limited use of it due to the right-side neglect, and therapy could not help. I wondered whether he was more aware of it than we suspected. Did he have to force it to work? Was it awkward or painful? "This is my sad limb" was the extent of what he told us. He also had lost a good bit of peripheral vision, which he phrased as, "The visibility on my right side isn't equal."

When I thought he could handle it, I showed him a photo of his crushed car, and briefly discussed the accident.

"I was in a triple accident," he said. This is true. He was hit from behind, then shoved into the car in front of him, then hit again when the thrust pushed him out onto the main road. Three hits, thus a "triple accident."

He looked at the photo of the demolished car and said, "I escaped that?"

He did accept what had happened – or gave the appearance of acceptance – and recognized there was still more work for him to do when he remarked, "I'm not regular all the way yet."

Yet.

There was a short respite of comic relief. Bill called from Idaho with the notion that he wanted to get a job and move to an apartment, but he would need a car. He did not seem to be plagued by school itself and told me that "studying was an eastern concept." When he called again a few days later to discuss buying a car (financed by us), I said no. Both my men were totally out of touch with reality, but Tom had a reason.

What I did not understand at the time was that Bill, in his own way, might be trying to exert a little control over his life in the face of the confusion he felt. Bill is a lot more sensitive than some of his remarks might lead one to believe, but he keeps a lot in. I was certain he did not want to trouble me, and equally certain that like many college kids, he was trying to find his place in the world, a world that held uncertainties and questions beyond our ability to answer.

At the end of October we accepted a contract for the house. It was much lower than I'd hoped, but apparently consistent with what I could expect based upon the assessment of our house. Tom expressed the idea that we should have held out for more money, and this was one of the thousands of times I wished I could get inside his head for just a minute. Did he have some understanding of the process but was unable to express it? Had some connection been made in his brain to last only an instant and fade away? Or was he automatically pulling out words from some previous event that he knew were appropriate? I had no answers and had to work with what was in front of me: his momentary response to a situation followed by an inability to explain further, and then confusion.

He was able in some way to let me know that he wanted me to be happy. I felt fine with the move. I had a chance to be happy. Just dreaming about the house, its refashioning and furnishing, sustained me through September and October. At the same time I realized my dreams might have to carry me quite a bit farther because we'd be pretty strapped after we bought the new house. I was alternately excited, then sick with worry that I was disappointing Tom, who loved the dome he and his father had built.

As if to justify my determination to leave the home we'd built and lived in for 20 years, I suddenly realized how painful it was to live there, with all its memories. But the wheels were in motion, and slow them down I could not do. We marched into November, heading fast and furiously toward the completion of our first post-accident year, for better or worse, and nothing could stop us.

CHAPTER 14

NOVEMBER 1994

I am going to share with you, in excruciating detail, one
month of our post-accident life: November 1994. As I write
this, I am asking myself why I have decided to present you
with a daily account of all our activities. Do I want you to feel
sorry for me? Not really. (But you can if you so choose.) No, I
think it's because I'd like to hearken back to the original purpose
of this book, which is to illustrate our life after traumatic brain
injury, and, I sincerely hope, to be of use to any family who might
be living through this kind of experience. As I've mentioned
earlier, there was no useful literature for me at the time; I like to
think our story will help others.

It is very important to me to let those who may also be
experiencing the struggle understand that life outside that
struggle goes relentlessly on, and must be dealt with. Maybe
under some circumstances life can be entirely devoted to the care
and comfort of the afflicted, but I did not find that to be the
case. My own energies, though curtailed and confined, refused to

be crushed. The world outside of our private concerns pressed us for decisions, resolutions and interactions. It may well be that I was not handling our situation as intelligently or as sacrificially as I might have done; I can only repeat once again: I did what I thought was right at the time.

Let me again make one thing clear: we were ordinary people undergoing an extraordinary experience, but it is not a tale of great adventure, nor is it a story recounting the conquest of adversity. People – ordinary people like us – have suffered more, endured more hardship, and fought more valiantly than we were called upon to do. We were not cast adrift in an open boat on the high seas. We were not trapped high in the Himalayas during a blizzard. We were never in the kind of situation where we had to consider eating our shoes to survive. More realistically, we were not forced to sustain great physical agony, or asked to watch a child suffer. We had a home, enough money to live modestly, food and hot water, and the support of friends and family. In many ways we were very fortunate. However, I believe that despite all the horror in the world, you can only truly know your own Worst Thing, and this was ours.

That being said, get ready for the sleigh ride. I am reporting directly from my diary. You will be spending a month with me, but in greater comfort! Incidentally, I stopped writing Tom's journal. There was no longer the kind of daily excitement that made good reading, which I thought he would enjoy when the day came for him to read it. I reconciled myself to the fact that he would probably never be able to read, nor, because of his memory losses, understand the events that actually happened. I returned to keeping my own diary in my voice, and it is from that I take the following saga.

TUESDAY, NOVEMBER 1 IS BUYING AND SELLING A HOUSE always this traumatic? Today I was *sick* – terrible muscle aches, which I've had since Sunday, all down my left side as if I had a pinched nerve in my neck; fever; headache and just generally just plain sickness. It took two doses of Theraflu and a couple of Excedrin before I got to rights by late evening.

Met Mom at 12:30 to show her the house. I don't think it spoke to her as it did to me.

WEDNESDAY, NOVEMBER 2 WE WERE UP EARLY AND WAITING for the bank to open by 9 AM, at which time we closed out some IRAs and now will have enough to purchase the house with a little cushion to float on.

Came home for my Italian group. Poor Tom was polite but insistent that he go to "school" at 11:30. We all explained that he didn't need to leave until 12:45 and he agreed to wait as long as he could "push it off on you." [blame us] He settled to watch television while the rest of us sat in the dining room for our lesson.

While he was at therapy, I did errands, came home, set some pachysandra to root, and then Barbara and Tracy came. We all visited Villa del Mare for the Italian Night 2-for-1. Back home, I started packing books (I had rooted through the dumpster behind the liquor store for boxes) but only filled three because I started feeling more like I did yesterday.

THURSDAY, NOVEMBER 3 SLEPT POORLY LAST NIGHT, DESPITE A dose of Theraflu. At some point I got up for Excedrin for a pounding headache, got up again to use the bathroom, and yet again to lower the heat. All the while a million little items needing attention flashed through my mind. Today I feel better, although I am feeling overwhelmed and probably won't be secure until the deed is done. (Get it? Deed. New house =deed.) All afternoon I packed books and art supplies. There's a *lot* to do .

FRIDAY, NOVEMBER 4 SOMETIMES I FORCE MYSELF TO HOLD back tears. Poor Tom will say or do something and it breaks my heart and could so easily lead to crying, but I won't allow myself to cry. Tonight it was just the words, "Two breakfasts," and a look of delight on his face. What he means is that tomorrow we'd go out twice to eat, beginning with breakfast.

I had a busy day at school, packed up Bill's room and a lot of art stuff all afternoon.

SATURDAY, NOVEMBER 5 BREAKFAST AT THE INNER CIRCLE AS usual. I was so hungry/tired from the pace of the last few days that I had the buffet. At 5:00 we went out again because Tom had been enjoying the Wendy's ads on TV. I had *their* buffet. Packed all day. Madli was able to give me an hour's help. Afflicted with headache and allergy problems; took medicine for each, which made me a zombie by mid-afternoon. Made plaster casts for school, all day. Zonked tonight.

SUNDAY, NOVEMBER 6 REALLY FEELING ILL TODAY. I'M TRYING to do some packing. It just tears me apart to go through Tom's school stuff – all his meticulous planning and the hours upon hours he put in.

I've been hot and cold all day, doing little chores, reading the paper, etc. but through it all feeling flu-ish. Slept poorly last night and for part of the night did not sleep at all. Tried to sleep sitting up in the living room to ease coughing, which is probably due to too much plaster dust yesterday.

MONDAY, NOVEMBER 7 I WAS LISTENING TO IRENE, ONE OF our girls at school who, between offensive words and in the grossest terms, was talking about her family: her grandmother, who went out at 2 AM, just home from Atlantic City, to find and pick up Irene's younger sister who, Irene expects (proudly) will be doing serious drugs by the time she's 10. I have to wonder, sometimes, why I even try.

I was sick most of today and even slept all afternoon. Bill called; he wished he could be here to help move and has a lot of questions about the new house. (So do I, like: will it go through?) No one was pleased with the buyer's lawyer, who was an obnoxious student when I had him at Lakewood High School, in my teaching-English days. He's still obnoxious but when I hinted at that, he said it was a good quality for a lawyer.

TUESDAY, NOVEMBER 8 DESPITE ALL THE SLOW, STEADY progress, there was a slight set-back this morning. Tom had been able to get his own socks and underwear from the closet, but today he forgot how to do it.

"All this space has nothing on it for..." he said, pointing to the bed. "There's nothing laid out..." He was remembering the way I had put out his clothing when he first returned home. I thought we were past that by now.

We drove into Point to leave $9,000 on the house. While Tom had therapy, I did food shopping. Nearly all the rest of the day was spent dealing with my nose, which was alternately running like a river or stuffed like a sausage. Took too much medicine; became a zombie.

WEDNESDAY, NOVEMBER 9 FEELING A LITTLE BETTER. THE Italian group was here this morning, then while Tom was at therapy I went to the mall and spent *big money* on a futon at This End Up. Do I know what I'm doing? Am I crazy?

Now tonight I am again dealing with The Nose and trying not to think about all the pressures closing in on me. The Nose is enough.

THURSDAY, NOVEMBER 10 THINKING ABOUT NOSES, AS I AM forced to do nearly all day and night, reminds me of Bill. While I cringe inwardly and try to keep a brave face when the kids at school make fun of my nose (they have an uncanny ability to home in on everybody's weakness), Bill in return memorized the Cyrano nose speech and makes people listen to it if they remark about *his* nose!

The day today got off to a low start: I was in the bathroom taking a shower when Tom got up and apparently was confused because the bathroom door was closed, and so had an accident on the kitchen floor. The poor man...yet he wasn't at all upset by it and had started to try to clean it up when I got out.

I emptied his desk, a sad thing for me because there were lists and lists of projections for the years ahead, all so carefully worked out. It just breaks my heart.

On the Italian TV station tonight a very pleasant and intelligent young man was reading long passages from literature and then illustrating their flow and rhythm with music and with just his way of speaking. It was lovely.

FRIDAY, NOVEMBER 11 I PACKED THIS MORNING WHILE TOM was in therapy. After lunch we went to the lawyer's to answer interrogatories from one of the opposing parties in Tom's accident. Marty, our lawyer, mentioned his poor opinion of our buyer's lawyer. According to Marty, the other lawyer is arrogant and obnoxious and should have learned more than he has in his five or so years as a lawyer. I hope he doesn't give us trouble.

SATURDAY, NOVEMBER 12 UP EARLY AGAIN WITH A HEADACHE; this is about the third day in a row. I probably won't feel well until this is over and we're in! Before my helpers came I unscrewed the plywood panels over our two windows by the front door to wipe away what might look to tomorrow's inspector like little piles of insect chewings. (Because they were...) Then Joey, Andrea, Jeff, and Danny came and we did the shed and the crawl space. Everyone went home with salvaged goodies. I'm nervous about tomorrow's inspection and will be glad when it's over.

SUNDAY, NOVEMBER 13 WOKE UP EARLY WITH ANOTHER headache, due to my worry about the house inspection. They arrived promptly at 10:00 − the engineer, the buyer, the realtor. The inspection did not reveal any problems; the engineer assured me "it looks good," and the buyer is a very sweet, laid-back fellow.

Of course, the fly in the ointment could still be his lawyer. The realtor called tonight to tell me the buyer almost pulled out because the lawyer was so irritating! But, I feel a bit more confident and less ill at ease.

Watching the Stones on 60 Minutes. They're my age and still going strong, but the clips of their early years are startling: they were babies when we were all young; was I a baby, too?

Bill spoke on the phone with Tom and then told me he thought he could tell there was great improvement. I suppose I'm too close to see it, hence some of my desperation.

MONDAY, NOVEMBER 14 ANOTHER MORNING, ANOTHER headache. I took medicine about 5:30 but between Tom's snoring and somebody's dog yapping, I never got back to sleep before it was time to get up. By 8:00 I was on the phone with the Board of Education to discuss Tom's retirement, and with Public Works to arrange pickup for our trash. Therapy for Tom, school for me, then I took Tom to his mother's and hied me off to our new house for its inspection at 3:00. It went pretty well. Dinner at Helen's, then home where I started my Italian homework, which is supposed to be ready for Wednesday, but I feel like it's all gliding over my head instead of being absorbed.

Tom has alluded under my questioning to something that maybe bothers him but he says he can't tell me what it is. He also said he is happier with this life than he was with his old one – but he has no specific information about his old life! I'm just glad to know he's happy.

Tuesday, November 15 I finally wrote to Pina in Italy and did my homework for our Italian group tomorrow. Took Tom to therapy, and then went down to the Toms River NJEA office to meet with the pension people. It looks like we'll do well on his Full Disability Pension; now I have to fill out more forms and gather more information. Helen had picked up Tom while I was in Toms River; all three of us carried out our junk to the curb for pickup tomorrow. I was pretty beat, but finished the night working on finances.

Tom has learned to knock on the door when the bathroom is occupied, so we've prevented two potential accidents this week!

Wednesday, November 16 Up early and out in the rain to empty out the Blazer, which is being bought by the fellow who has been fixing it the past few years. (You'd think he'd know better!) I made some calls to straighten out some financial kinks. Tom got up and agreed to take a shower, which he does completely alone now, although it still takes some work to get him in.

The Italian group came at 10:00 and we had our lesson. While Tom was in therapy I ran errands. When we got home the garage guy was loading the Blazer onto a trailer. It was kind of sad, despite all the trouble we'd been through together, to see it hauled away. I had hoped we could save it for when Tom was ready to drive again. Another dream evaporates with the Demon's passage. I did a little packing, got us some supper and tonight we watched *Moonstruck*.

Poor Tom began a request this afternoon: "Would you consider the bill we have to pay in October or August..." He went on with paying bills, naming various months. Then, when he pointed to the kitchen, I caught on – he wanted to know when he was going to have supper!

But he *is* at least trying and his categories (time, cost) were sensible. That's all improvement, right?

THURSDAY, NOVEMBER 17 FOR SOME REASON I FEEL A VAGUE disquiet tonight. Maybe it's the move and all it entails and my controlled anger at the buyer's lawyer, who's playing games and slowing the whole thing down. I should have failed him back in Lakewood High School when I had the chance. I wonder if the statute of limitations has run out yet on his English grade...

Perhaps I'm worried about my mother, who, with Chuck, has fled Florida because of the storm. She called from South Carolina last night, which means they and the storm are marching up the coast together.

Maybe it's because I feel a little out of step with real life. I'm living so intensely in the future of our new house that daily life seems unreal."If I am convinced that reality is unreal, how can I be certain that dreams are dreams?"

There's a Zen koan for every contingency.

But probably the unrest is because I finally gave in when Frank Hunter called yesterday and invited him to stop by tomorrow. He has kept on calling even though Tracy asked him not to.

FRIDAY, NOVEMBER 18 SCHOOL AND THERAPY IN THE morning, then home to pack and await the dreaded visitation of Frank Hunter. We had a plan that after he was here a little while, I'd ask Tom if he was tired and wanted a nap. He'd say yes, go off

I DON'T WHETHER MYSELF

to bed, and Hunter would leave. As it happened, the poor pest popped up at the very moment my mother, just back safely from Florida, called on the phone. I took the call while Tom was supposed to be "visiting" with the old man. Soon I heard Hunter calling, "Tom! Tom!" and I peeked in. Tom was already asleep! I thought he understood our plan and just started faking sleep too soon, so I went in and tried to wake him, but he was no longer pretending – unless the snores were also faked. That left me to deal with the pest until he finally left.

Joyce and Lisa came by about 4:30; we had a lot of laughs and a piece of cake. Lisa loved the afghan I finally just finished up for her engagement, which was about two years ago. Tonight I spent about an hour on some Italian worksheets for our group.

SATURDAY, NOVEMBER 19 THIS MORNING I WAS UP AT 7:00 with a wicked headache. More Excedrin, coffee, sitting up to rest and about three hours later it was mostly gone. Out for our usual Saturday breakfast, then home for the day's work. Basically, I cleaned Bill's bunk bed mattresses outside, and began to disassemble the bed itself. I made 48 plaster objects for school and did a lot of packing. Also laundry. I dug up a little tree to take with us and planted it in a pot. Supper and a bath. Tom slept and ate all day, perfectly content to do so.

SUNDAY, NOVEMBER 20 I WAS UP EARLY TO CONTINUE cleaning the mattresses. Then Mark and Madli came and for four hours we worked like crazy dismantling Bill's bunk bed and hutch, loading them onto a truck, then reassembling them at Helen's. Very heavy work. As soon as we got back, Mom came over with my contributions for our school's Thanksgiving baskets. I have no idea how I could have managed without her – we're doing 10 baskets this year. (We hold a "lottery" but because of the needs and circumstances of our special population, the winners are pre-selected.) Packed, then led the realtor through the house to help me check for fire alarms and so on. Phone calls. More work and I was zonked.

MONDAY, NOVEMBER 21 EXHAUSTED. SCHOOL, A QUICK TRIP TO the lawyer's to sign something, then to pick up Tom at therapy. Lunch, packing, nothing in particular but I was and am very tired. (Wait! Maybe it's the allergy pill!) Very stuffy nose all morning; exhausted breathing through my mouth. One of Tom's colleagues stopped by to pick up a box I'd put together of his lesson plans and books. He had such detailed plans and such creative teaching ideas – it's just heartbreaking. Now I'm so tired.

TUESDAY, NOVEMBER 22 ROZ AND BERNIE CAME OVER EARLY to help me carry the boxes of books down from the loft. We moved about 30 boxes. Then we had our Italian study group and after that Tom's therapy. I ran errands until it was time to pick him up. More packing and time set aside to look at the new books I bought on landscape gardening.

And, of course, another hot bath to prevent (or lessen) soreness.

WEDNESDAY, NOVEMBER 23 PACKING AND SUCH THIS morning; this afternoon another run of errands – things for the

I DON'T WHETHER MYSELF

new house and Christmas gifts. A little drift of snow tonight. Bill called; I spoke to him, Kathea, and Cassie. It was so "homey" to have them on the phone, to hear them. I guess I miss them all, especially my Bill. Cassie says he really "fills up the house."

THURSDAY, NOVEMBER 21 THANKSGIVING. WE WERE AT Paula's today. Tom did well; he had at least 12 hours of sleep, then rested the few hours he was up until we left, so he managed to stay awake the whole time.

We were discussing History; I asked what happened in 1776 and Tom said, "The English went their way."

"What about Napoleon?" I asked. I asked this because certain specific words seemed to trigger immediate and correct responses from Tom.

"He was involved in the second tryst," he replied. If the American Revolution was Number One, then the French Revolution would be the "second tryst." Close enough!

FRIDAY, NOVEMBER 25 ONE MONTH TILL CHRISTMAS, AND I can't see it, can't see where we'll be or how we're going to get there. Tom had therapy this morning. I went food shopping. Packing and sorting this afternoon and panicking because the county water people had to test the water and I know it won't pass. It's very annoying to realize that I've got to pay to correct a water problem we've been living with just fine! People are telling me horror stories about being unable to rent moving trucks, so now I have to get that in motion, which is a difficult thing to do without a moving date. We watched *A Home of Their Own*, a true story about a mother and her six kids who bought a shack in

Idaho and fixed it up. I kept assuring Tom that at least our house in Idaho was in better condition than theirs!

SATURDAY, NOVEMBER 26 OUTSIDE THE RESTAURANT WHERE we had our usual Saturday breakfast, Tom pointed to the newspaper kiosk and said, "Let's do this bit of shopping."

A bittersweet remark given his inability to read coupled with his insistence on pretending he can. He also looked at the sales receipt for gas, pointed to the date, and said, "Excuse me, but is this today's date?"

How hard he tries to appear "normal" and the frequency of those appearances still gives us hope, although I have to accept that an hour later all will be forgotten.

Tom slept most of the day. I packed, made and answered phone calls relative to the move.

SUNDAY, NOVEMBER 27 MOM CAME AND WE SORTED OUT THE shed. The weather's getting bad and I'm dreading the winter. I'm not really prepared for it.

MONDAY, NOVEMBER 28 THERE'S A NEW LITTLE RASH ON MY arm and I think it's nerves. The two houses, Tom's pension papers to be sorted out, Christmas, packing, my job, and of course ol' Tom himself and the topsy-turvy nature of our lives – all of these are doing it. Take today: there was school, always tough on a Monday and especially tough today because I've been off for a week. A major headache developed by the time I had to pick up Tom.

I began making calls when I got home: both realtors, a piano mover, insurance company and the lawyer. The secretary there told us we had to come in right away. Now, get this. The lawyer for the buyer's pension company wouldn't release funds to him because he, the lawyer, questioned our signatures on the contract. He felt my name was written too short and narrow to contain all the right letters, and suspected that one person – Tom! – had written both signatures! For a year I've been writing Tom's name on everything and now, when he had both signatures before him, he thought Tom had forged mine!

So, in the rain, we went out to sign an affidavit. What a nuisance! I didn't think Tom understood what was happening, but when we all signed the papers, Tom noticed our lawyer's scrawled name, pointed to it, and said, "Look at that!" – with a sense of proper indignation! He certainly did understand.

TUESDAY, NOVEMBER 29 I THINK I AM COMING CLOSE TO losing it – at least as close as I've come so far. I was up early, finishing finances and some correspondence, and making phone calls. Rushed out at 11:45, hoping to do three errands in 45 minutes before our team meeting at the Therapy Center. However, poor ol' Tom had an accident, which involved a bit of time in the bathroom and a bit of laundry. We got it all taken care of but I did not have enough time to do all the errands; all I got to do was go to the town hall to pay $25.00 for an inspection of smoke alarms which I have not yet bought. We had the team meeting, which went well.

At home, I continued trying to reach a phone number to order Mom's Christmas gift; the number had been busy all day. I was expecting her to stop by, and of course the number answered just as she pulled up. The poor lady had to wait out in the cold while I placed the order with the world's most careful order-taker: "That's S as in Sam...R as in Robert?"

The rest of the afternoon I tried to locate stick-on smoke alarms over the phone with no success. I have a real problem regarding the placement of the alarms because the dome is largely open-plan and does not conform to the usual locations in a standard house.

We watched *The Bicycle Thief,* which Tom followed as I read him the subtitles. However, three minutes before the end, he walked out to start his dinner routine of setting the table. I tried to tell him we had just eaten lunch three hours ago, and I went off to see the end of the film. Tom was upset, but forgot and recovered quickly.

I'm exhausted. And, oh yes, the car is making noise! A grinding, metal-scraping noise. Shades of the Blazer, the Demon Truck is having its revenge! That is what really makes me weak in the innards.

WEDNESDAY, NOVEMBER 30 I THINK TODAY'S FEELING OF defeat was worse than yesterday's because I started out more optimistically. The Sears Man, in whom I had placed all my hopes, called early and said he'd be here between 11 and 1:00. One o'clock came; Roz and Bernie took Tom to his therapy after our Italian group this morning. A little after 2:00, Sears Man showed up, took a water test, spent a minute in the laundry room, and was gone. A nice man; he found no iron, said the PH was the problem and our equipment doesn't solve it.

I left at 3:00, got Tom from therapy and raided the liquor store for packing boxes. (Perhaps I should consider the liquor itself and forget the boxes...my problems might not look so hopeless.) Between yesterday's team meeting and today's Sears Man, all my hours to run errands were used up, so I'm backlogged. We got home and ...a puddle on the laundry room floor! The equipment was leaking! I called Sears many times over the next few hours and finally got our own plumber to fix it, at 8 PM. We'd been without water all afternoon, which is a problem for frequent-flusher Tom. We had to run to fast food for supper. Tom, of course, did well all through it. He used the toilet at McDonald's several times, he ate well, he didn't worry. Me? I held it in, ate half my fish sandwich and worried very much.

I had to delegate the purchase of the smoke alarms and Velcro to Mom, after I checked with the fellow at the town hall who said Velcroed attachment would be okay.

Exhausted again, mostly from aggravation. I see now that this is all a process in motion, I'm a little shell that has lain quietly on the ocean floor for decades; now I've suddenly decided to seek new quarters and am being swept on by a tsunami of realtors, lawyers, and inspectors. There's been a lot of pummeling and plummeting on the way, but the shore is at least within sight and soon we'll be in our new home, although the stickiness of the salt water and the goo from the ocean will still be on us for a while.

I think a buyer should be able to just go buy a house without a horde of "We're here for your protection" people hovering around. Then, if the buyer wants to hire inspectors and whatnot, he should just do it. The seller should be able to just *sell*. What about caveat emptor? Save me the protectors – let me take a risk! Life on the edge! It sounds good about now.

YOU HAVE SPENT A MONTH WITH ME, AND I AM THE FIRST TO admit that most of the narrative has been about me, as opposed to detailing Tom's progress. There are several reasons for this. First of all, Tom had reached a plateau of sorts, which we were warned about all the way back in the ICU. He did exhibit sporadic bursts of brilliance, or such speech as we were willing to interpret as brilliant, but these were few and far between and neither consistent nor a base for further exposition. His life was smooth and comfortable for him, and that was as expected. This was, after all, what we had been working toward all year. But the second reason I have devoted this chapter to my own machinations is that this was what happened. This important month made a bridge between the life we had lived thus far, and the new life we were undertaking. Crossing this bridge meant we accepted Tom as he was, and, while we always hoped for a miracle, we were now facing reality. Our life, such as it was, was moving in a new direction and November opened the door to our new path. Yes, I was turning the knob on that door, but Tom would be by my side as we stepped through it together.

CHAPTER 15

ONE YEAR

And so we arrived at December 2, 1994, one year post accident. That time period, the first 12 months, marked the most dramatic improvements we could hope to see from Tom. Although the possibility of "miracles" would not be completely ruled out, the reality of our situation was something we were learning to accept, despite the fact that it was not the reality we'd hoped for so many months ago.

We had a walking, talking, happy eight-year-old in the body of a person 40 years older than that. We had a gentle soul, a harmless and content person whose life satisfied him. He occasionally chafed under the supervision he had to endure ("Tom, you cannot go out without a jacket; it's cold out") and tried to assert a bit of opposition, but always his good nature prevailed – or he forgot the issue entirely.

As the first year progressed we accepted that we would not have the former Tom Sorrentino back with us any time soon – if at all. Bill would grow into a man without his father's advice and support; I would not have a husband or even an adult companion. These were the harshest realities of our lives; we could accept them and still hope for slow, steady improvement.

The year had seen us through all the normal problems of everyday life. To me, those problems loomed large because I was facing them alone, and in addition dealing with the uncertainties of Tom's recovery and all the situations it produced.

Would it have been healthier for the family had we *not* so encapsulated ourselves in shells of hope that we could not see where the tide was taking us? Ought someone to have told us at the onset that the outlook was bleak and we should be prepared? Should we have relegated Tom to an institution and gone on with our lives?

It is impossible to answer these questions. I believe we did everything right. I'm not sure I could have carried on with my little attempts to help Tom, with the demands of school and with the problems of house, weather and vehicles had I not had the hope, at least in the beginning, that all would eventually be well. The other end of hope is despair. What would our lives have been like if we'd given in to despair? I can't imagine living that way.

And so I bring you to the conclusion of the first year. We were still looking ahead with optimism, we were still trying, every day, to keep Tom happy, motivated, stimulated, and headed toward further recovery. We looked back to the coma, to Tom's early attempts to make sense of his world, and to communicate and we realized how far he had traveled. Of course, we could not know what lay ahead, but I believe the 12 months after those few seconds that changed our lives prepared us to handle whatever it might be.

The move to the new house proceeded. Friends came to help us load and unload the truck I rented. Joey Kiernan agreed to drive the truck, totally setting aside his inexperience in handling such a large vehicle. Joey was not one to let inexperience get in his way. When he arrived at the new house he told me he'd had qualms about crossing a little wooden bridge where signs were posted warning how many tons the bridge would support.

"I had no idea how many tons the truck was," he said. "What do I know about trucks and tonnage? I didn't know if we could make the bridge or not."

"Well, thank you for being brave and worrying about our stuff," I told him.

"Your stuff?" He laughed. "I was worried about me! I had the driver's door open a little so if we went down, I could jump out."

We were unpacked and settled in before Christmas. Bill and Kathea arrived to spend the Christmas break with us. I sensed that Tom was not happy with the move, but when I questioned him he was unable to frame an answer. He seemed moody during the first few days in Point Pleasant and could not be as easily diverted as he had been back at the dome. I understood the change might be difficult, and he didn't understand my reasons for making that change. I also understood – or at least hoped – he would eventually accept the new house and our life there. If his past behavior was any indication, he would soon forget the dome and find happiness in his new situation. Until that occurred, I felt guilty and morose myself, wondering whether I'd done the right thing and whether he would ever forgive me for the re-location and the desertion of his beloved dome. For both of us, this colored the early excitement of the move.

PART IV

Life is not a spectacle or a feast; it is a predicament.

– George Santayana

CHAPTER 16

1995

T hey were right, of course. They who told us Tom would make most of his progress in his first year were spot on, and we, who hoped for a full recovery, were wrong. We had Tom with us for six years more during which he never recovered to any greater degree than he had in his first post-accident year. As time unfolded this condition became more apparent, and devastating as it was, we had no choice but to accept it.

This does not mean we ceased our efforts to keep him happy, healthy, and stimulated. Nor did we stop rejoicing over every perceived improvement, every little step we continued to hope would lead to a more robust recovery. For as long as Tom was with us, he was still the focus of our lives. Gradually, as he attained a more or less permanent stasis, we circled his tenuous stability with little movements of our own, our personal attempts at building a life around his. Reminiscent of my earlier imagery, he was still the stone thrown to the center of the pond and we were still circling around him, but this time our circles did not fade out as quickly or disappear as they once had. It was important for Bill, Helen, and me, as well as our family and friends, to find a place for ourselves in Tom's world, and this we did with varying degrees of success.

Helen continued to be devastated by the condition of her oldest child, but she never stopped prompting him, setting him little mental exercises, and providing day care for him when I needed time. She was a strong presence in his life, and stalwart enough to keep her worries and fears to herself. It had to be difficult for her, but she never complained. She was essentially a robust woman to begin with, and she found additional stamina and comfort in her religion. Tom had five brothers and sisters whose lives quite naturally continued along their paths as we were journeying with him. These siblings and their children, the events of their lives, and visits back and forth also helped sustain Helen and offered her a bit of distraction from the otherwise unsettling state of Tom's condition.

Bill was more affected by his father's situation than he was willing to express. He had returned to the University of Idaho in early 1994, but never got back on a sure footing. At the time he returned, he had to make up first semester exams, formulate a second semester schedule, and enter his classes after they had already begun. Not a strong student at the time, this presented quite an obstacle for him and for the balance of his stay in Moscow, one-and-a-half more years, he toyed with a major-of-the-month, unsure of what direction he wanted to take. He finally finished the second year, in a manner of speaking, and came home to stay. He wanted to be an essential part of his father's recovery, and he was. Tom was very proud of him, often becoming visibly cheerful if we returned from an outing and Bill's car was parked outside: "Bill's home! My son is home!"

Bill was also a great support to me, I gladly put up with the vicissitudes of his life: girlfriends, the boys he hung out with, classes at the community college, jobs, cars – all the normal comings and goings of a healthy and popular young man. He was certainly entitled to his life and I did not begrudge him a moment of it, although at times I found his struggles almost as frustrating as Tom's. But we all tumbled on, and sharing the path with Bill was definitely a more pleasant way for me to travel than trodding beside Tom alone.

I did my best to keep Tom healthy and occupied. Believing that supplements from the Health Food store might be of use, I loaded Tom up with gingko biloba, pycnogenol, grape seed extract, CoQ10, and anything else anyone suggested. You name it, I bought it; Tom swallowed it. And who is to say these did not help? Those who studied the MRI of his brain and those who worked with him in therapies were often amazed at the progress he'd made, given the extent of his injury. Whether or not the supplements were responsible is a moot point; I felt they might be beneficial and I was willing to try anything.

The little house in Point Pleasant Beach sat only two blocks from town. I could make quick forays on foot to the library, supermarket and post office, leaving Tom with his TV in relative safety for thirty minutes. Bill and I painted the walls. I was referred to a superb craftsman, Mike Yaccarino, who built bookshelves in the study and created a huge bedroom for Bill out of the attached garage.

My pride and joy was the "discovery" garden created by Bill and me in the backyard. What others might justifiably view as a landscape nightmare, I saw as a delightful arrangement of paths, patios and greenery. We dug a fish pond. Bill made wooden boardwalks which invited a walker to stroll around the many splendors of our garden. He built a lattice arbor at the back door. The idea was that a casual rambler (which seemed to consist of mainly me; other folks were too polite to comment) might meander along the boardwalk's twisting paths, discovering at each turn a new delight. Mind you, this was not acreage; this was a tiny yard but we doubled paths beside themselves, with plantings in between them, and we did all the work ourselves. I was mighty pleased with the effort and the effect.

Besides being able to walk into town, we were only a mile from the beach and the boardwalk, more places to walk. I really loved this little house and once Tom forgot about the dome, he was happy there as well.

We learned a lot, Bill and I did. We learned that expensive koi did not survive in our little pond, but feeder goldfish, ten for a dollar, were invincible, possibly even immortal. Bill learned a bit about woodworking. Once the garage was converted into his room, he began to develop what would become a life-long avocation - painting 3-D effects and murals on walls. I resumed flute lessons and Bill for some reason bought an accordion. Life moved along.

As whimsical as some of our diversions may seem, there was a concurrent growth and a better grasp of reality for us. Bill made the decision to remain in New Jersey rather than return to Idaho, which meant he had to sever the somewhat fragile engagement to Kathea. He found work and began classes at a community college. Tom attended therapies, but on a reduced schedule now and my school schedule was adapted to meet his needs. He slowly developed some degree of independence.

Tom's speech therapist, of whom he was very fond and for

whom he had a great deal of respect, came to our house for his sessions. He began to keep a spiral notebook which he filled with speech exercises, names and addresses of friends and family, names of characters on TV, and advertisements from the newspaper for restaurants or movies. He could not read, but he managed a form of word recognition to help him select the advertisements. He might have recognized the names on his lists, but not enough to pronounce them or indicate that he remembered to whom they referred. This procedure was a shadow of old Tom, who kept meticulous records, as well as a pocket notebook of daily tasks and reminders.

This time the tasks were simplistic, the writing all in large capital letters; it was the notebook of a child. But Tom saw his therapies as "classes" and something deeply ingrained in him understood that one took a notebook to class, therefore his red spiral notebook became a compendium of the exercises in speech class as well as a scrapbook of meaningful listings.

One such exercise was recorded by the therapist in Tom's notebook. She offered him a word and he was to respond with a word or phrase related to the stimulus word. Here below the stimulus word is in capitals and Tom's response follows it:

BANK – Money
RESTAURANT – I like to eat Italian food.
AIRPORT – [no response]
HOSPITAL – Go there for treatment
SCHOOL – Get an education
LIBRARY – Get a book
VACATION – They're a lot of fun.
GRADUATION – You succeed
WEDDING – They're a lot of fun,
ELECTION – Choices

POLICEMAN – Two people together in a ...[he motioned his hands as if driving a car]

BIRTHDAY – a good time

His responses were miles ahead of the feeble replies he was able to give in speech therapy at Jackson, but they were still very childish. He did not identify the bank, restaurant, hospital, school or library as places or buildings. He could express the purpose of each location but could not group them into general categories, or even make a statement beginning with "It's a place where..." No doubt the reference to Policeman was triggered by a TV show. He understood the concept, but faltered in searching for the word "car". Similarly, the wedding, vacation, and birthday answers were indistinguishable from one another. His immediate reactions were not incorrect, but certainly not specific, and left us wondering whether he knew the differences among the various celebrations. Airport meant nothing to him, but he'd had no recent experience with one.

On the plus side, I loved his reply to Graduation – You succeed. It spoke so much of the old Tom, whose enthusiasm for education was an integral part of his persona. We had come a long way, though, just to arrive at these simple responses, so we were not discouraged.

The therapist requested photographs of familiar people or objects to use as points of discussion with Tom. She recorded his responses in his notebook:

My son smiles.

My wife's artwork. Oh yeah, she's good. She's an artist.

This is in the old house. This is upstairs. Oh, yeah, my spot. [his desk in the loft]

It's ours. I don't know how to describe it to you. You use this as an output. Fireplace or woodstove. [It was the woodstove]

A new house. It's in... we own it but I don't remember too much. It's where we moved. But I don't know too much about it. It's in a different state. It's – Idaho.

This is the vehicle that gave us a life as we lived it. It's dead now. [Demon, of course]

And that's the house. We built that house.

That's my picture. [He laughs] It's me, this was before the accident. In Idaho.

I saw this and I know he was someone from the past. A teacher. I knew him, in my department, but I couldn't identify his name. [Rich MacFarland, who was a History teacher with Tom]

ONCE AGAIN, THE RESPONSES WERE MUCH MORE ACCURATE than they had ever been, but still simple and shallow. However, many of them seemed to be evocative of memory, which was very encouraging. He remembered Idaho, certain features of the dome house, and family members. He was able to correctly attach labels to people. A definite sign of continued improvement.

Life in Point Pleasant Beach settled into a comfortable routine. Bill was living with us. Though grateful for his company and his help, I also worried that having abandoned the University of Idaho, he might not complete college at all. He worked at various jobs, mostly up at the Boardwalk. He liked riding my 10-speed bike up to work and then coming home through misty, deserted streets late at night. He reconnected with a group of friends who all met together in the diner at various odd hours. He enjoyed fixing up his room and doing the woodworking projects in the garden. There were girls who came and went. He was busy and I believed he was happy.

One day in June Bill gave up his day off to be with his father, freeing me to take my mother up to North Jersey for our twice-annual excursion to the cemetery to place flowers on my father's grave. When we got home in the late afternoon, Tom greeted us, very obviously distressed.

"Tom, what's wrong?" I had to ask several times, and each time he replied, "I can't tell you."

He was ashen, his eyes wild and he could not settle down to TV. He could not – or would not – tell us what was wrong. Bill had spent most of the day in his room and had no clue.

We began a barrage of simple questions: "Do you hurt anywhere?" "Are you sick?" He answered "no" to each one. When we finally arrived through a series of deductions, to "Did you receive a phone call from someone in the family?" he hesitated.

We then suggested names, knowing that "a phone call" to Tom could mean any sort of communication or even a thought about a person not necessarily involving the telephone. None of our suggestions resonated with him. Then, very suddenly he pointed to my mother and said, "It was your first husband!" My mother's only husband and my father. Tom was referencing my mother's friend Chuck as a second husband.

"Tom," I said, "you could not have heard from my father. He died long before I met you."

"He was right there," Tom insisted, and pointed out the living room window, which faced the street. "He walked right there." He was adamant, more adamant than I'd ever seen him.

"How do you know it was my father?" I asked. "You never knew him. You don't even know what he looked like."

"It was this father," he said, and walked over to the drawing I had done of my father which was hanging among other paintings and drawings on the wall. I had never seen Tom pay any attention to these pictures. "This father," he said again, pointing determinedly to the drawing.

"But Tom, my father has been dead for thirty years. You could not have seen him."

"I know. That's what worries me."

"You saw someone who looked like my father."

"No."

Eventually we calmed him down and got him settled. We decided the impression created by our trip to the cemetery and the presence of the drawing had convinced him a passing stranger was my father. He remained absolutely certain that my father, although dead, walked past our house. And he was understandably upset by the experience.

When my mother was ready to leave, Tom came out of the TV room with a very serious face and directed himself to her. "Take good care of yourself." Then he added, "Because you're going to die. I don't want you to, but you are."

He was as certain of this as he had been about my father. Against all reason, we felt a little tinge of alarm. He was convinced – and convincing.

My mother called later to tell me she arrived home safely.

Television continued to be the main source of entertainment for Tom and indeed, the chief occupation of his day. With the help of clever Mike Yaccarino I had a drawing table and shelving for my art supplies in the TV room, which meant I could follow my own pursuits and also keep Tom company, and continue to pepper him with questions or urge him to comment on the shows.

For example, I asked him why one of the characters in a particular program always spoke in such a loud and annoying voice.

He told me, "She had to build her character. She's an external," which meant the actress had to develop her characterization as an extraterrestrial on the program.

"Why do they extend their voices like that?" He referred to a loud commercial.

"They hope people will pay more attention," I replied. "But most of the time people don't pay attention."

"That's what intelligent people do. But the ignorant's attention is paid to the media."

Once in a while we even – intentionally or not – got a little joke from Tom. Referring to Clint Eastwood, Tom observed, "He's a man I look up to."

"Why?"

"Because he's taller than me."

Other than enjoying the pleasures of watching television and eating, Tom was also very much absorbed with Bill and tried to be a father figure. One morning I started in on Bill with questions and plans while the lad was still in bed. Tom overheard me and asked me, "Did you give him a good introduction to the day?"

He was asking if I had at least said "Good morning" before I began talking. I was chastened and rebuked, but it was a pleasure!

PROTECTIVE AS HE WAS, HE WAS ALSO REALISTIC – DESPITE ALL his brain befuddlement. "You poor thing," he told me. "Because you have all these expectations for your son and he often upsets them."

With a great deal of patience we could actually play Scrabble. Tom was able to form small words even though he could not pronounce the word or name the letters.

"Did you deposit this?" He wondered if I put down a word on the board.

We played nearly every day. I sensed that these games gave him a feeling of normality, that he was doing what other people do, what we used to do, assuming he remembered. Occasionally he would ask for assistance. "You've got to help me. I don't know the recipe."

He was able to laugh at his own mistakes. "I used the word 'goopy'. There's no trade-off for that word."

What a long way we had come!

Tom made a show of looking at the newspaper each day, but was not able to read it. When he was involved with the paper one morning, I asked him if he was ready to go out. "When I finish judging this literature," was his reply.

Tom was not happy with what he wore. "I want to trade this outfit," he announced. I helped him find new clothes.

While we watched "The Coneheads" I asked Tom why the characters were so out-of-touch with reality. We had come quite a long way indeed if I could put a question like that to Tom, whose own hold on reality had been tenuous for so long

"Everything's by a standard definition," he explained.

He was correct. The Conehead characters took everything that was said quite literally. They did indeed follow a "standard definition."

Columbo was a favorite program of Tom's. How well he understood the plot was evidenced in a statement he made regarding a character in an episode who had "book knowledge" but not common sense – a trait that was only implied, not stated in the program. Tom explained, "He knows it all as he reads it but he doesn't know it in his head." Right on, Tom!

Tom set his coffee aside. When I asked him why he explained

that he must "wait until it softens." I assumed he meant "cools" but "softens" works.

Sometimes I wanted to punch a subject further, even though I knew was a futile exercise. Generally, he could not go beyond his original statement and I was only setting myself up for disappointment. The song *Carrie Ann* was playing. The lyrics tell about the subject's life from childhood to adulthood.

"I like this song because it extends the whole circuit," Tom reported.

Of course, he is correct, but I wanted to ask how he knew this. What parts of the song related to which parts of Carrie Ann's life? I knew he could not tell me, yet I was intrigued by his immediate and intuitive grasp of the meaning. Did he also understand he was unable to explain beyond the simple statement? Our new and improved Tom was still quite a mystery.

I showed Tom some cancelled checks and asked if he knew what they were. "They represent deductions from our inventory," he said. But look, they "represent," they are not actually the deductions themselves. He was so precise. Of course they did involve deductions and "inventory" is a fine word for "checking account." Maybe even better, simpler.

It was often difficult to get Tom out the house to take a walk. I learned he would happily move himself up and out if food was promised. I suggested a walk on the boardwalk; he was unwilling until I suggested we could have a cup of coffee. Then he was ready! As we walked, I asked him what made him change his mind. He answered, "I was thinking of doing it because you gave the prospect of pouring some liquid."

We were in the kitchen on a Sunday morning, already late for a breakfast gathering at a diner with the Italian group. I was trying to rush Tom along but he was intent upon organizing the Sunday Times according to the alphabetical section letters, carefully adding each section, folded neatly, inside the previous one. He was confused by the Magazine and Book Review sections, which did not belong anywhere, alphabetically. I was losing my temper with him, really losing it, for the first time since this adventure began.

"It doesn't matter where the damn sections go! [You can see I was out of control here. I never say, "Damn"] Just put them anywhere! We're late!"

Tom looked up. I may have surprised him with my vehemence; I certainly disturbed his sense of the order of things. He made a waving gesture over the papers. Clearly it did matter very much how the sections went together.

He continued to organize.

I grabbed the paper from his hands and slammed it on the floor. He had never seen me like this before. Indeed, I had never seen me like this before. "We're leaving!"

When we got to the diner I explained our lateness. Tom had forgotten the entire incident and was happily looking at the menu. "I think I need a break," I told my friends. "I'm going to ask Helen to take care of Tom for a few days and just check into a hotel somewhere."

Most of the group agreed it was about time.

Bernie's daughter Lise, who was visiting from her home in England, had an idea. "Fares are really cheap right now. Why don't you come and spend a week with me?"

And just like that, the deed was done. In one week's time all the arrangements were made. Helen had Tom. I had a round-trip ticket to Manchester.

Lise was pleasant and obliging; despite her work schedule she planned a lovely week for me. I returned rested and ready to resume our adventure.

FOOD WAS HIGH ON TOM'S DAILY AGENDA. HE CONTINUED THE small mealtime preparations he had begun back when we lived in the dome. Once in a while he needed a little help.

"Are these relevant?" he asked, wondering if the plates he had in his hands were the right ones for lunch.

Once seated, he was momentarily confused as he held the bottle of ketchup. "Where shall I distribute this?" he wanted to know.

Television ads spiked his desire to eat at Red Lobster. Sometimes, just dinner out was not enough. "I want to be able to afford to get in and out of two places." He wanted us to carry enough money for Red Lobster and also the movies.

Our sweet Tom had come such a distance. He had developed his language skills to the point he not only could be understood, but also could offer tantalizing glimpses into the workings of his intellect. If only, if only, if only these little glimpses, these charming gems of wisdom would continue to develop, be remembered and retrieved, and would lead him back to the man we lost. If only.

Our second post-accident year ended in December 1995. We were by now more realistic about Tom's recovery and were forming a life based more on what we had than on what we hoped for. The interior and exterior housework was a pleasure for me and kept my body busy and my mind off our reality. That reality, while not exactly grim, was now emphatic in its evidence: Tom was not going to make much more progress. We passed the six-month, the one-year, and the eighteen-month hurdles with little significant change. He could express himself clearly but without depth. He needed constant supervision. He could toilet and dress himself but his clothes had to be put out for him. He had no concept of dressing for the weather. The kitchen remained mostly out of bounds; he had no idea how to regulate the stove or prepare foods. He could not read, write or do math. However, he kept himself happily occupied and never seemed to be bored or discontent. (Is this not a goal for all of us?)

Our second year was definitely less of a roller coaster ride than our first had been. We had all grown in our knowledge of Tom and of our own strengths and weaknesses. But, except for those moments Lin Yutang promised, I cannot say it was a happy year.

CHAPTER 17

THE INVISIBLE DISABILITY

The fact Tom had achieved a kind of stasis and was not destined to make much more progress in his recovery did not mean our adventure was over. We still had six years before us. (Although, of course, we did not know the time frame.) There is no point in recounting all of those years in detail because, in contrast to his first post-accident year, they lacked both the drama and the excitement of his steady growth as he initially sped toward recovery.

If this narrative is to be of use, however, it is important to understand the kinds of situations that might occur as you steer a brain-injured person through the waters of life. Here, you will find a variety of events that sparked the remaining years of Tom's life, some of the adventures we undertook, and the little changes we encountered as we moved along. Bear in mind, we still had an eye out for a miracle. We continued to believe every returning memory, no matter how short-lived, was evidence of brain strength. We always looked for new words, better forms of expression, greater independence, and we took heart from each instance. No one was giving up on Tom.

One of the difficulties with brain injury – or at least with Tom's form of injury – is that to all external appearances, the victim seems quite normal, therefore the expectation of an onlooker is for "normal" behavior. And yet, as the persons closest to him, we knew Tom had serious problems when he confronted the greater world. And sometimes the problems were exacerbated by his complete ignorance of them.

It was natural to want to help him, and at the same time to assist his independence. We wanted to protect him, but also to encourage him to try new experiences, much the same philosophy as a parent would use in raising a child. This conflict sometimes led to episodes of different descriptions: "interesting" at worst, "amusing" at best, but generally "frustrating."

We did our best to guide him, but many times we were helpless in the face of circumstances none of us had foreseen or could control. If he had been battling demons, we would have fought them. But what we had was an absence of demons. He struggled against shadows instead.

Tom loved to sing and had a wonderful voice. After his accident he still loved to sing, but usually could not remember the words to the songs. He was undeterred. We would walk into a diner or restaurant and if there were music playing in the background, he would immediately go into show mode: a correct, if somewhat exuberant hum or collection of "doo-doo-doos" to make up for the lack of lyrics, accompanied by broad gestures, both arms outspread. Rather alarmingly at times, his theatrics were visited on unsuspecting diners whose dining enjoyment was suddenly overshadowed by Tom looming over their table, arms out wide as he favored them with a personal serenade. Should we have to walk any distance to our table, all the folks between the door and our booth were serenaded. I was the person hurrying him along from in front, or pushing him along from behind and trying not to make eye contact with anyone in the diner.

On the Point Pleasant boardwalk where we frequently walked when I could lure Tom outside with a promise of coffee or a hamburger, there was a large house whose resident blared Frank Sinatra's songs over a loudspeaker for all to hear, all day long. It was Tom's custom to step up to the porch of the house, his stage, and sing (hum or doo-doo) along with Frank. It did not affect his performance one little bit when three young Japanese girls were trying to take pictures of each other on the steps of this house. He stepped right behind them as they posed for each other, and began the show. There was no way I could explain and equally no way I could get Tom off the porch. "I'm a good singer," he would reply to my futile insistence for him to step down. There must be some interesting photos being shown in Japan of a crazy man standing behind the girls, singing his heart out.

With the Italian group, we went to the Opera Cafe in Philadelphia. This was an interesting place masquerading as a restaurant where, following a clank of spoons against glasses, all conversation would cease and the wait staff would burst into an aria. Tom came along with the group; beginning days ahead, we warned him that he was absolutely *not* to sing along with the waiters. My delicious mushroom risotto did not sit as well as it should have because I got so nervous every time I heard the glasses ring. Tom, however, understood and remained quiet But the strain on him was evident when we left. He marched atop the first stoop we came to outside someone's house, and treated the street to his own renditions.

We flew out to Idaho one summer for a brief stay. Despite all my worries, we got to the airport on time and were safely strapped into the plane when I thought of his bathroom problems. He had gone to the bathroom before we left at several stops along the way to the airport and a few times while we waited to board, all necessitated by his "immature bladder." I called the stewardess over and explained his situation. Should he feel the urge, it would have to be acted upon immediately. She was very helpful and led him to the head of the line in the less-crowded first class compartment each time he wanted to go. Perhaps the fact that he was escorted by airline personnel clued in the other people waiting, but no one complained. Incidentally, this toilet was the closest any of us had ever got to first class!

But who knew that the escalator and the moving sidewalk in the airport would terrify him? As he stood at the top of the escalator, tentatively reaching out and then withdrawing his foot, the line formed behind us and we realized we had another unusual situation – a grown man, seemingly normal, who was afraid to entrust his admittedly rather large foot to the narrow moving steps regurgitating from the maws of the machine. Finally, Bill turned around in front of Tom and I stood beside him. With the vocal, if somewhat surly encouragement of the crowd behind us, we got him down the stairs. This happened again at the moving sidewalk in the terminal. I could see the terror wash across his face, but I must give him credit. We were victorious – although a little slow.

We live in a very frightened world. Parents are completely protective of their children and the children, no doubt quite sensibly, are wary of strangers. New Tom loved little children. I think he may have understood them on some intuitive level as less threatening than adults, less judgmental. He gravitated toward them – anywhere, anytime – and had a habit of wiggling his fingers near their faces, bending his six-two body if necessary, and greeting them. "Hello! How are you today?"

The child would cower behind its parent, the parent would encircle it in protection and glower at me: why is this obviously perverted man being allowed to accost my child? It was too difficult to explain; I simply avoided eye contact and kept pushing Tom along.

But these scenes kind of isolated us. I felt like we didn't belong out in the world, that it was too complicated and too critical for us. Other people just walked through it unencumbered or, if they were managing a handicap, had a visible manifestation of it. We had no crutches, no wheelchair, nothing in the way of a signal to prepare people for our presence. We had only a nervous, small woman behind a tall man with a friendly smile who was wagging his fingers at small children. Clearly, we did not belong in this setting, but only Tom was unaware. We had an invisible disability and it was our secret.

Twice, I must admit, his disability saved me from traffic tickets. In each case I was hurrying to get Tom home to a bathroom and somewhat overstepped the speed limit. Each time, as the policeman stood next to the car window, I explained, "Officer, I have a brain-injured man here who needs a bathroom and can't control himself."

And each time, bless his heart, Tom replied from the passenger seat, "I'm not brain injured!"

SOME OF TOM'S RESPONSES WERE SO UNUSUAL THAT THEY bordered on savant-ism. For example, shortly after the move to Point Pleasant, I tried to teach him our new phone number.

"I know it," he assured me.

"What is it then?"

"It's 477-3628."

I was astounded. That was my mother's number, a number he never dialed post-accident and very seldom ever called before that! I was so amazed that I asked him to repeat it – and he did, correctly.

Fifteen minutes later I asked him again and it was gone. To test whatever prompted this recollection, I asked him his mother's number, which he had used frequently since the accident and which was posted on the wall above the phone. He could not remember her number.

Although we were used to the stimulus-response reaction in cases where the stimulus of a question or a word produced an immediate and generally correct response from Tom, this telephone number recall came as a surprise. I expected him to know his mother's number if he remembered any number at all, but was shocked when he produced my mother's, which was so unfamiliar to him.

Another interesting puzzle popped up here: if the primary stimulus immediately produced my mother's number, had the fifteen-minute interval before the question was put to him again erased the stimulus-response reaction completely? If so, why? Where had that answer been hiding until he brought it out for display, and where did it go?

We were watching *Jeopardy*. Alex Trebek stated: "He was the last President born in the nineteenth century."

Tom immediately replied, "Eisenhower," which turned out to be correct.

I asked Tom how he knew. "I know my history," he told me.

Yes, he did. The pre-accident Tom was an encyclopedia of historical knowledge. Often, when we checked out at a supermarket and the total of the bill came to a number that represented any year in the past, Tom would start listing the significant events of that year. The clerk at the register might not have been interested in the Battle of Agincourt or the Treaty of Aix-la-Chapelle, but it was an impressive stunt, nonetheless. The man did know his history.

After the Eisenhower answer, thinking we might be on a memory roll, I asked Tom what we had just eaten for supper an hour earlier.

"Little things," he said.

Save us from those who would protect us. I had to do a bit of business over the phone and in the process I had to request that Tom's name be replaced with mine. I explained to the fellow on the other end that my husband had suffered a brain injury and was no longer capable of making financial decisions.

"May I speak with your husband, please?" the man asked.

"He won't understand what you are talking about," I told him. "He has lost the use of nouns, numbers and any kind of financial understanding." I was calm at this point, thinking this would be a very simple procedure.

"I just need to ask him a few questions, ma'am."

"He cannot understand the questions. He's had a brain injury."

"Mrs. Sorrentino, I cannot make this transaction without his permission and without having him answer a few simple questions"

Maybe I should have just put Tom on the phone, but that was a risky prospect. I had no way of knowing how he would come across. Instead, I persisted. "You don't understand. He cannot answer questions or give you valid answers."

"I' m sorry," he replied. "I cannot help you."

Where I might have cried in the past, a sudden, wonderful, totally underhanded idea occurred to me. "Thank you for your time," I stated as sweetly and calmly as I could, considering I was about to enter the world of High Crime. I hung up.

Bill came home an hour later. "Bill, be your father," I said. I instructed him in how to be fraudulent without fear as I dialed the number again. This time when someone whom I hoped was a different fellow answered, I repeated my request and we danced along all the way up to our previous impasse.

"May I speak with your husband? I need his permission."

"Of course you may." I handed the phone to Bill.

The transaction was completed with no further problems.

Frequently, it was difficult to find the balance between thinking I had to explain something to Tom or draw out nouns that had eluded him on the one hand, and his sudden, intrinsic expressions of comprehension on the other. There was no way to determine in any given circumstance whether he would understand the matter and contribute, or be confused and need assistance.

Bill needed to buy new tires for his car. I felt sorry for him because his job did not pay enough for that kind of expense. I mentioned the problem to Tom, and finished with, "Poor kid."

Tom looked at me in surprise. "He's got two parents, a father and mother."

I was sure he meant we would take care of Bill, and he was surprised I hadn't grasped that.

The subtleties of Tom's thought processes were sometimes presented to us as tantalizing nuggets of information, just out of reach or slightly askew in terms of explanation. With perseverance we were often able to understand his intention.

At the Philadelphia Art Museum with our Italian group, Tom

spotted a face in a café scene painted by Joan Miro. Thoroughly pleased with himself, evidenced by a satisfied smile, he announced, "I know this man!"

"Who is it" we all asked at once.

"He's on every bill. He's Uncle Sam."

We all pulled out bills of various denominations. "Can you find him on these bills?" Bernie asked.

Tom looked at the money and then at us, almost in exasperation. "It's a symbol," he said. "It's invisible."

Yes, Uncle Sam is a symbol of the United States, and our printed money is also a symbol. Tom saw the connection even if Uncle Sam did not appear on the bills – or in Miro's painting. It was an astute observation and a plausible connection. He used the words "bill," "symbol," and "Uncle Sam" all correctly. As with so many of his pronouncements, he had pulled these terms out of their hiding places in his brain and put them to use this one time. We knew by now not to expect further explanation or a repeat performance, but the one time was interesting in and of itself.

On the same excursion, it was a great thrill for Tom to stand in Rocky's footprints which are engraved on the top landing of the steps leading up to the museum. Lunch, of course, was an added attraction.

We moved again, to Leisure Village, a gated adult community. It was a positive move in some ways. Tom had escaped the Point Pleasant house twice when Bill was supposed to be watching him. He'd gone into town, problematic because he did not know how to return home, and could not explain himself to any useful degree. He did manage to buy himself a cup of coffee at a nearby restaurant; I could only hope the money transaction was handled fairly. In discussion with Tom's cognitive therapist, we all concluded that a quiet, secure setting such as a gated community would best serve Tom's growing independence, and offer him the opportunity to participate in such activities as singing groups, pool, and horseshoes, all of which he enjoyed.

Our new condo was a short distance from the clubhouse; I walked him back and forth every day until he learned his way and could go by himself. He had never seemed happier than when he had packed a gym bag with his cassettes, and slung his cue stick case over his shoulder to head off to play pool. A few times he did get lost, but either I found him or one of the residents read the identity card I'd made for him and steered him home. I learned that just about every household in Leisure Village had a story: death of a spouse, a crippling last disease, or simply the infirmities of age. For that reason, many residents were disposed to understand and to help others.

It transpired that the other pool players in the clubhouse were less than enchanted by Tom's singing, which accompanied his games as he listened to oldies on his Walkman. He never regained the ability to follow the rules and none of the other players offered to play with him, which did not bother him. He contented himself by merely hitting the balls around on the table. There were those in the hall who played tournament pool but I learned not to worry about them. If his singing were a distraction, it was an equal opportunity distraction. Both teams playing in the tournament had the same opportunity at the same time of missing their shot thanks to Tom's vocalizing. He only stayed in the hall for about an hour, anyway.

A BRAIN INJURY WILL RESULT IN AN EXAGGERATED EXHIBIT OF some character trait that the victim had displayed to a lesser degree before his injury. This could be a positive or a negative trait. A previously violent person might become more volatile while a gentle soul could become cripplingly timid. All things considered, we were fortunate in this respect. Tom was previously organized to an amazing degree, perhaps bordering on the pathological. After the accident he developed his organizational skills until they reached unforeseen heights.

I could live with his meticulous table setting. In fact, that was a pleasure. I could live with his persistence in laying out his toothpaste, cap unscrewed and placed neatly above the mouth of the tube. There was no real problem in his arrangement of tooth brush, shaving cream, razor, shampoo, and soap all laid out neatly in a row. I did learn, however, that if he had one or more tubes of toothpaste in his bathroom cabinet, all of them would be laid out each day, all in preparation for use. But these did no one any harm and anyone needing to use the bathroom in our house was aware of his tendencies.

But the men in public restrooms were neither aware nor appreciative of their perceived need to employ the neat stacks of accordion-pleated toilet paper that Tom left out for them on every available flat surface in every restroom. These stacks were placed next to carefully folded paper towels, ever handy for the next customer. No amount of persuasion on my part could convince Tom that people using public toilets did not want anybody to pleat their paper or touch their towels. It was organization and he knew organization.

If Tom overstayed his visit in a "one seater," I had no qualms about marching to the head of the line and telling the men waiting that I was going in.

We had one bit of wonderful news from the outside world. Poor old Frank Hunter had retired and was now living on the

West Coast with his daughter. I was happy for him, but a lot happier for us.

My hopes for Tom in the chorus at Leisure Village were dashed as soon as I learned this was a semi-professional group with a modest, local tour schedule. I knew he could not read the words to songs or remember them. Nor was he able to tolerate the discipline of rehearsal, and it was doubtful that he could participate in any activity for long without needing to use the bathroom. Touring was completely out of the question.

Instead, I took him to the Music Lover's Club, a large group of people who enjoyed singing but were not necessarily good at it. Tom and I sat among them for the duration of a few songs, then, in a quiet moment between songs (a very, very quiet moment) Tom announced very, very, loudly, "These people have terrible voices!" I hid behind him as I pushed him out of the room.

By contrast to Tom's singing ability, my own four-note range fell a little short.

We were visiting at my sister's house; Tom was unusually lucid. At some point I joked about my singing. He began to laugh in a rather exaggerated fashion, then tried to stop. "I love you too much to laugh at you," he said. "It's not within me."

Amazed at this well-put-together sentence, I tried to continue the conversation by saying, "It's okay, I know I have a four-note range."

"You shouldn't sing in this country," he remarked.

"Where should I sing?"

"Down the street." He traced a large letter "C" in the air with his finger. "You know the place very well. I go there with you and my mother."

I knew exactly what he meant. He was referring to a Chinese

restaurant that was indeed down the street from where we lived, and we had gone there a few times with Helen.

Was Tom telling me my voice was better suited to Chinese music?

Early on, I learned it was useless to try to explain Tom's behavior to the public. It wasted time and engendered no result. His disability was invisible; my explanation would not render it more visible. Moreover, I sensed the response would be natural and logical: if he is brain-damaged, why did you bring him here?

I cannot say I hardened to his public behavior; I definitely cannot say I found it amusing at the time. It was tempting, however, to picture the expression on the next guy's face when he walked into the restroom to be confronted with the neat little stacks of folded toilet paper. I often felt momentarily uncomfortable, but Tom did not. Should anyone have asked, I was prepared to explain. But no one ever did. They recovered from whatever little annoyance Tom had caused and forgot it.

I did not.

Therapy continued for several years more, but eventually stabilized and would no longer be supported by our insurance. We'd been there before! Once blocks of time were no longer occupied by Tom's therapies, I left my job to be with him full-time.

I stubbornly believed I could be a help to him and to his intellectual development. We continued every form of cognitive stimulation I could devise – primary workbooks, *Scrabble*, conversation, visits and small trips. When it became apparent there was very little progress, my focus gradually shifted to just keeping Tom safe and happy. I never completely gave up, to be sure, but I eased up. Tom, for the most part, asked for nothing more than his meals, TV and visitors.

Devastated as she was by Tom's condition, Helen nonetheless readily agreed to sit with him frequently. Twice she kept him for a full week while I visited friends in Europe. She never gave up on him, continuing to ply him with questions, photos, little chores. Anything to keep his mind stimulated. Thankfully, Tom was amenable to every effort made on his behalf, although he sometimes balked at the pre-reading workbooks.

Day to day there was not much to memorialize. There were no sudden breakthroughs, no miracles (yet) and little hope of our ever returning to the life we once enjoyed and the plans we'd made for our future. However, we did attempt a few adventures and they were stories in themselves. I brought Tom on a circle tour to visit various friends in Connecticut. We spent a few days in South Jersey exploring gardens and glass works. We went to Provincetown for a long weekend. Truth to tell, none of this made much of an impression on Tom but he appreciated the food, and the people, and it was diverting for me.

CHAPTER 18

SCENES FROM THE REST STOP
TOUR OF AMERICA

I n a fit of probable insanity (which is being generous), I had decided to drive out to Idaho with Tom. I tried to think of every problem we might encounter along the way, and to plan for every contingency. Ha! Once again, I afforded the gods an opportunity to have a good, long howl.

Since Tom's chief activity, post-accident, was watching television, I bought a little TV to plug into the car's cigarette lighter. At a great expense of time, money, and our friends' energy, I also had a small solar panel installation put up at the Idaho house where there was no electricity. It would easily run the little TV and enable Tom to watch any of the dozens of video tapes I'd packed.

We were ready! The TV and Tom were in the back seat of our Chevy Lumina, (a new – used – car to better accommodate Tom's size) with his supply of Betty Boop videos and a set of earphones. The front passenger seat and the trunk held all our gear. We were as ready as ready could be, and off we went. We left Lakewood,

New Jersey early one morning in the middle of June. Three thousand miles stretched before us.

Tom was watching Betty Boop in the back seat, and I was listening to Merle or Waylon or Andrea Bocelli in the front. We had not been on the road ten minutes when he said, "Where can I go to the bathroom?" and The Plan immediately began to disintegrate.

Post-accident Tom had what the urologist called an infantile or immature bladder, a misdirection in his brain which left him with the very frequent feeling that he had to urinate and when he felt the need to urinate, he was unable to postpone it. We tried to have this tested further, but the test involved drinking – and holding – a vast amount of water for a certain period of time so the bladder could be examined full and empty. Needless to say, Tom was never able to complete the test because after drinking just a portion of the required water, he felt the need to urinate.

I have to ask myself how in the world I ever expected to get him across country when we had not been out ten minutes and he already needed the bathroom. I quickly resolved that we would simply stop at every other rest stop all the way out, and visit the men's room. A New Plan! Were the gods tittering?

After a bathroom stop at my sister's, we were off again. This time we got to the bridge into Pennsylvania without incident, except that it was around 9 AM and we were buried among commuters, the very situation I'd hoped to avoid by leaving early. Packed within the morning rush hour traffic, I paid my toll and noticed the toll-taker-lady looking startled, and directly into the back seat. I turned. There was Tom, almost green, with his hands over his mouth. Motion sickness! Who knew?

As quickly as I could manage on a bridge in very heavy traffic,

I emptied the plastic shoe box holding my cassettes and passed it back to Tom.

"Throw up in this," I ordered.

He obeyed.

Now we were winding around Philadelphia, trying to find the Turnpike and transporting a sloshing box of vomit. The trip was barely an hour old, and I suppose anyone less insane than I would have turned back. But no – we soldiered on to the first rest stop, where I washed the shoebox at the outdoor dog-watering faucet while Tom visited the men's room.

You might think I'd postpone lunch until lunchtime, but I really needed a break, so we stopped at a diner. Tom got out in a hurry, sooner than I could excavate my pocketbook from under the pile of cassettes that were now scattered on the floor and seat. He was heading up the steps to the diner entrance but I didn't want him to go in alone because he wouldn't be able to explain what he wanted.

I dashed out of the car, tripped over the concrete car stop at the edge of the parking spot, and lunged for the stair railing with an outspread left hand. Instead of grabbing the railing, however, I pushed my hand straight into it, jamming two fingers. One of them began to swell immediately.

And yet, with only hours behind us and days ahead, did I resolve to head home?

No, indeed. I altered The Plan.

On previous trips we'd always stayed at a Motel 6, a decent enough chain for our purposes (and a step up from our tenting days), but one that usually came equipped with stall showers only, not bathtubs. I decided on the spot to upgrade to Holiday Inn – I knew more than anything that I wanted a nice, hot bath.

Several hours short of our planned destination, but desperate to end the day, we stopped in Breezewood, PA., bought Dramamine for Tom, a finger splint and bubble bath for me, and checked into the Holiday Inn.

We managed, slowly, thereafter, to creep along to Idaho. We stopped at rest stops all along the Interstates; the Dramamine completely cured Tom's car sickness and he thoroughly enjoyed his tapes. As I drove along with a hand and a half, I had the consolation of knowing that a beautiful bubble bath awaited me each night. The rest of the trip was not without incident, however.

There was the Event in Effington, Illinois, at a very busy rest stop. Tom was taking rather a long time in the bathroom, so I decided to investigate — or rather, to ask some fine fellow to check. As soon as I got into the lobby, I discovered I'd left my pocketbook in the car. I went right out and of course, the car was locked.

Fortunately, I belong to AAA; I joined right after the accident when I realized the responsibility of the vehicles would now rest on my incapable shoulders (one of which is higher than the other, as a friend pointed out — shouldering new responsibilities on uneven shoulders was a feat I hadn't quite mastered). But how was I to contact AAA? I'll tell you: I begged. I walked right up to a truck driver parked next to us and asked for 35 cents, the going rate for a pay phone call. Coins in hand, I returned to the rest stop, where Tom was now wading through lines of teenagers who had just been disgorged from a bus trip. He was content to sit nearby while I took my place in line behind dozens of kids who were all shouting variations of "Ma, we're in the middle of nowhere!" into the phones.

The Triple-A number was in the phone book hanging from the phone stand. I called and asked for road service.

"I locked my pocketbook in the car and I'm traveling with a brain-injured man who doesn't understand what's happening. I need help fast!" I think I managed to stay calm, but I had to shout because of all the kids in the lobby.

"Yes, ma'am," AAA answered. "Would you please give me your AAA number?"

"I can't. It's in my pocketbook and it's locked in the car. That's why I need help."

"I understand. But we do need that number."

"How about I give you 1-2-3-4 for now, and when you get here to open the car, we can find the real number. I can give you my name and address; I'm sure you can look up my number."

It was eventually arranged, although I suspect not happily on the part of Ms. Triple-A. I left the line, but my end of the conversation had been overheard by a man in the next line. "You're locked out of your car?" he asked.

I nodded.

"I wish I had my break-in kit with me," he said.

"Are you a burglar?" I asked. Are you a burglar? Was I totally crazy? It was the first thing that entered my mind and I said it. It was a measure of how distraught I was. Or how stupid.

"I'm a policeman," he said. He did not seem amused.

But he opened the car. I thanked him and promised that, in return, I would not speed, a promise I kept all the way to Malad, Idaho, where our urgent need for a bathroom necessitated a lead-foot approach. Fortunately, the policeman who stopped us there was also understanding.

I had to reconnect with AAA and call off the rescue. By that time, Tom needed the bathroom again.

On a different day we were stopped somewhere for a 15-minute construction delay with our motel in sight. Fifteen minutes was too long and resulted in wet pants and a wet seat in the car. Leaving Tom in the car when we finally got to the motel, I assured the receptionist we planned to stay the night, but first I had a little problem. She gave me a blanket to wrap around Tom, which would presumably be less embarrassing for him than walking in with wet pants. While I can easily pass for a Native American, Tom, with his mustache and curly Italian hair, could not. Chief Couldn't-Hold-It made it to the room wearing his "robe." Once he was settled, the receptionist fixed me up with cleaning supplies for the car. People are very nice. All it takes is a pseudo-Indian with wet pants.

Tom needed a change of clothes at another rest stop after another accident. (Memo to the Interstate Highway Department: we need more rest-stops!) This one was located somewhere in the wilderness and seemed to be populated by the kind of truckers who give rise to the stereotypes – big, tough and suspicious. I sent Tom ahead and followed him several minutes later with clothes and a plastic bag. A big, tough, suspicious-looking guy was standing outside.

"Is this the men's room?" I asked.

He nodded. The sign reading "MEN" was pretty obvious.

"Are there any men in there now?" Never let it be said I'm at a loss for words – stupid words that let themselves out with no control on my part.

"Yeah," he kind of drawled. The suspicion was kicking in – on his part.

Did he think, perhaps, that I was a working girl, plying my trade? What better way to find johns than in a men's room? (Get it? Johns!)

But I was equal to him. "I've got to ask you to help me," I

said. "My husband is in there and needs a change of clothes. His name is Tom. Would you please take these in to him?"

The man looked not pleased, but grabbed the clothes. I held out the plastic bag. "Oh, and the soiled ones have to go in this bag."

Notice I did _not_ ask him to handle the soiled clothing, but from the look on his face, I might as well have. I'm sure that's what he thought.

Minutes later I heard "Tom? Tom?" echoing through the tiled chamber, and Tom's good-natured laugh. We got *that* event sorted out!

Another time I needed to put my camping skills into use. We required too serious a change of clothes to attempt walking into the bathroom at the rest stop. Instead, with a blanket and the open car door, I fashioned a tent of sorts and at the farthest reaches of the parking lot, Tom changed. Before he did so, I soaked some towels in the sink of the Ladies' Room. We managed this one as well.

In general, I found it effective to stop at every other rest stop along the Interstates. For the most part, the plan succeeded, although it did add considerable time to the trip. As I write this in retrospect, the entire venture seems foolhardy and I wonder that I ever attempted it in the first place. I can't even admit that "it seemed like a good idea at the time," because I started out with some trepidation and realized within the first hour the jaunt was going to be a challenge. Put it down to cockeyed optimism if you will. Put it down to my own restlessness and naivete. But we did it, and that ought to count for something.

CHAPTER 19

THE CHARGE (WE GOT) FROM
THE LIGHT BRIGADE

We had always been campers flattering ourselves that we were *real* campers – tents, backpacks, hiking boots, blisters – genuine outdoorsmen, proud of our ability to survive in the wilderness.

Well, okay, we did carry an impressive array of vacuum-packed or freeze-dried foodstuffs, and although we sometimes had to contend with the complete lack of sanitary facilities, Tom was able to construct a decent outdoor toilet from flat rocks. Not for us the decadent summers on the Continent, idling on the Via Veneto with an espresso and a panini. Mind you, a bit of decadence might have been a lovely thing, certainly as far as I was concerned, but it didn't happen.

When Bill was a little boy, we graduated to a room-sized tent, large enough for our double bed air mattress, Bill's air mattress, and a spiffy little table and chair arrangement that collapsed into itself and became a large, heavy, awkward suitcase. We thought we were quite special, indeed – comfortable but still rugged enough to consider ourselves real campers. We imagined we were a step above back-packers and certainly not associated in any way with the people who "roughed it" in trailers or RVs. *They* were truly beneath contempt. I specifically remember an experience in the desert outside Las Vegas when we sat under water spigots all night long trying not to die from the heat, while the contemptible RV people slept peacefully in air-conditioned comfort. Ah, yes, we were tough.

And then we discovered Idaho. Robert Redford is directly responsible. We watched his movie, *The Electric Horseman*, and were thoroughly captivated by the scenery. We decided we were going to situate our summer and retirement home wherever the movie had been filmed. I sat through all the credits and am perfectly certain, to this day, that near the end of the credit roll I read the sentence, "Filmed in Idaho." I am so certain because why else would I ever have thought about The Gem State? I don't know about you but whenever I was called upon in my youth to list state capitals, Boise was always the one I forgot. Who raised in the general environs of Newark, New Jersey, has ever even heard of Boise? And who could pronounce it? The state itself gets mixed up with Iowa and even Idahoans have told us they have two capitals, Boise and Des Moines.

During the summer following our Electric Horseman Resolution, we camped in Idaho along the beautiful, wild, scenic Salmon River. We were enchanted. We were also certain at every bend of the river that some shot or other from the movie was filmed *right there*! Our little Toyota Corolla sub-compact couldn't make it into the back country, so during the next school year, Tom bought a used Chevy Blazer (which you now know as the Demon) and we wrote to realtors in the Salmon area. We warned them that we were coming and hoped to rent a house in a remote area for the summer.

Since we were from New Jersey, most of the realtors assumed a decrepit trailer on the highway three miles outside of town would satisfy our notion of "remote." No way. Thankfully, one realtor owned a hunting cabin about 60 miles off-road, but he wouldn't rent it to us until we went out to look it over. He figured: New Jersey – what do they really know from remote? We drove on mountain roads through steep canyons of yellow and orange rocks, past deep, dark pines, along the edges of massive piles of shale where nothing separated us from a precarious plunge into peril. (No New Jersey Highway Department guard rails here!) We drove through herds of cattle, past two bulls with locked horns fighting, presumably, over the cattle. We survived a couple of roof-denting hailstorms – but we found the cabin and rented it for the next five summers.

There are about ten cabins scattered along a two-mile stretch of our hidden valley, and eventually one of these was available to buy. We bought it to use for summers and as part of our retirement plan and our legacy to Bill. It was our "Idahome," and we loved it! The school year became just a prolonged interval between summers in Idaho.

I suppose I must tell you, if you haven't already figured it out, that years after we had settled so happily into our cabin, we learned *The Electric Horseman* was actually filmed in Utah! Oh, well...

After the accident, the cabin became a difficult issue. Bill and I loved it and were not prepared to give it up. Confident that Tom was going to improve and would someday want to return to Idaho, I continued to pay the taxes and mourn the loss of our beautiful summers, a situation I accepted because I truly believed it would only be temporary.

Driving Tom out on this particular summer was probably not one of my better ideas, and I cannot even ask to be excused for it on the grounds of being young and foolish. Foolish, perhaps. Young, no. However, you must understand that in any given year, around March, the sights, sounds, and smells of Idaho always began to tantalize us. We'd drive around town in New Jersey but we'd see the Morgan Creek Road ahead of us. We could breathe the fresh, clean air, feel the hot, dry heat and see the sun sparkling on our lake. To go was a compulsion, a need beyond merely escaping the noise, confusion, and humidity of New Jersey. Idaho was *right; it* was the right place to live, the only place that made sense.

During the preceding year I had arranged with our dear friends, Jim and Connie Sugden who live in Challis, the nearest town, and who also have a cabin in the valley, to install solar panels on our cabin so we could run a TV/ VCR for Tom to watch video tapes. There is no electricity in the valley, no phone lines, no paved roads, and mail delivery only twice a week to our box about a mile away. I know you are wondering: *What in the world was she thinking, to take him out there?*

Maybe I wasn't thinking. Nevertheless, out we went.

What I really needed was some sort of idea about the future of the cabin, and us. Could we continue with it? Should we? Was the trek out, with all its attendant problems, worth the limited use we could now make of the wilderness setting? Would Tom be safe and happy there?

Luckily, as it turned out, Tom was quite content to watch his *Betty Boop* and *Columbo* tapes on the little portable TV/ VCR. The house had a large play room when we bought it, complete with a regulation-size pool table, to Tom's delight both pre- and post- accident. He was occupied and happy and I was able to do some sorely needed maintenance work on the house. Many of our friends came by often. They were encouraged and heartened by his jovial attitude and apparent improvement.

The summer was, for the most part, sunny and slow and satisfactory. Bill and his girlfriend Melissa flew out to Idaho Falls, where we picked them up. Bill marched Melissa up a mountain and proposed to her there. She told us she cried all the way up because it was a tough climb for a girl from sea level at the Jersey Shore, and then she cried all the way back down because she was so happy. Tom was thrilled with her. "He's marrying a good woman." They stayed a week; Melissa was as delighted with the Idaho setting as Bill was – a very good thing!

Shortly after they left, we were having breakfast at the kitchen table. Tom, as always, was enjoying his meal. I, as always, was looking for a way to get his mind working and keep mine sane – which is to say, to prevent myself from observing and dwelling on the true nature of our situation. Desperate for the diversion and apparent normality of conversation, I noticed two hummingbirds fighting with each other at our feeder hanging out on the porch, and decided that would do for a topic.

"Look, Tom," I said, "two hummingbirds are fighting for the feeder, but there are four spouts. You'd think they could see that and share."

Tom didn't bother to look; generally when he had food in front of him he wasn't interested in anything else. I often suspected I talked chiefly for my own entertainment, and to keep up the pretense that everything was normal and fine, and only secondarily in the desperate hope that he might respond.

This time, however, he surprised me. "Well, they're not human beings, so they don't share," he said.

I was floored. He was not often given to such clear, rational, and relevant replies. In my recollection of the moment, I was too stunned to reply.

But he surprised me again. "Of course," he added, "not all human beings share."

Now I was really amazed. This was a breakthrough conversation. It was entirely apropos, perfectly reasonable, and it sent my hopes soaring over the mountains. Could we have just made a giant leap on his road to recovery? I sat there, transfixed, ascending into dreams of wonderful possibilities (and I do mean "wonderful" in the sense of "full of wonder" because I was, and he was, full of wonder at that moment.) Then, still attending to his breakfast, he finished up with another observation, spoken quietly and calmly.

"It reminds me of the Crimean War," he said. "Everybody lost their lives."

Where did *that* come from? I was stunned. It's not as if we discussed the Crimean War frequently – or at all, for that matter.

True, he had been a history major in college and he had possessed an encyclopedic memory for facts, dates, and personalities, but most of his memory was lost in the accident. How did he go from the hummingbirds to the Crimean tragedy? What synapses fired off in his brain to make the connection? From what depths did he retrieve the information?

Our nearest neighbors, Jim and Connie, were about a quarter of a mile away. I raced over after breakfast to tell them about this fantastic conversation. Tom did not come with me; he found walking on our stony roads slow and difficult and I was too impatient this time to wait for him. Jim and Connie had guests who also knew Tom. I told them all what had happened and they were properly amazed. They are such good friends. They had known and loved the old Tom and had been devastated when they heard about the accident.

Desperate to see improvement, we took the little conversation as a sign of hope, a prefigure of recovery. We took to speculation: where in his battered brain had the Crimean War been lurking all these years? What brought it to the surface? Was this just the beginning? We tried to link up tiny fighting birds with the slaughter of the Light Brigade to discover plausible relationships between the two. We discussed "not sharing" and its possible connection to the historical drama. But mostly we marveled at Tom and his astonishing revelation. Only Tom himself seemed unimpressed.

Later, when we were again at the table, having supper this time, I thought I'd resurrect the subject and see where he'd go with it.

"Do you think the hummingbirds will fight again tonight, Tom?" I asked.

No response.

"Do you think they've learned to share by now?"

No response. Tom carried on happily with his meal.

"Tom, tell me about the Crimean War," I asked.

No response.

It was over...gone...lost.

CHAPTER 20

PROGRESS AS SEEN IN THE HISTORY OF HAIRCUTS

In the beginning, I had to make the decision about when Tom needed a haircut. I took him to his former salon, a unisex beauty shop, until we moved and there was a barber just up the street.

Gradually, he became aware of the need for a haircut and would point to his head, saying, "I need to do this." Or, he would say he wanted to go see his "friend up the street," who was Jimmy Cox, the barber.

As his ability to express himself became more exact, he would point to his head and say, "This needs to be made shorter."

Finally, using Jimmy's business card for the phone number, he was able to make his own appointment. "This is Tom George Sorrentino. When are you coming to see me?"

He needed my help to fix a time. I always spoke to Jimmy after Tom's call, but he continued to make his own decision about the need for a haircut, and he made his own calls.

Tom liked to go to Jimmy's because, "He only does men's

hair," and because he was as much a fan of Oldies music as Tom was.

It became possible to send him alone to the barber shop, as it was located at the end of the block and he did not have to cross any streets. I would call Jimmy and alert him when Tom was on his way, and he would alert me as Tom left the shop.

These trips to the barber were a big step for Tom. It was his first independent, if closely supervised, journey. I think he was pleased with the little excursions; I know we were pleased for him.

CHAPTER 21

CHRISTMAS DISCUSSIONS

As the Christmas holidays approached, I was curious to find out what Tom remembered – or could discuss – about the meaning of the season. I proposed a short dialogue of questions to test his memory, and was delighted to learn that despite his enormous loss of memory, he did retain some information. Whether this was evidence of deep and significant memories, or the result of recent television programs is not possible to determine. At home we did not discuss the meaning of Christmas prior to the dialogues. If anyone else had had a conversation with Tom about the holiday, or if he had remembered something from TV, then his answers would be proof of some sort of memory, perhaps a recollection of recent origin, which would be lovely.

§§

1994

Joanna: What is the meaning of Christmas?

Tom: It's about three people – E, B, C.

Joanna: Who are they?

Tom: One is a young man who doesn't speak and the other two speak their own language but not English.

Joanna: What do they say?

Tom: It's a privilege to understand what they're saying and it's an...I don't know how to say it so I'll just say it: I'm given the opportunity to speak that language. Not everybody understands that language but...[here he put his hand to the side of his mouth and whispered]...I do. It's a different kind of language.

Joanna: And this is what Christmas means?

Tom: Yes and no. I really don't want to think much about it.

Joanna: What about Christmas presents. Why do we give them?

Tom: That has nothing to do with it.

Joanna: How about Christmas carols? Christmas music?

Tom: That's nonsense...[In a whisper again] When you really talk about the message, the message is that three people can see the message and understand it and they're very good in what they understand.

Joanna: What about Jesus?

Tom: He comes along at the beginning. He doesn't even speak. He's young. He doesn't have any voice. No, it's the other two that bring his message across.

Joanna: Who are they?

Tom: The mother and the father?

Joanna: Mary and Joseph?

Tom: Exactly. But they don't *know* they're Mary and Joseph yet. They're not looking ahead.

Joanna: When did all this happen?

Tom: It began at the beginning of the old semester.

Joanna: What about the Three Wise Men?

Tom: They didn't understand what the hell was going on and they understood about the beginning and the middle and the end and then they understood the real meaning of Christmas but this took a long time. They didn't understand right away. They looked, and they said, "What the hell is going on here?" – They didn't say it that way – and then, "Oh, my God, so this is what he meant." And then they understood the real meaning of Christmas.

Joanna: What is the real meaning of Christmas?

Tom: The real meaning of Christmas is understanding what goes on, silently. That he can understand what goes on in the dead of night and he can look forward to that understanding.

Joanna: He?

Tom: Well...he's the little baby.

Something about Christmas stayed with Tom after his accident, his replies indicated a basic understanding. He noted that a different language was spoken among the participants, thus realizing that the events took place somewhere other than here in the United States. In his way, Tom made it plain that at first the significance of the event is not truly known. Mary and Joseph had no particular fame yet. ("They don't know they're Mary and Joseph.") and the Wise Men had yet to see the purpose of their journey.

Moreover, he dismissed the commercial sides of Christmas, the gifts, and music as having "nothing to do with it," as "nonsense." I wondered whether former-History-teacher Tom was responding to the historical event as opposed to the present-day celebration of Christmas as a family-friendly holiday with some religious significance. His use of "the old semester" was evidence he still referred to time units in term of his academic background and experience. He explained that the method of reckoning time was affected by Christmas, as indeed it was.

Please notice a wonderful line here, almost a poem: "He can understand what goes on in the dead of night and he can look forward to that understanding."

Could Tom be expressing a metaphor about himself?

§§

1995

Because I had started what I thought might become a tradition last year, in December of 1995 I again asked Tom to talk about the meaning of Christmas. Until this dialogue we had not discussed the holiday, and he was not in any way caught up in the season – he showed not the slightest interest in the tree, or gift giving or holiday music. He would brighten a bit when I discussed holiday social plans that involved food, however!

Joanna: What is Christmas?

Tom: Christmas is the opportunity that Christ has to come to the public.

Joanna: What do people do?

Tom: They sing – indoors. They have a good time.

Joanna: Why?

Tom: To understand Christ a little better.

Joanna: What is that understanding?

Tom: Well, there are parts of Christmas and everybody understands it differently.

Joanna: How do children understand it?

Tom: Well, I like adults better.

Joanna: How do adults understand it?

Tom: They sing, they dance.

Joanna: What is the Christmas story?

Tom: Well, there are two people and they live intelligently and then all of a sudden there's a little baby that comes upon them and they don't understand him at first and he has to give them a message and he gives them a message.

Joanna: What is that message?

Tom: Well, he's very intelligent and he talks to them and they at first don't understand him because he's speaking a different language. They don't understand him because he speaks differently to them – different ideas – biblical messages. How to behave, how to be people. They didn't understand that. They had to be taught that.

Although clearly stated, the content of Tom's answers had not improved in depth or color since the previous year. I had to admit I'd hoped for more, but at least it was not regression.

§§

1996

For the third year, as Christmas approached, I attempted to engage Tom in our "traditional" discussion, our Christmas dialogue.

Joanna: What does Christmas mean to you?

Tom: I'm going to see the female god.

Joanna: What is Christmas about?

Tom: Jesus Christ – but it's not really about Jesus Christ.

Joanna: What is the meaning of Christmas?

Tom: It's about how he became a priest.

Joanna: How did that happen?

Tom: He rose from the dead and became alive. He became a god.

Joanna: Tell me more.

Tom: All his Apostles except the bad one who didn't pray for Jesus Christ – he became one of the fifth aliens.

Joanna: Who were the people involved in Christmas?

Tom: Father and son - no – father and – they were both married. They helped him become a good male but he was already a good male but they didn't know that yet.

Joanna: Where did all this happen?

Tom: To our west. There was no United States then. In Israel.

I think more than any other yardstick, our Christmas dialogues illustrated Tom's lack of progress. His explanations never developed more fully over the three years and in fact, the final dialogue demonstrated less concentration on the topic plus some interference from the science-fiction programs he watched on television. Each dialogue presented an interesting array of answers but there were no signs of growth. This rather discouraging conclusion led me to abandon the project.

CHAPTER 22

SIX YEARS OF VARYING LENGTH

S ix years passed, some parts of them moved very slowly, indeed, and at other times they seemed to speed along. We marked special occasions, the date of the accident, the date Tom regained consciousness, the dates he was released from the hospitals and therapies, and on those occasions we tried to mark his progress. Look how much better he was doing!

Tom continued to be a content person, easy to please and easy enough to take care of, but neither his behavior nor his vocabulary developed much further than they had at the end of his first year. There were, to be sure, small gains, and we rejoiced at each one. But added together, they did not result in the kind of independence or intelligence we hoped to see. It was clear he often understood and could express his comprehension, but there was no depth to it. He spoke in simplistic terms and continued to use his strange, but correct vocabulary, pulling words and phrases out from his private thesaurus.

On the other hand, he still needed constant supervision. He

could toilet and dress himself, but clothes had to be put out for him or he would wear the same things every day. He had no concept of dressing for the weather, so had to be told to add a jacket or take one off. The kitchen was mostly out-of-bounds; he had no idea how to regulate the stove or how to prepare food. Once his therapies ended, his day revolved around television, the visits to and from friends and family, and whatever diversions we could try. Walks to town or on the boardwalk were fine if a meal was involved. He was able to play Scrabble, placing down words he could neither read nor pronounce − an intriguing feat! We played nearly every day and I know these games gave him a sense of normality, a feeling he was doing what other adults did. He made a show of looking through the newspaper each day, but he was not able to read it. He kept himself happily occupied and never seemed to be bored or discontent.

Tom's therapy continued for several years more, but eventually stabilized and would no longer be supported by our insurance. Once there were no blocks of time occupied by his therapy, I left my job to be with him full-time.

One of Tom's psychologists tried to make Medicare understand that because I saved the government a sizeable amount of money by keeping Tom at home rather than placing him in a residential institution, it would be a fine gesture on their part to support a few hours each week of respite care, to give me a little break. Such a plan, which exists in many European countries, was not part of Medicare's scheme of things, alas.

I could distort the truth and paint a saintly portrait of myself as an unselfish, gracious, caregiver during those six years, but it was not always the case. Depression sat on me often, veering close to a clinical stage. If I looked at life as a day-to-day journey, it was not difficult to get through any 24-hour period. But when I looked ahead, to possibly thirty more years of the life we were living, I became scared and depressed. It was still almost impossible to accept this "happy eight-year-old" as an avatar of our intelligent, independent, and determined Tom. It was still painful to look at him as he was, and to realize that whole dimensions of life were forever closed to him.

After the two attempts to take him to Idaho, I gave up the trek as not worth the time, money, and energy we needed to expend. The aura of the mountains was lost on him and in fact, often scared him. He was incapable of tending to the needs of the cabin. So was I in some ways, and I depended on the help of our friends to open it up and close it down. Beyond sitting on the porch and admiring the view, I was not able to do very much. I could not hike any distance or take him away from a bathroom for any prolonged period of time. He no longer enjoyed fishing and his television viewing was limited to the tapes we brought with us. The days there were long and the peace we once found there was elusive. It seemed the best idea just not to go.

I met a few other women who were also managing lives with brain-injured spouses, or women whose husbands had dementia of one sort or another, but I took no heart from them. The dementia cases, as difficult as they were – and in the end they were *much* more difficult to handle than Tom was – had a known life span. They were terminal. Perhaps my comment sounds harsh and cruel, but I believe that with dementia, the lost person is mourned while he is still living (as we mourned the old Tom), but the difficulties of his and his caregivers' lives make his passing welcome.

Of course, no one wills death for another person. I am sure no caregiver will say outright, "I wish he would die." No; what we wish for is recovery. In the absence of that possibility, our concern becomes his care and comfort until he expires, however far away the event may be.

I certainly did not want Tom to die. But I did get a bit frustrated as I looked ahead. Would I have the fortitude, the courage, the strength to go on for thirty or more years with our situation as it was?

I met two women whose husbands were twenty years post-injury, and both of these encounters scared me. Neither injury had been as serious as Tom's, yet both men, in different ways, did not present as the man I wanted to envision ahead for Tom. They were helpless in some ways, inarticulate in some ways, not well-kept and completely without the spark of life Tom still retained. (All head injuries are different, remember?) The wives seemed to be adjusted to a life bordered by their front street and back yard. (Or, I wonder, did they just give up?)

I CANNOT REALLY COMPLAIN ABOUT THE SIX YEARS LEFT TO US, except to characterize them as somewhat jagged. There were wonderful times with generous, obvious love and concern shown by family and friends. We enjoyed meals at various homes and restaurants. We took Tom to concerts and museums and on short road trips. Helen was always agreeable to keeping him for a day if I needed to be out and about. Tom was never forgotten or ignored by those who had been with us all along, and for that attention I am forever grateful.

To balance those times, there were the bouts of depression I endured, feeling an entrapment from which I could not free myself. I would look at Tom, study his face, and try to convince myself that this was the same man I married, just in a different form. That did not really work. I told myself how other people put up with a great deal more hardship than we were enduring. That did not work, either.

As I have said before, you only *really* know your own worst thing, and this was ours. I got angry with myself for lacking grace under pressure. But most of all, I could not loosen a deep and abiding sorrow for Tom, old Tom whom we'd lost, and all of life he would never again experience or appreciate. He had done nothing to deserve such a devastating sentence; my only consolation was (and still is) that he was unaware of his own losses. I mourned for Tom, for the students he would never teach, for the son and grandchildren he would never counsel, and for all the hopes and dreams that would never see the light of day. I could not shake the sorrow.

The business of life went on around us. There were deaths to contend with: an aunt and a family friend that deeply affected us. Tom understood and genuinely mourned the sudden death of our dear friend Bernie Ressner, who had been so good to him through this ordeal. A good friend in Idaho died in a snow machine accident, but he did not remember her. My mother's health was precarious and we were losing Chuck to dementia. I needed to have an operation on my hand. Bill's life wove in and around ours with all the usual vigor of a young man. Like any normal life, there was happiness and sorrow, hope and disappointment, trouble and peace.

But we put one foot in front of the other and marched along, learning that despite the seeming banality of our everyday existence, there were indeed, meaningful consequences to be gleaned from this life of ours. Tom had become a kind of catalyst, or perhaps a filter through which the interest and administration of so many others would pass. We noticed which people could visit Tom and deal with his condition and which people could not. We learned what the words "help" and "support" meant, and who were the providers. There were those who did not invoke deities, but were there with Tom constantly, and there were religious people who totally ignored him. Bill and I discovered our own strengths and our abilities to face calamity. Many people saw our situation as a call to organize their own affairs, to be sure they had emergency contingencies in place, and that each member of their family knew how to run the house should one of them become incapacitated. Yes, there were lessons to be learned from our adventure, but need Tom have been so grievously injured for those lesson to be learned? And were they of such importance that a good and innocent man had to be brought down? Questions, no answers.

Life moved on. We did with it what we could. I wrote about our adventure; I lived it but to be honest I have to tell you that I'd rather have read about it as written and lived by someone else.

In his previous life Tom had earned a Master's Degree in Educational Media Technology; he was as much at home in a library or media center as in his own home. At the conclusion of his cognitive therapy, his therapist arranged for him to volunteer at the Lakewood Public Library where he was able to shelve books for a couple of hours a few times a week. The fascinating thing here, for us, was that Tom could not read, could not recite the alphabet, could not count, yet he was completely capable of organizing books on the shelving carts in either alphabetical order or according to the Dewey Decimal System, and then placing the books in their proper positions in the stacks. For him this was an important job and he took it seriously. It gave him, we supposed, a sense of worth and dignity that he could present to the outside world.

We started him out in the Children's Section, where the books were filed only by the last name initials of the authors. He let us know immediately that he wanted to be out on the main floor. Like so much else in his rehabilitative experience, he intuitively understood work which he considered childish or beneath him. Whether he could actually do the work (and he could not) was not an issue for him. He knew that stacking rings of different sizes or doing simple math was not on his intellectual level. And so with the Children's Section. We moved him to the main floor where he quite happily went about his work.

He did work slowly and carefully and no doubt did not realize that it took him longer to sort and stack one cart than it did the other volunteers to finish several. None of that mattered to him, to us, or to the library. He was useful and happy, which was all that mattered.

In the course of his library work Tom noticed a number of special needs adults frequenting the open spaces. They usually settled at tables for several hours at a time, where they played cards or sorted through their belongings which they carried around in an assortment of Shop-Rite plastic bags, or they rested. I explained to him that these people lived in sheltered housing but were independent enough to be allowed to walk through town on their own. They used the library as a meeting place, a place to be warm in winter and cool in summer, but they were not interested in the reading materials.

Tom assumed a protective attitude toward them. "We take them in. After all, they can't help it."

Crying time for me.

Tom saw himself as part of that "we," the library staff, and understood the misfortune of these people. He was completely unaware that in many ways he was one of them, one who had not even achieved the independence they were allowed to find their way around town. I was happy for him in that he made a distinction between himself and these challenged adults, although I could not help but wonder if the distinction was a false bravado, a persona he was clever enough to assume for his own peace of mind. An intriguing question, another one without an answer.

Tom was satisfied with his life, which was the really important thing. The concerns felt by the rest of us did not affect his own happy existence. He was completely unaware of the person he had been, the things he had known, and the things he had lost. I can tell you with truth and satisfaction that we did our best for him every day. Having never been faced with anything like this, and having no playbook, friends and family alike stepped up and we wrote our own rules, and together we created a new game for Tom, and for me, and we were willing to play that game to the best of our abilities, for as long as it might take.

PART V

When you have done your best, await the result in peace.

– John Lubbock

CHAPTER 23

SUNSET

N early seven years passed. Some parts of them moved
very slowly, indeed; others sped along. We had taken
Tom from the dome house he built and loved, and
moved him into two new houses, and back and forth twice to
Idaho. He managed to find his way in all the new settings and
seemed to have been happy in all environments.

Tom found a measure of independence in his library work, in
his ability to go back and forth to the barber by himself, and to
the clubhouse all alone, and in the little chores he performed
around the house. He was a happy eight-year-old, a fact we
accepted and built a life around. The devastation was always
present; the sorrow was always present; and the hope was always
present.

This was how we planned to go on. As long as Tom remained
healthy and happy, this was the life we would have for as long as
we could. If we allowed ourselves to forget the life we had once

experienced, and the life we had once planned, we could embrace the one we'd been given. Live in the moment. Very Zen.

The path we trod had been uneven, rife with twists, turns, unexpected barriers and detours, but we had come a long way and we saw it stretching a long way ahead of us.

Yes, we even said it was "fine." We were sure of our footing and knew our direction. What we did not know was the "End of the Trail" sign just around the next curve.

THE END CAME SNEAKING UP ON US, BUT EVEN AS IT STEALTHILY approached, we were as unprepared for it as we had been at the beginning, seven years earlier. Every end has a beginning. Ours began in October of 2000, around the time of Bill and Melissa's wedding, with all of the attendant frenzy, and included the mechanics of another house move, this one to include my mother, who was in increasingly fragile health. I found myself dealing with Tom's rapid deterioration, the wedding, getting my mother settled and seeing her through her doctor and hospital stays, and moving to another house. However, I was never alone. All along, I had the wonderful support of the same people, family members, and friends who continued to extend hands, time, and effort throughout our final ordeal.

Instead of summarizing the time, I have decided to take you through it as I recorded it in my journal. Even now as I look back at the entries, I find they are charged with a certain immediacy, energy, and fullness I could not give them should I write in retrospect. We pick up in early October.

THURSDAY, OCTOBER 5, 2000: TOM HAS BEGUN SOME NEW obsessions which I'm trying to quell. A couple of times he got up and got himself fully dressed around midnight, while I was still up, reading. He didn't know why.

THURSDAY, OCTOBER 26, 2000: TOM HAS HAD A FEW STRANGE days. I think he's feeling a bit of the wedding and home hunting upheaval and as a result becomes a bit confused himself.

FRIDAY, OCTOBER 27,2000: (BILL AND MELISSA'S WEDDING. I am sparing you the tales of the flat tire we experienced on the drive up, our late arrival, the cousins' little brawl in the parking lot, and all the usual events that make any wedding so cheerful and delightful.) Tom was well-behaved during the ceremony, but became a wild man at the reception. He was all over the cocktail hour, happily eating his way through the crowd. I left the table for a minute to get my camera from an anteroom and on the way back I heard a microphoned voice that was clearly Tom's. He was working the room, microphone in hand like a sleazy nightclub singer. Unfortunately, he didn't know the lyrics, but that didn't stop him. His eyes were wild – I saw that. Then, against the wishes of the bride and groom, the DJ began those group dances – the electric slide and conga line and so on – and Tom was out there, dancing frenetically. Then he crashed. He sat at the table and said he wanted to go home. But we were prepared. Richard and I went out to the car and got his portable TV, his *Betty Boop* tapes, a change of clothes, and set him up in the little anteroom, where he was given his meals and was visited throughout the evening by family and friends. Helen was feeling ill, so Richard took her home early and they kept Tom with them until the wedding was over and I picked him up at Helen's house.

SUNDAY, OCTOBER 29, 2000: TOM HAS BEEN BIZARRE AND confused since the wedding. He can't remember his morning routine; he doesn't know where dishes and pans go, the same ones he's put away for over two years. We've had wet underwear, wet spots on the rug in the bedroom and on the bathroom floor. He puts his cue stick case and the pack holding his Walkman on his back and then walks around looking for it. (And they are a *heavy* presence; hard to ignore there on his back.) One day he brought home two cue stick cases, his own and someone else's. If this doesn't settle down soon, I'll have to call a doctor.

WEDNESDAY, NOVEMBER 8, 2000: I CONTINUE TO CLEAN UP after Tom and direct him through his basic hygiene, which he seems to have forgotten – or else remembers at 2 AM when I find him with shaving cream on his shoulders and chest as well as face. Today he wet a chair. I found his socks neatly folded on the kitchen counter by the toaster, and two decks of cards in the refrigerator!

SUNDAY, NOVEMBER 12, 2000: TOM IS LOSING GROUND EVERY day. He has spells of incontinence about twice daily. I find I'm washing sheets and scrubbing the bedroom rug every night, every day. He is totally unaware. His speech is slurred. Today he mangled, "Sorrentino" several times before he got it right. He is increasingly confused and that increment moves along rapidly;

every day is less good than the previous one. I'm hoping he can stay as mobile and tractable as he is until Wednesday when we see the doctor. Today, Paula, Mom, and Helen saw him; Friday, Richard saw him – all agree there's been deterioration. He is losing interest in, or the ability to enjoy TV, and he seldom smiles or laughs. It's very frightening.

MONDAY, NOVEMBER 13, 2000: THE ITALIAN GROUP SAW TOM today and were shocked and heartbroken. Today's adventures included an afternoon attempt to shave, but with toothpaste on his face instead of shaving cream. He went to bed at 5:30, without supper, and slept soundly until he wet the bed at 11:00. Last night he was up around 3 AM – putting the TV on...I'm scared about our financial future should he continue in this vein and require institutionalization. Unless I have a house in my name alone, I could lose everything. Bill is my strength; thank goodness for him.

TUESDAY, NOVEMBER 14, 2000: TOM CONTINUES TO DRIFT away from us. This morning I left him with only his pants and shoes to put on and when I returned after a small bit of time, he had one leg in the wrong pant leg and was fiddling with his watch, unable to put it on. I helped him and he shook his head, his face clouding up as if to *cry*. I asked him if he was a little confused and he said yes. I reminded him we were all trying to help him and we'd see the doctor tomorrow.

THURSDAY, NOVEMBER 16, 2000: I HOPE WHOEVER READS THIS in the future will be dealing with a better organized health care system than the one we presently have. Yesterday we took Tom to the doctor, (his former psychologist and the head of the last therapies Tom was given) who confirmed our suspicion that Tom had endured a stroke or a series of small strokes. He sent us down the hall to the neurologist for an appointment and a new MRI. They had nothing for two weeks. I went back to the doctor and explained that if we had to wait another two weeks at the rate of deterioration we witnessed in the past two weeks, I'll be bringing Tom in in a wheelbarrow. The doctor said he'd see if he could get it moved up. Today I heard from no one. I called the neurologist's office; they seemed concerned that we see our "family doctor" first. We don't have a family doctor. I used to have one, but he retired. I called the fellow who had taken over his office. Nothing open until mid-December.

Meanwhile, Tom has become almost a stranger; I feel more desperate about this new fellow than I did about the post-accident one because where that one was happy with his life and made steady, minuscule improvements, this one is confused and disintegrates daily. The nighttime incontinence has me worried. Today I spent $70 on incontinence products and he wet through them all. (I even got "heavy duty" padded underpants – by 10 PM they were as soaked through as any of his regular ones ever were.) I do two loads of bedding a day – I guess tomorrow we buy the rubber sheets.

I felt unsure about our future at the time of the accident, but I anticipated recovery and improvement. This time I don't know what to expect.

(I moved into the second bedroom by this time. There had been too many accidents to warrant sharing a bed.)

FRIDAY, NOVEMBER 17, 2000: I WONDER IF I'LL EVER LAUGH again. After the accident I never cried – I never let myself cry for fear of not being able to stop, of becoming too weak for whatever was ahead. Well, today I cried. Since yesterday Tom has disappeared much more, and yesterday was a decrease from the day before. This morning he got "stuck" and wouldn't move into the shower or out of the bathroom to dress. I almost had to push him, and he is too large for me to manage, especially at a dead weight.

My $100 investment in pads and padded underwear was an exercise in futility – he soaked right through it all, which meant an entire change of bedding around 11 PM and another this morning. Richard came over and then later Roz came. It felt good to have people around. I called Bill and told him he'd better come now, or the shock of what has happened might be overwhelming. He had previously visited in the evenings (after work) when Tom was in bed. Later, Melissa told me Bill had cried as well.

Bill and Melissa came at lunchtime. I made a big pot of soup but we'd only had about two spoonfuls when Tom dropped his spoon and his left hand began to shake, his fist clenched. Alarmed and probably panicky, I wanted to go to the emergency room, but calmer heads (notably Melissa's) prevailed and convinced me to go to the doctor first. We left right away, expecting to get there within 15 minutes. However, a dandy of an accident on Route 88 slowed us down and when we did get to the doctor's office, it was closed for lunch.

When the office reopened, we brought Tom in and the doctor sent us to the hospital for a CAT scan, which took all afternoon. We are still in limbo, just waiting to see what's next. Each day seems to bring a lessening and a diminishing. The Tom of only a month ago seems a fit fellow compared to the poor man we have now.

SATURDAY, NOVEMBER 18, 2000: ALL OF TOM'S FAMILY WAS IN and out today. Bob called from Colorado. Everyone is subdued by this awful thing. And the losses continue daily. Today he got the toothbrush in his mouth only after a random attempt to figure out what to do after I spent about 15 minutes demonstrating...Sometimes I can't believe this. This is the worst. The poor man now can't be understood, but he doesn't seem distressed. We are, very much so...

TUESDAY, NOVEMBER 21, 2000: THE POOR MAN IS deteriorating daily right in front of me and I can't seem to get any professional to be alarmed. Our new family doctor saw the neurologist this morning in the hospital and asked her to make Tom a priority. I know this only because I called the doctor twice today. The neurologist never called. You can be sure I will call her office tomorrow.

Tom has lost all his self-care abilities except eating, and even that is not without some confusion and a little instruction in the use of utensils. He got "stuck" with a loaded fork, in the air but not going anywhere. He has begun "tongue-flicking," a sign of a neurological disorder. He cannot dress himself and his speech is chiefly babble. My heart is aching but we've got to take him to someone tomorrow – even if it's the emergency room.

WEDNESDAY, NOVEMBER 22, 2000: AH, WHAT A WONDERFUL health care system we have – once you can get into it. I determined last night that if no appointment had been made with the neurologist for today, I would take him to the hospital ER. It wasn't, so I did. Richard and I took him there and all who saw him agreed it was the right thing to do. So why, eleven-and- a-half hours later, did we have to take him home? Because no doctor would/could admit him. A neurologist won't see him unless his family doctor admits him; our new family doctor doesn't work out of Jersey Shore, where we went, expecting that the neurologist would see him. A day full of phone calls among doctors produced no admission. Tom was discharged.

However, he wouldn't get dressed, then he hit and pushed me – with great strength – when I was trying to help, and wandered out into the corridors shirtless and shoeless. Security came, and also the doctor with a shot of Haldol to subdue him. *Now* they agreed he should be admitted! But no one could be found to admit him, so by 9:30 we came home, and with difficulty, Richard and I got him into bed. Bill and Melissa are staying here overnight and will help me in the morning. We will start out by contacting our family doctor (who had turned him over to the neurologist anyway).

THURSDAY, NOVEMBER 23, 2000: THANKSGIVING. EACH DAY IS more disheartening than the one before. This one began at 6:45 when Tom got up. I coaxed him back to bed, went back myself for a few minutes, and then heard a crash. I ran in to see glass splinters and shards all over the rug – he'd probably "adjusted" the light fixture on the ceiling, and it fell. The problem was to keep him off the rug, and pick up the glass, and decide whether I could run the vacuum cleaner at 6:45 without disturbing the very ill couple on the other side of the wall. I ran it briefly and put towels down, and then Tom urinated on the towels. That set the tone for the rest of the day, a great deal of which was spent in the bathroom. He has lost nearly all control and is just about completely incontinent. His speech is a babble. Worst of all, I think he has some awareness of his difficulties.

Pat and Richard came over this morning to shower and shave him. It took both of them about an hour and a half – and I've been trying to do it all alone. While they helped with Tom, I made preparations for Thanksgiving dinner. We had a nice dinner, 11 family for the meal, later joined by others. Tom and his massive confusion dominated the day...This is the saddest, most awful thing any of us has seen. After seven years of such remarkable progress – to come down so fast.

Today I almost broke down when I moved the case he always took with him, with his cassettes, playing cards, notebook – all his little treasures – and I remembered how content he'd been with his life, his food, his pool games. Despite his limitations he had built a secure and comfortable life for himself and was happy with it. And *that* Tom was only a dim shadow of the old Tom; and now *this* Tom is but a shadow of that one.

SUNDAY, NOVEMBER 26, 2000: THE LAST IMPRESSIONS OF TOM II flickered across his face on Friday and by 3 AM the next day that Tom was gone and a new, unknown, and unreachable one had taken his place. On the Friday after Thanksgiving Pat and Dennis came to shower and shave him. Richard came and I went out to buy the hygiene supplies he'd need for home care. When Richard left, Andrea and Joey came over because I felt I couldn't be left alone with Tom. Tom wandered and sat, and spoke very little; when he did speak it was mostly babble. He joined us between walking huge circles through the house, and it was then that old Tom II made his last appearance with a soft, sweet smile and an intelligent gaze.

(I'd like to interrupt here to tell you about his smile because it is with me still. It was, as I mentioned before, soft and sweet, and his face held, momentarily, a last glimmer of intelligence. He was seated in a big easy chair; I was kneeling beside him on the rug, holding his hands, and talking to him. He smiled down on me, and to this day I believe he was telling me not to worry, that it would somehow be all right in the end. There was a rare confidence in his face, a gift of assurance to me. I really do not know of any other way to describe it, or its effect on me, except to tell you that I thought he might know what was happening, what was going to happen, and wanted me to know we'd both get through it. Forgive me, religious people, but I think Jesus would have smiled at his mother in the same way just before he went off to create mayhem with the money changers, which led to his ultimate demise. Or perhaps it was like Lawrence Oates when he left the tent in Antarctica, knowing his injuries were slowing down his teammates, and told the others on the ill-fated expedition, "I'm just going outside and may be some time." That was Tom, perhaps also knowing he would soon be going out for a while and we were not to look for him. The moment was his last gift and I treasure it.)

It was a quiet day. He refused food but I woke him from a short nap to have him join us for coffee and cake. He ate most of his lunch. Spying the pizza box Joey had brought, he tried three times to open it; when he had been successful, he carried a slice of pizza to the table.

After they left we were alone for a short time and Tom was pretty calm, mostly watching TV in the kitchen and wandering. Bill came to help me with getting him to bed. I called him earlier than I'd expected because Tom refused to go near supper and began dragging chairs all over the kitchen and placing, then repositioning them. It took us a while to get him into bed and Bill realized it was unlikely I could handle Tom alone.

Once Bill left, Tom was up four times. Twice, he had pulled the "fitted brief diapers" down and was walking with all of that round his ankles, a very dangerous situation that could send him crashing down. Once, he had taken the pillowcase off, was swinging the pillow and knocked over the large picture over the bed. This was followed by a little bit of quiet but hysterical laughter. Later, about 11:00, I heard a crash and found him on the floor wedged between the bed and dresser, but sitting up. While I was calling Richard for help, Tom managed to get himself up on the bed and I settled him in again.

(I did not always call Bill when I needed help because I preserved the notion that maybe I could prevent him from seeing his father in the worst of circumstances, so he might not have to think back on this time in their lives and only remember the gruesome encounters. I wanted Bill to have the most decent memories he could, despite what was happening to his father. I can only imagine how difficult a time this was for Bill.)

At 3 AM I heard him chanting "pu-pu-pu-pu-pu" and laughing. He was stretched diagonally across the bed with his feet hanging over, his head raised against the headboard, bedding all awry, and the pillow on the floor. He seemed amused by this situation, as if to say, "How did I get into this crazy position?" and, "Look at this absurdity" at the same time. He was determined to get off the bed and I couldn't keep him on it.

Finally, his size alone demanded that I give up. He got to the little section of the hallway between the kitchen and the bathroom and began to turn in a circle with his hands raised rigidly in place. They only became unstuck when he pushed me away each time I tried to lead him back to bed. Concerned that he might fall, I called Richard, who came over and also had no success in getting him out of the hall. Finally, we had to call 911 and an ambulance arrived. Two big, burly guys easily got him on to the stretcher, and we followed the ambulance to the hospital.

This time we went to the closest hospital, Brick Hospital, and this time he was admitted from the ER to a floor. Most of yesterday he was sedated. The family doctor saw him as did someone from neurology who seemed to be under the delusion this was perhaps a psychiatric problem.

When I got home, it was like Tom's presence was still here. Every sound seemed to be him – in the bedroom were his clothes, all the hygienic supplies, in the hall all his things – his black carrying case and cue stick and jacket, ready to go. He was very much here, although I knew by the time the EMTs had gotten here yesterday morning, all the Toms we knew were gone.

Can they bring back Tom II? That's what we have to find out.

TUESDAY, NOVEMBER 28, 2000: MY GREATEST HOPE FOR HIM now is that he is unaware of the difficulty he's in. Helen thought he was crying today; I can't be certain. Last night on the phone and this morning at the hospital I spoke – finally! – with the neurologist who – finally! – got to see him. Yesterday's EEG revealed great abnormality. Tom is being given Dilantin for seizure-like activity. It's seven years ago all over, and that's a very disheartening thought.

THURSDAY, NOVEMBER 30, 2000: TOM IS STILL ASLEEP, snoring so loudly that even my "world's best" earplugs didn't help. I had to go to the day room. But oh, how grim he looks, so completely expressionless – we're really back seven years.

SUNDAY, DECEMBER 3, 2000: YESTERDAY WAS TOM'S SEVENTH anniversary. We were supposed to be at Red Lobster celebrating his survival. As you can imagine, it was a pretty gloomy day. With my help, he was calm for another EEG, but so far they've been unable to do another MRI because he gets too restless and confused. I offered to help there if I could. Unfortunately, there is a team of neurologists and I get the feeling they barely speak to each other. Yesterday they ordered medicine by mouth when we all know he can't take it. Why isn't that on the chart? So, time is wasted while the doctor is contacted, the prescription changed, etc., etc. Our doctor said so far his diagnosis is "seizures" – but there's no reason yet to explain why he's having them.

MONDAY, DECEMBER 4, 2000: WE HAD A LITTLE TALK WITH the doctor and he was not very optimistic. He believes Tom will not improve. I asked him if he thought Tom was aware of what was happening to him; the doctor does not think so, but by then I was a bit misty, so he may have known it was not what I wanted to hear. He softened it by saying he wasn't a neurologist, the new MRIs hadn't been done yet, and he wasn't God.

Helen was at the hospital today and she washed Tom and did his hair and mouth. Fortunately, she noticed that his right arm was red, hot, and swollen and demanded that the IV and block be removed. The arm does look bad; she kept a cold compress on it.

Tom looked more rested and quieter. He's receiving nutrition through an NG tube, just as he did seven years ago. Perhaps the food is helping to calm him; I did not see any spasms or tremors today and he looked peacefully asleep.

I think the Friday after Thanksgiving was our last visit with Tom II – at least for the time being. At 3 AM on Saturday, when I discovered an hysterical person stretched diagonally across the bed, shaking his head and laughing and saying "pu-pu-pu-pu," I had no sense of his being Tom. When he went out into the hall and froze in a mime (or Tai Chi) position and began turning circles, he was definitely someone else. I guess that's when Tom III came to see us.

TUESDAY, DECEMBER 5, 2000: NOT A GOOD DAY. THE DOCTOR called me this morning and said Tom was not doing well. I had the choice of either having him kept on the floor and "made comfortable" or moving him to Critical Care. That's where he is now. He has pneumonia, had fever through the night, and is altogether in critical condition. Both mothers came to the hospital, Paula and Dominick, Bill and Melissa arrived. Helen wants Pat, who is supposed to go to Maine with Dennis, and Richard, who is supposed to attend a class in California, to all stay home this weekend. I don't know what they'll decide to do. She got the priest in.

We've been here before – he was critical seven years ago and came back. I'm trying to hold on to that thought.

WEDNESDAY, DECEMBER 6, 2000: I FEEL BETTER ABOUT leaving him in the CCU. He is getting wonderful care there; it's just too bad he had to get to the brink of extinction before these services were available. Here there is one nurse for every two patients. She tends exclusively to their needs and is always on hand, as opposed to the floor where nurses are sometimes difficult to find. I found Tom neat, clean, well-attended to, and seemingly peaceful. A procedure was done to insert the IV into his chest because his arms are sore and infected. He's going to be given some nutrition through the NG tube, and the seizures seem to be somewhat under control. Let's hope all continues as well.

I called the CCU just before 11 PM and was told he showed no change, which is good – at least he's not worse. Richard was alarmed by all the equipment surrounding Tom, but it looks familiar to us. Now there's a computer at his bedside; the doctor can access it from home.

SATURDAY, DECEMBER 9, 2000: HOW COULD THINGS GET A BIT WORSE? Well, Mom could have a car accident, which she did. She is shaken, but basically unhurt, although the car is probably totaled. This is going to make things a little confusing for a while.

Tom has made no progress. I have a sick feeling in my stomach when I think of what has happened to him in the two weeks he's been in the hospital – seizures out of control, cellulitis from an unmonitored IV, pneumonia – and still no MRI, no diagnosis, no prognosis. We are trying to see if he can be moved to Robert Wood Johnson. People who see him are urging me to have him moved. Helen is also pushing for a move. I feel caught – I don't know what is best, but something must be done. I'm very distressed tonight and feeling helpless.

WEDNESDAY, DECEMBER 13, 2000: NO, NO BETTER; MAYBE worse. I spent all morning yesterday trying to get Tom into Robert Wood Johnson. Eventually I found someone who would accept a call from our neurology team, but after the phone call, Tom was rejected. We had great hopes for Tom at the Open MRI across the street from the hospital, but when he was taken there yesterday they wouldn't admit him on a stretcher! Now we're back to the beginning. He's been moved to a telemetry floor, which means his life is not in danger, but we are still without a diagnosis.

THURSDAY, DECEMBER 14, 2000: YES! TODAY THE MRI WAS finally done. It was late in the day, so I have no results yet. The poor man opened his eyes and looked around once in obvious alarm while we were there; the nurses said he'd done that earlier today as well. We tried to explain his situation to him and he quickly fell asleep again. But he did send out some cries of terror and confusion for a few awful minutes.

FRIDAY, DECEMBER 15, 2000: I ALMOST HATE TO GET UP IN THE morning because each day brings new horrors. We learned today that the new MRI for which we had such high hopes showed no essential difference from the one three years ago. This means there is still no diagnosis, no explanation. Tom was moved to yet another room, this time an isolation room, but obviously he has it to himself, which is nice. Sadly, his roommates have been locked in their own crises. Of course I cannot blame them, but the ambiance was less than cheerful.

I'm so discouraged about everything – it looks like so much

work to get this house sale settled and the outlook for Tom seems so dismal. I'm tired by and of it all.

SATURDAY, DECEMBER 16, 2000: HE LOOKS A LITTLE LIGHTER today, a little more alert at moments and less deeply into the roaring, snoring sleep he'd been in the past few weeks. But still we know nothing. In a few days, the NG tube will be removed and the stomach feeding tube inserted, so Tom ought to be more comfortable.

It seems longer than three weeks ago since we called the ambulance. I am still haunted by the vision of the strange, lost and laughing creature stretched across his bed that night, off in some other world where we couldn't reach him. And that same person, who was not-Tom, turning those little circles in the hall, his arms poised and rigid. Who was he and what did he do with Tom II?

TUESDAY, DECEMBER 19, 2000: TOM CONTINUES AS HE WAS, although the NG tube has been removed, so he should be more comfortable. The cisternography has begun; we should know in a few days whether hydrocephaly is the problem – or one of the problems. He lies there mostly asleep. When his eyes are open it's hard to tell whether they're focused. Sometimes he cries out, but if it is pain or anger or frustration is impossible to tell. This is a very difficult time for us.

FRIDAY, DECEMBER 22, 2000: WE'RE NO CLOSER TO anything. Tom's test for hydrocephaly, the cisternogram, proved normal; that is not the answer. The poor man is racked with seizures; he's had new and increased dosages of medicines but there's no improvement. We see increased awareness in the form of open eyes, but still no evidence of focusing or recognition.

SATURDAY, DECEMBER 23, 2000: A GRIM DAY. I SAW THE doctor at the hospital and we had this conversation:

Me: Do you think Tom's condition is reversible?

Doc: No.

Me: No, that's not the right answer. I'll try again. Do you think Tom's condition is reversible?

Doc: You never know. I see miracles every day.

He did finish up with the old line about God never giving us more than we can handle, to which I replied with *my* old line, "Then there wouldn't be any suicides."

The hospital is about finished with Tom since he is now medically stable. Next week we'll have to consider the next place – rehab for now unless another hospital will look at him.

It looks like the mental impairment has set upon him with a vengeance. I'm reminded of photos I've seen of victims of mercury poisoning in Japan, especially one picture of a mother cradling her adult son, and bathing him, he with his mouth open, eyes unfocused, and hands contorted backwards – the very posture Tom has developed. Can he be brought back? That is our hope. I try to be optimistic but the outlook is grim.

Always my thoughts come back to Tom, to the poor demented not-Tom for whom we called the ambulance and for the pitiful, lost man in that hospital bed, neither of which is the real Tom, who left seven years ago, or Tom II, who left a month ago. Who is this one?

MONDAY, DECEMBER 25, 2000: CHRISTMAS DAY. MOM STAYED overnight with me and today we made the rounds: Helen's, Bill's, the hospital. Barbara and Tracy met us at the hospital and we ate dinner at the only place open, the Crystal Palace Diner. It was a good enough meal and we got through Christmas, which we postponed celebrating.

WEDNESDAY, DECEMBER 27, 2000: TOM IS STILL A MYSTERY. The official diagnosis is "seizure activity," there is no explanation of how they began, or whether they are related to the deterioration. The hospital is beginning to talk about discharging him. Our neurologist is trying to locate a placement at JFK or Robert Wood Johnson now that all the tests are finished and we have a diagnosis – reasons why he'd been rejected by those institutions earlier. However, they do not have to accept him. I'm learning that nothing succeeds like success – these places with wonderful reputations are very selective about who they take in so they can have success stories. Remember our first rehab hospital? Poor Tom might not fit their criteria. It's so sad to watch him, losing ground daily but still looking so like Tom. It's also very difficult.

THURSDAY, DECEMBER 28, 2000: JUST WHEN YOU THINK IT'S impossible for things to get worse, etc., etc. Mom and I got to the hospital and it all got quite awful. Tom's EEG was worse than the past one; the neurologist spent all morning trying to get him into Hahnemann University Hospital in Philadelphia. Helen, Mom, and I waited with Tom until his transport arrived; he is now at Hahnemann in the Neurology Unit.

Tonight I am at Mom's because the closings are tomorrow, and my stuff is all on a truck . It is bitterly cold and a blizzard is predicted, which could mean days before I find my way to Philadelphia. Things are looking a bit glum right now.

SATURDAY, DECEMBER 30, 2000: MY BIRTHDAY. YESTERDAY the closing went well enough, although I was so tense that I cried through most of it. That hurried up the process – everyone was anxious to get me out of there! Tom is in the ICU at Hahnemann. Yesterday Helen and Richard went out there and were very pleased with his care and the hospital itself. I am pleased it is a teaching hospital. Maybe Tom's plight will at least be of use to medical students; his travail will not have been in vain. We had the blizzard all day.

SUNDAY, DECEMBER 31, 2000: HELEN AND I WENT TO SEE TOM today. The poor man was extensively wired to a great jungle of machinery, He's heavily sedated and was probably not aware of us. The care seems to be excellent but we still have no diagnosis and therefore no prognosis. Nobody cares about the New Year and its nonsense.

SATURDAY, JANUARY 6, 2001: THE PROBLEM WITH GOING TO Hahnemann is that it involves the whole day. We went Sunday, Wednesday, and today. Tom is heavily sedated; they are still trying to control the seizures. We have no answers yet. The hospital has been good about keeping in touch; the doctors are always around, but none of them has an explanation. Poor Tom. It's so sad to see him all wired up and motionless.

SUNDAY, JANUARY 7, 2001: NOTHING SEEMS QUITE RIGHT. I look at myself in the mirror and am not sure who I am. The phone startles me and I'm not sure where it is, or where I am. I think of Tom, lying amidst all the machinery so far away and I wonder where he really is, and who will come back to us. Will it be that affable fellow, Tom II? I also worry because the smoke from someone's woodstove fire in the neighborhood is infiltrating my house and making me ill. Will I survive the night?

I need to tell you here that, yes, I have moved house again, this time to a charming cottage in Point Pleasant Beach. My mother, who is in failing health, has to come to live with me. She was very reluctant to sell her house, so at first we told ourselves she would be with me to help me take care of Tom when he returns to us. I think we knew we were fooling ourselves. My mother can no longer live safely on her own and she is in too much pain to attend to her house. We sold the Leisure Village house with no difficulty, and put my mother's house up for sale.

MONDAY, JANUARY 8, 2001: A RATHER GLOOMY DAY, although I suppose I should be grateful I didn't die of smoke inhalation last night. This was a rainy day; Bill and Melissa gave up their day off to drive to Hahnemann to see Tom. It took us two soaking hours each way. There was a team in his room and most of the members took time to talk with us. I just called. His temperature is low and the echocardiogram was not done because his blood culture indicated no need. Maybe we'll see some changes for the better in the next few days.

FRIDAY, JANUARY 12, 2001: MOM, HELEN, AND I WENT TO Philadelphia to see Tom. He had a tracheotomy and we waited until he was safely out of it, which meant not getting home until 6:30 – a long day. We hope to see improvement in Tom in a few days; I just spoke to the nurse (11:30 PM) and he told me Tom has been seizure-free. Let's hope he continues to do so well.

TUESDAY, JANUARY 16, 2001: HELEN AND I WENT IN TO Philadelphia today. Tom certainly looked better and opened his eyes rather frequently. The seizures seem to be under control.

SATURDAY, JANUARY 20, 2001: YESTERDAY RICHARD, HELEN, and I braved nasty rains to go see Tom. I was a bit upset; to me, he didn't look as well as he had a few days ago. There was a little twitching, some drooling, and not as much open-eye time. The doctor assured us all was well. Tonight, however, they called to notify me of new problems: blood in the urine, hopefully only from a catheter problem earlier this week. Also, there was a little seizure early this morning. He has edema, retaining water horribly, although still expelling a good deal of it. It's quite upsetting.

THURSDAY, JANUARY 25, 2001: TWO MONTHS SINCE THAT awful day we had to call the ambulance to cart away a poor, out-of-touch stranger we now call Tom III. Two days ago, Bill, Melissa, Helen and I went to the hospital. It was still as upsetting for me as the last visit; tomorrow we will go again.

I'm trying to get rid of all my old *Logic Puzzle* magazines and I now find myself finishing up a book I'd begun in the summer of 1993, which was Before. It's as if I could communicate with the old me, the last happy me, as I look at all the pages filled in and puzzles finished back in such an innocent time, before it all happened. The Me of Now is reaching out to the Me of Then, wishing I could hold back the march, settle into the puzzles still undone, and just stay there.

SUNDAY, JANUARY 28, 2001: LAST FRIDAY OUR VISIT TO TOM was rather gloomy – the chief of the neurology group and the two doctors we usually see all came to talk to us, an impromptu family conference. The topics: do we want resuscitation, and what the next placement will be. Too much reality for me. For the first time, they talked about a prognosis, and it wasn't a good one – always tempered, however, by wait-and-see, you-never-know, and so on. Just Helen and I were there and we tried to be brave. All I can think of is poor, poor Tom. Not the man in the bed – Tom III – but Tom I who was gone forever seven years ago and Tom II who made and enjoyed a happy little life and made everyone around him happy. Tom III, so far, doesn't seem to be trying hard enough, but then he's been sedated so long and so heavily that he's hardly been given a chance. Maybe when we next see him there will be improvements. Meanwhile, more than ever I can't bear to see his clothes, his few things that gave him such pleasure.

THURSDAY, FEBRUARY 1, 2001: TOM IS SUPPOSED TO BE MOVED to the floor out of the ICU, but only because he is off the ventilator. The idea is to wean him off the machinery, decrease the medication, and hope he will become alert with the seizures controlled. I've been crying a bit over him – over his destroyed dreams and the awful tragedy of it. This is not other people; this is us! This is a man like any of us who had hopes and plans and great intelligence, and now all of that is gone. The full horror of it comes sneaking up behind me more frequently than before and I feel like I'm smothering. Poor, poor Tom who is way beyond us, as Tom III, and whom we want back. And yet, I'm a little afraid of who Tom IV might be. Please, let's hope things get better soon.

MONDAY, FEBRUARY 5, 2001: TOM IS NOW ON A REGULAR floor in the neurology ward, but in an isolation room. The resident doctor started talking about the "case manager," which means trouble. Sure enough, she called me today to start her little wheels in motion to carry him out – propelled, of course, by the insurance companies. I agonized over the two choices she asked us to consider: have him home, or place him in a nursing home. Now, I know it's impossible to have him home. It takes two people just to turn him, and it would be a 24/7 job, one for which I am and have always been constitutionally unsuited – but still I felt guilty. Bill made me feel the case worker is immune to other people's agonies because she must be to perform her job, therefore I shouldn't let her make me feel guilty. And, he asked how guilty would I feel if Tom were at home and something went wrong with his hookups and I couldn't fix it. Still, the nursing home is a grim alternative. Also, I'm so afraid we'll lose the Idaho house if he goes into residence because the government takes everything in his name to pay for his support. The only consolation I have regarding nursing home placement is that he did well seven years ago in Jackson Health Care, so there is the hope he might do well again, this time. But he is so different now.

TUESDAY, FEBRUARY 6, 2001: YESTERDAY, HELEN AND I WENT to see Tom; we met the case worker and the medical team. Tom is still not medically stable; he has infections again. Tonight they called me for permission to put in a central line (again) and give him blood (again). He has lost hemoglobin but no one knows where it is. He looked so pale and so sick; I hated to leave him. He seems now to be more ill than disabled; and he's slipping away from us. Still, I can't say there's no hope – even the doctors admit that no one knows enough to say what will happen, how he'll run the course.

However, I do have to begin research on skilled nursing facilities, and the little I've done has been discouraging. He's going to be discharged with too much equipment, too many needs, to be accepted in most places. I'm so, so depressed and sad about him; he looks so lost and alone and helpless in the isolation room, and so far away...

SUNDAY, FEBRUARY 11, 2001: TOM LOOKED A LITTLE BETTER today and kept his eyes open much, much longer. It seemed as if he were working his mouth in an attempt to form words. However, he is swollen again – arms, mostly – and pale. But when he opens those beautiful gray eyes, it does seem as if he's with us for the moment. Mom, Helen, and I spent last Friday afternoon looking at nursing homes, a mentally exhausting experience for all of us and a physically exhausting one as well for Mom. She is in increasingly fragile condition, but bravely soldiers on.

WEDNESDAY, FEBRUARY 14, 2001: EVERY DAY SEEMS TO BRING a fresh disaster, although there may be a glimmer of hope that Mom at least might be beginning to feel better. On Monday she saw one doctor in the morning and we looked at three nursing homes in the afternoon. The next day we saw a different doctor, then went to the hospital with Helen. The trip was too much for Mom, who was weak and sick the entire time. During each elevator trip, as she paled from nausea and gripped the handrails, several doctors riding with us were already fingering their stethoscopes, ready to check her.

Tom showed no change and did not seem as "lively" as at our last visit. His arms were swollen again. And now today – a real blow. I saw an Elder Law lawyer this afternoon and was devastated by the prospect of losing our house in Idaho – a very real prospect. And no one other than myself and Bill seems to care, or to understand how much that house means to us. The whole system stinks, which I said to the lawyer when I wasn't crying.

And then there's Helen, who is already talking about letting God take Tom, if it comes to us having to choose or reject resuscitation. I've got to find a way to tell Helen that I don't feel very personally connected to God at this moment. Neither Bill nor I are ready to surrender – as long as Tom is not in pain and has the barest of chances to pull out of this. But today, he had a fever again and they have to find a new place to put in another new central line. It's been a discouraging day.

THURSDAY, FEBRUARY 22, 2001: LAST TUESDAY PAT AND I went into Philadelphia. The neurology team told us Tom was ready for discharge. Since I had given a list of eight acceptable (to us) nursing homes to the case manager last Friday, when Madli and I had gone to the hospital, I expected rather immediate action. Hah! Yesterday we saw a new lawyer. She was wonderful! I was determined not to cry this time, but I did get a bit misty when I talked about saving the cabin – and when she said we could keep it, I wept with relief; I couldn't help it. Today there were flurries of phone calls and for a while I was very happy because Hahnemann called to say Tom would be transferred to our first choice nursing home either this afternoon or tomorrow. About an hour or so later, they called back to tell us that hospital had rejected him: he needs more skilled care than they can offer. What a disappointment! I'm still upset over it because now I'm afraid this might be the situation with all of them on the list and he'll end up in that really depressing coma facility in Toms River (#8 on our list of 8).

Mom is not improving; she refuses to take more medicine. I'm just getting tired of it all – between Mom and Tom and Medicaid, I have too much right now. And on top of it all, we're having another major blizzard as I write this.

SUNDAY, FEBRUARY 25, 2001: YESTERDAY'S VISIT WAS A REALLY dolorous one. In the first place, neither Helen nor I wanted to go to Philadelphia because we'd hoped Tom would be locally situated by now, and secondly, once we got there, he seemed very much the same and for some reason so piteous, so helpless. His eyes opened a bit but he doesn't move his body at all. And for the past week, there's been a strong urine odor, which doesn't help. I felt miserable the whole trip. Then tonight Mom was watching a movie with a character named Lila and it reminded me of Tom singing *Lida Rose*; it made me really, deeply sad to think we may never hear his voice again. During the same show an ad came on for a Platters CD with snippets of all the Platters' songs that Tom sang so beautifully. A few bad minutes there for me.

SUNDAY, MARCH 4, 2001: IT HASN'T BEEN THE BEST WEEK. I felt very down. Mom is a little better, but cold inside out, and blue at the fingertips, numb hands. Very scary! I took her to the hematologist as usual on Wednesday and he wants her to see an orthopedic doctor for her back pain, but she refuses..... Helen and I went in on Friday to see poor Tom. Lots of phone calls with the case manager; he might be moved to the nursing home tomorrow (our second choice) except that a monster storm has been predicted. It's been *the* news topic for the past three days and New Jersey has already declared a state of emergency. The blizzard was supposed to begin at 5 PM today but it's midnight now and all we've had has been rain and wind.

TUESDAY, MARCH 6, 2001: DESPITE ALL THE MEDIA HOOPLA that preceded it for days, the "monster storm of the century" never materialized. The other thing that never materialized was Tom's move to the nursing home. It now seems he has an infection and thus cannot be put into the room reserved for him, lest his waste, dumped into a shared bathroom, contaminate the other residents. However, one of the doctors feels he might not have an infection after all. If he can produce three negative cultures in the next six days, he'll be good to go. Will our #2 choice still have a bed?

WEDNESDAY, MARCH 7, 2001: TOM IS NOW IN JERSEY SHORE Center, a sister facility of our #2 choice, in Eatontown. Our second choice referred the case manager to Jersey Shore Center and she found they had a bed, and informed us we'd have to take it if Medicare is going to pay for it. No one seems to be concerned any longer about the infection...Fortunately, it's a very nice place and the staff has been more than kind to us. The doctor gave me a hug when we left at 6 PM after spending a long time talking with us. (The nurses told me they had *never* seen her hug anyone; she's just not the emotional type!) I'm a little angry with the case manager at Hahnemann because she did very little of the work. It was we who traipsed around to the nursing homes, wrote up the preferred list, and it was I who had to tell them yesterday that a bed was available at our second choice home. I certainly do not mind doing the work, but we might have been less hampered if we eliminated the case worker and just went out on our own to begin with. Maybe I'm just tired; she was probably only doing her job and there are usually lots of things going on in the background of which we are not aware regarding the arrangement of these things.

Today's transfer was not without tears. I cried when I saw the room – not that there was anything wrong with it except the finality – and cried much more later when the doctor and the social worker tried to impress me with the fact that he was "very sick". He arrived with a fever of 103° and they offered me the opportunity to have him sent to the hospital. (So why did a hospital discharge him?) They are asking me to make decisions that are much too difficult right now. The doctor asked me what I wanted her to do. How am I supposed to know? All of this comes from the very complicated medical system we have (only #13 in the civilized world) and from fear of lawsuits and consequent unwillingness on the part of the medical team to take responsibility.

THURSDAY, MARCH 8, 2001: TOM IS NOT DOING WELL. IT'S been a difficult day, a lot of tears. When Mom and I were at the lawyer's to begin Medicaid procedures for Tom's long-term care, the nursing home called there. The doctor wanted my decision immediately about taking Tom to the hospital. I asked what we were talking about – hours, days, weeks, months – and the social worker said it could be days. We raced right over. Bill and Melissa came. There was a lot of discussion, more than I can talk about now because my eyes are so sore I cannot let myself cry any more today. It comes to this: he is resistant to all forms of antibiotics, especially the Big One: vancomycin. He is full of infection, the coma is not lifting, prospects are not good. I really can't say any more now...

SATURDAY, MARCH 10, 2001: THE MAN IN THE BED IS LOOKING less and less like Tom. Yesterday he did, a little, but today less so. We were there yesterday in the afternoon, Helen in the morning. The social worker even called me from a convention she was attending to see how I was doing. Bill and Melissa went to the hospital about 5 PM, then we all came here for a little birthday supper for Bill. We weren't in a festive mood, but I guess we tried. Today Helen, Pat, Mom, and I went. He doesn't look the same. He's still feverish and comatose although he had his eyes open for quite a while, but they were unseeing – or so it appeared. I brought him some music, some of his oldies, but I had to keep leaving the room because I really can't let myself cry so much. I try not to think about Toms I and II; Tom III is a stranger we never quite got to know, yet he has made a lasting impression on us.

SUNDAY, MARCH 11, 2001: PAULA CAME WITH ME TO THE hospital. Tom had no fever today; he had bursts of open eye time but otherwise no motion, no change. His unseeing eyes looked up at the ceiling, his lips and arms twitched from the myoclonus, and he was just there with his face a bit altered, his legs bone-thin, his arms swollen. I don't know who he is, but I cannot spend much time with whoever he is before I have to walk away for a little while, because I am trying not to cry.

MONDAY, MARCH 12, 2001: TOM WAS THE SAME. I THINK HIS legs moved when I played some music – not the myoclonus, tic-like movement, but more an actual, purposeful movement. Could he be responding to the music? He is still unfamiliar, but I find myself crying over a stranger.

TUESDAY, MARCH 13, 2001: TOM LOOKED A LITTLE MORE ALERT today. His eyes were open all the while I was there, but not as open as they had been, in unblinking, unseeing blankness. Today they seemed to be moving around, looking, and he was blinking. It made him appear much more normal.

I've got to liquidate all our monies and spend big before I lose it all to Medicaid. And yet, I don't know what I want or need. Or rather, what I want and need – the full restoration of Tom – can't be bought.

THURSDAY, MARCH 15, 2001: TOM LOOKED LESS ALERT TODAY and yesterday, in fact he seemed to be almost entirely asleep the whole time, with a few, very brief moments of eye opening. Otherwise, just comatose. Bill and Melissa met me at the nursing home and we went out for supper. I don't know why, but it broke my heart to hear Bill say, "Good night, Dad" to poor Tom. Bill deserves a father; he's still just a child (though he'd argue the point!) and although he's trying and learning, he could have benefited from Tom's advice. And how Tom II, even in his fragile condition, loved him and would hear no criticism about him. What a shame all around.

Florence took Mom to the orthopedic doctor after her hematologist yesterday offered to get down on his knees to entreat her to go. (I had asked him to impress her with the importance of making the appointment when I took her for her usual Procrit shot.) Well – she has a broken rib! It is probably from her car accident back in December.

TUESDAY, MARCH 20, 2001: I'M FEELING A BIT OPTIMISTIC. Yesterday, it took all day but I finally unraveled the mysteries of the relationship between Medicare and Blue Cross/Shield. Today I saw the lawyer and am beginning to understand the Medicaid puzzle. Tom had no fever today. Even Mom says she felt a little better. I believe I may be teetering on the brink of a breakthrough like Gautami the Frail after she realizes no home is without sorrow, and life must therefore continue.

THURSDAY, MARCH 22, 2001: TOMORROW IS TOM'S BIRTHDAY; it's so unbearably sad. He is still fever-free, but very much asleep; his eyes never open at all. The man in the bed now looks more like Tom I than Tom II; I keep expecting him to wake up and ask what's for dinner.

FRIDAY: MARCH 23, 2001: WHEN I GOT TO THE NURSING home, the head nurse told me there was quite a crowd in Tom's room. I said, "I know – it's his birthday" – and immediately started crying. In the room, Pat, Helen, and Richard were trying to be jolly. The home had put a sign on the door and brought in balloons. Someone brought flowers. All this made me feel immeasurably sad. I'm just glad I missed their singing "Happy Birthday".

An obvious strain of optimism was still running through our family; perhaps I should better term it "strained optimism." We were facing a very sick man with a very short span of time left, but we couldn't see that. I had gone into the protective numbness I first experienced immediately after the accident. I was just walking through life, letting it hit me as it would, and trying to keep to my path. With the lawyer, we were doing the spend-down of our assets so Tom would be eligible for long-term care under Medicaid. If I thought about the future at all, I saw a stretch of long-term care that would eventually result in some sort of recovery. After all, it happened before and I saw no reason why it couldn't happen again. No one spoke to us about the possibility that he might die. I don't know if we were supposed to intuit the truth, or if, because of the variable nature of his afflictions, no one could or would make the pronouncement.

It is difficult, even from this far reach of time, to put words to the feeling we experienced toward the end of Tom's life. I certainly was not prepared for him to die. I was prepared to spend whatever time it took to pull him out of this crisis, and then make an assessment of our future. My mother had come to live with me and her care was more physically demanding for me than was Tom's, although his was more emotionally draining. No doubt there was a ton of denial in my attitude toward our situation. Yet, in the absence of more specific information from his medical team, I had to assume Tom had reached some kind of stasis and from here would either remain stable, or get better. Even at this late period, we looked for improvement. No one was yet prepared to give up on him. That's not who we are.

MONDAY, APRIL 2, 2001: TOM HAS BEEN MOVED UPSTAIRS TO A private room. The night they moved him (Friday) he had a temperature of 104°. A chest X-ray was done. He has pneumonia in part of one lung. He's in complete isolation; tonight they told Bill, Melissa, and me that we have to gown up with mask and gloves when we visit. He looks good, peaceful, and comfortable and still very much like Tom I. Without the rounded and cherubic face and shallow eyes of Tom II, his condition seems more profound – as if Tom II never existed and this is Tom I, the original, in a coma.

The second floor is much more depressing than the first, which was a rehab wing. Now he is housed with patients suffering from forms of dementia.

I've been working on the financial and legal stuff for Medicaid. It's very complicated but I'm beginning to get some control over it.

FRIDAY, APRIL 6, 2001: THE PAST COUPLE OF DAYS HAVE BEEN very difficult. The horror of Tom's situation is settling in around me. I think the move to the long-term wing amongst the Alzheimer's and dementia patients adds to the general depressing atmosphere. He is running temperatures of 98-101°, up and down. He can't throw off the infections and the pneumonia. We have to suit up fully to visit. His eyes open, but they are still unfocused. I wish I knew what to wish for. Could he/should he recover? Who would he be then? Tom I, II, or III? If he cannot, what is next? The person in the bed is not anyone we know, and he's so entrapped. He has the trach tube, the feeding tube, and the catheter all going in and out of him. He has splints on both hands and forearms to prevent his fingers from becoming permanently clenched; he has foot-drop boots on each foot to keep them from contracting. He has a host of infections in addition to the pneumonia. The situation is dreadful.

WEDNESDAY, APRIL 11, 2001: TOM CONTINUES TO HAVE FEVERS and remain comatose. There is less eye opening, it seems to me. I don't feel very much at ease.

THURSDAY, APRIL 12, 2001: WORKED ON TAXES, DID ERRANDS for Medicaid, then went to see Tom. Now they have him up in a jerry chair, where he looks good, peaceful, asleep – but is not well.

His fever was 101° again last night. He opened his eyes a little more today than in the past few days, but not with any focusing. I wonder what it is like for him. I hope it's not bad – maybe a peaceful, dream-like state. He doesn't seem to be in distress, but he is unable to move at all of his own doing – deep in a coma. I'm becoming very depressed over it all.

I look at my husband. We are alone in his room. It is a soft day. The staff here has placed him a recliner; he is semi-sitting up, but his head is strangely to the side at a sharp angle. It looks uncomfortable. He is deep in a coma.

I talk to him, telling him the words that will haunt me the rest of my life. "Tom, you know that we love you and all we want is for you to recover to be anyone of your iterations. If we can't have the original Tom back safely with us, then the happy eight-year-old will do. We'd be delighted even to have him back. But if you can't come back, then go away. We can't go on like this. Neither of us can go on like this."

I know – I believe – I believe I know that he cannot hear or understand me – that he is in a place already far away. I believe this because in his last few days of wakefulness, his last days at home, and throughout all of his hospitalizations since then, he did not seem to understand anything we said and was unable to communicate with us. Did not *seem* to.

I have to believe this because the words have already been spoken, have been flung into his space and are circling him. In all my days, I will worry about having said them.

I ask the God in whom I do not believe to be kind to him. My spoken words to Tom, too late to call back, echo through my head. Will they have done any harm? I look at my husband and I wonder where he is and if he is happy there. I hope so.

Oh, how I hope so – and this hope actually hurts.

FRIDAY, APRIL 13, 2001: TOM DIED THIS MORNING AT 8:35. IT was probably fast, and painless. He was discovered by the morning staff only minutes afterward, and I was called. It's difficult to talk about now; the next few days will show what all of today's anguish was about. The poor man's walk is over and if rest is at the end of the trek, then he's at rest. He was well-loved and well-cared-for and now it's over.

Goodbye, Tom. I hope you're whole again, and happy. More we cannot do.

And so our long walk together, mine and Tom's and Bill's, came to an end. I write his story ten years later, and it is as fresh as ever. I relive the joys, the worries, the pain, the frustration, the celebrations, and the hope. Always there was hope and it did not run out until his days did.

Yes, Tom died on a Friday the 13th – Good Friday. He would have appreciated the irony.

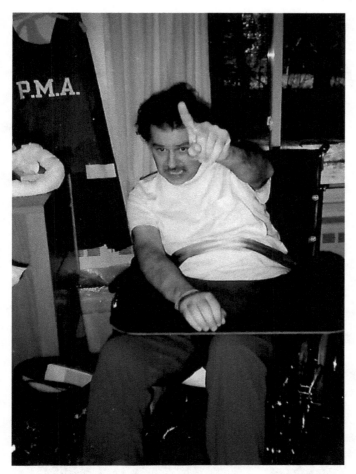

January, 1964 Tom, just emerged from the coma, is still non-verbal, but is trying to make a point.

June, 1964 Tom is ready for discharge from rehabilitation.

ABOUT THE AUTHOR

Having started life in Newark, New Jersey, Joanna Sorrentino considers herself American by birth and Italian by Nature. She was a career educator, holding teaching certificates in four subject areas. Although fond of adventure, she chronicles one she never expected to have in I DON'T WHETHER MYSELF, which was written as a tribute to her husband and in the hope it might help others traveling on a similar journey.

Joanna lives at the Jersey Shore, next-door to her son, daughter-in-law and their three children who are, like all grandchildren, brilliant and beautiful. This story is their legacy.

She can be reached at josorr1241@gmail.com